CAVALRY
OF THE CLOUDS

CAVALRY
OF THE CLOUDS

AIR WAR OVER EUROPE 1914–1918

JOHN SWEETMAN

SPELLMOUNT

'They are the cavalry of the clouds. High above the squalor and the mud ... they fight out the eternal issues of right and wrong ... They are the knighthood of this war, without fear and without reproach. They recall the old legends of chivalry, not merely by daring individually, but by the nobility of their spirit.'
(David Lloyd George, British Prime Minster)

'Of the chivalry of the air, which is so fatuously and ignorantly written about, neither side could afford to indulge in.'
(Harold Harrington Balfour, Western Front pilot)

'[War] is not as the people at home imagine it, with a hurrah and a roar; it is very serious, very grim.'
(Manfred von Richthofen, German ace)

First published 2010
by Spellmount, an imprint of
The History Press
The Mill, Brimscombe Port
Stroud, Gloucestershire, GL5 2QG
www.thehistorypress.co.uk

© John Sweetman, 2010

The right of John Sweetman to be identified as the Author
of this work has been asserted in accordance with the
Copyrights, Designs and Patents Act 1988.

British Library Cataloguing in Publication Data.
A catalogue record for this book is available from the British Library.

ISBN 978 0 7524 5503 7

Typesetting and origination by The History Press
Cartography by Martin Brown © The History Press
Manufacturing managed by Jellyfish Print Solutions Ltd
Printed in Great Britain

Contents

Abbreviations

ack ack	anti-aircraft (usually referring to fire)
ADC	aide-de-camp
AEG	Allgemeine Elektrizitäts Gesellschaft: German aviation firm and aeroplane
AFC	Air Force Cross
archie	German anti-aircraft fire
adolphus	British anti-aircraft fire
Air Cdre	air commodore
Avro(s)	A.V. Roe & Co. Ltd or aeroplane
AW	Armstrong Whitworth aeroplane
BE	Blériot Experimental aeroplane
Brig Gen	Brigadier-General
Capt	Captain
CAS	Chief of the Air Staff
CID	Committee of Imperial Defence
C-in-C	Commander in Chief
CO	Commanding Officer
Col	Colonel
DFC	Distinguished Flying Cross
DFW	Deutsche Flugzeugwerke: German aviation firm and aeroplane
DGMA	Director-General of Military Aeronautics, War Office
DH	de Havilland aeroplane
DSC	Distinguished Service Cross
DSO	Distinguished Service Order
FB	Fighting Biplane
FE	Farman Experimental aeroplane
Fg Off	Flying Officer
Flt Cdr	Flight Commander
Flt Lt	Flight Lieutenant
F/Sgt	Flight Sergeant
FSL	Flight Sub Lieutenant
GAF	German Air Force
GHQ	General Headquarters
GOC	General Officer Commanding
Gp Capt	Group Captain

HE	High Explosive
HP	Handley Page aeroplane
HQ	Headquarters
IAAF	Inter-Allied Independent Air Force
JWAC	Joint War Air Committee
KCB	Knight Commander of the Bath
kg	kilogramme
km	kilometre
kph	kilometres per hour
Lt	Lieutenant
2/Lt	Second Lieutenant
Lt Col	Lieutenant-Colonel
Lt Gen	Lieutenant-General
LVG	Luft Verkehrs Gesellschaft: German aviation firm and aeroplane
mag	magneto
Maj	Major
Maj Gen	Major-General
MM	Military Medal
mph	miles per hour
NCO	Non-Commissioned Officer
NPL	National Physical Laboratory
OBE	Officer of the Order of the British Empire
OC	Officer Commanding
Op	operation
ORB	operations record book
OTC	officers' training corps
Plt Off	Pilot Officer
PoW	Prisoner of War
PR	photographic reconnaissance
pusher	aeroplane with engine behind wings
RA	Royal Artillery
RAF	Royal Aircraft Factory *or* Royal Air Force
RAFVR	Royal Air Force Volunteer Reserve
RAE	Royal Aircraft Establishment
RE	Royal Engineers *or* Reconnaissance Experimental aeroplane
revs	revolutions
RFA	Royal Field Artillery
RFC	Royal Flying Corps
RFC HQ	Royal Flying Corps Headquarters
RGA	Royal Garrison Artillery
RN	Royal Navy
RNAS	Royal Naval Air Service
RNVR	Royal Naval Volunteer Reserve
rpm	revolutions per minute
RSM	regimental sergeant major
R/T	radio-telephony
SASO	senior air staff officer

SE	Scout Experimental aeroplane
Sgt	sergeant
sortie	single operational flight
SPAD	Société pour Aviation et ses Dérives: French aircraft firm or French aeroplane
Sqn	squadron
Sqn Cdr	Squadron Commander
Sqn Ldr	Squadron Leader
tractor	aeroplane with engine in front of wings
VC	Victoria Cross
WAAC	Women's Auxiliary Air Force
Wg Cdr	Wing Commander
WO	War Office
W/T	wireless telegraphy

List of Maps

Preface

Aerial Warfare
'High Above the Squalor and the Mud'

During the First World War, the air emerged as a third dimension to armed conflict, and this new form of fighting was dramatically illustrated in North-West Europe, where Britain's confrontation with Germany and defence of her homeland against airship and aeroplane attack took place. Beyond the more measured pages of official reports and statistical analyses, powerful images of the personal impact, sometimes exhilarating but often tragic, are contained in letters between combatants of both the British and German air forces and their anxious families at home.

With the passage of time, however, the dangerous aspects of operations have been overshadowed by colourful misrepresentation of the reality of aerial warfare. After the Armistice, writers of articles in lurid 'penny dreadfuls', as well as authors of full-length adventure stories, concocted audacious tales of clashes in the sky. William Earl Johns wrote stirring novels involving his fictional hero Biggles, and contributed to a wide range of weekly or monthly publications such as *The Gem* and *Boy's Own*, which idealised heroism, patriotism and pluck. Covington Clarke promised 'a story of young warriors in the air, who thunder aloft to dizzy, breathtaking conflicts'. In the United States, Elliott White Springs, an American Western Front aviator, produced entertaining volumes about 'those gallant adventurers *The War Birds* … packed with exciting episodes … dog-fights, 5,000 feet above the lines … six Camels attacking ten Fokkers'.

Hollywood soon discovered that cinema audiences preferred scenes of aircraft wheeling and spiralling overhead to ranks of mud-spattered infantry advancing towards rolls of barbed wire in the face of lethal machine-guns. The silver screen has even trivialised the perilous and often fatal efforts of aviation pioneers in such epics as *Those Magnificent Men in their Flying Machines*. Evidently, flying before and during the First World War was rather fun, and to some extent aerobatic performances and wing-walking stunts at post-war public displays heightened the aura of retrospective levity. Today, spectators at air shows frequently break into applause at the approach of a 'vintage' biplane, the relic of a curious past. Maurice Baring, who served on the Western Front, reflected that 'the image of goggle-clad aces peering over machine-guns or discharging revolvers as they wove across the sky had become ingrained in popular mythology.'

The fiction that airborne activity somehow constituted a detached, romantic adjunct to the traditional forms of warfare gained momentum while hostilities were in progress. In October 1917 the British Prime Minister, David Lloyd George, proclaimed airmen 'the cavalry of the clouds. High above the squalor and the mud … they fight out the eternal issues of right and wrong … They are the knighthood of this war … They recall the old legends of chivalry.'

Such idealistic bombast airbrushed 'the turmoil and sweat of actual combat' according to Sholto Douglas, decorated airman and future high-ranking officer. As the British official history, *The War in the Air*, observed: 'Life in the Service was lived at high pressure and was commonly short.' Aviators dreaded fire, bone-crushing crashes caused by mechanical failure, the deadly impact of multiple-fighter clashes, or the prospect of being set upon by a swarm of enemy machines. Cecil Lewis, pilot of a slow reconnaissance aeroplane, recalled: 'It's no joke to be shot up by a dozen machine guns for half an hour, engaged in a running fight in which the enemy can outpace you, outclimb you and outturn you.'

Patrick Huskinson, who would survive to become an air commodore, expressed serious misgivings about the structural integrity of his biplane. Attacking a train near Le Cateau in north-eastern France from 200ft, to his acute discomfort the bomb-load exploded instantaneously on impact, 'flinging me high like a jack-in-the-box. My wings … were nothing but a blur of flapping fabric, what I could see of the fuselage too closely resembled a sieve.' On landing, 'my aircraft … fell to pieces.' Charles Portal, destined to command the RAF during the Second World War, was similarly unimpressed with the qualities of his monoplane. Take-off and landing, he discovered, could be hair-raising, and 'the chances of death by misadventure on the aerodrome were infinitely greater than by enemy action.'

Once aloft, the vagaries of the weather in the absence of reliable navigational instruments proved a constant danger, and sheer fatigue caused by up to four operations daily quickly drained the first flush of innocence. The greatest fear of all was knowledge that, with no parachutes for aircrew, terminal damage to an airborne machine meant a long and terrifying plunge to crippling injury or death. Among the enemy, famous personalities like Manfred von Richthofen, Oswald Boelcke and Max Immelmann admitted to these same life-threatening concerns.

The hopes, fears and in so many cases, grief experienced by loved ones underlines the unending strain placed upon relatives left behind. Douglas Joy, Canadian-born pilot of English parents, acknowledged 'the huge number of families that have been separated, and widely too'. To reassure his wife, when he was at the Front Joy wrote to her daily. His mother-in-law fought tenaciously to ensure that her sole surviving son did not even cross the Channel; the loss of his two brothers in action sufficient sacrifice. Philip Joubert de la Ferté, who would achieve high rank in the RAF, reflected on a particular aspect of marital stress: 'my wife found her existence in hotels and lodging-houses when I was on home service, and with her relations when I was abroad, very little to her taste.' Margaret Douglas, like the mothers of Richthofen and Immelmann, had two sons in her country's air service, and Frau Boelcke had three. Each would lose one of them. Three of Mrs Amelie McCudden's four boys, who served in the RFC or RAF were killed, and many families endured the despair of losing an only child. Sholto Douglas reflected too, on 'the very high stress' put on his former headmaster, many of whose former pupils were flying operationally.

Evidence of the appalling conditions on the ground and devastating losses incurred in repeated 'pushes' to break the trench deadlock on the Western Front (almost 60,000 casualties on the first day of the 1916 Battle of the Somme being but one depressing figure) is now well-known. So many writers, organisers of commemorative events and producers of television documentaries focus on the undoubted horrors of the land warfare without recognising, often without even mentioning, the contribution of airmen to the Allied cause.

Initially, British aeroplanes had a single 70hp engine, and their one- or two-man crew had only rifles, revolvers or shotguns for self-defence. Within four years, machines with four 375hp engines capable of reaching Berlin from England were ready for action, modified hand-grenades tossed over the side had given way to 1,650lb bombs dropped with the guidance of bomb-sights honed for accuracy, and machine-guns were synchronised to fire forward through propeller blades to enhance the aggressive potential of fighters. Such technical advances, however, were often matched and at times outpaced by the Germans, the progress of military aviation being by no means one-sided.

In the closing months of 1914, British airmen tracked the path of enemy troops advancing through Belgium towards Paris and crucially, detected their alterations of direction or tactical redeployment. The commander of the British forces at the time, as would his successor and subordinate commanders in the field, paid generous tribute to their valuable contributions to the campaign. When the number of British Army units multiplied, so squadrons expanded to become an accepted, integral part of warfare. In addition to reconnaissance, aeroplanes came to patrol the forward trench-lines, protect troops from hostile aircraft and liaise closely with the artillery, infantry and tanks. They bombed targets on the battlefield and attacked balloons from which observers directed German guns onto Allied positions. As early as November 1914, bombers attacked the Zeppelin works at Friedrichshafen inside enemy territory, and in 1916 they began systematic, long-distance raids against enemy manufacturing facilities; the forerunner of a more sustained bombing campaign two years later on Germany's industrial heartland.

Whether by doing this 'high above the squalor and the mud', airmen recreated the legend of medieval chivalry is debatable.

DH9 bomber deliveries only began in January 1918. Its Siddley Puma engine had to be de-rated from 300 hp to 230 hp. Trenchard commented 'I do not know who is responsible for deciding upon the DH9 but I would have thought that no-one would imagine that we should be able to carry out long distance bombing raids with machines inferior in performance to those we use at present.' The learning curve was steep and occasionally punctuated with failures. (*Spellmount*)

I

Countdown to Conflict
'Are you ready for War?'

On 24 November 1906, before either an airship (lighter-than-air machine) or aeroplane (heavier-than-air machine) had flown in the United Kingdom, the *Daily Mail* proclaimed:

> Great Britain and the British Empire stand in the van of progress. We know more about the science of aeronautics than any other country in the world. As yet we have not attempted to apply our knowledge but silently and quietly we have been studying the subject.

At first sight, the newspaper's claim appears outrageous, given that Ferdinand Count von Zeppelin's airship, powered by two Daimler engines, had successfully taken to the air in 1900 and three years afterwards the Wright brothers flew an aeroplane. However, for almost two centuries, Britain had been actively involved in efforts to conquer the air, and the Royal Engineers been prominent in seeking to exploit its military potential. In 1784 a Royal Engineer officer ascended in a hot-air balloon from Moorfields in London, and British interest in aeronautical research gathered pace during the nineteenth century, Henry Coxwell and James Glaisher reached 37,000ft in a balloon. Sir George Cayley defined the fundamental requirements for an aeroplane to fly: the curvature and angle of its wings, lateral and horizontal controls, streamlining of the body, the ability to gain and maintain lift. He experimented with non-powered, man-lifting gliders, but died before invention of an efficient internal combustion engine. Orville Wright believed that Cayley, 'knew more of the principles of aeronautics than any of his predecessors, and as much as any that followed him up to the end of the nineteenth century'. Wright also paid special tribute to the work of an earlier British scientist, John Smeaton, in connection with air pressure.

Operationally, during the nineteenth century, a British officer served with a Federal balloon unit in the American Civil War and observation balloons were used during British military expeditions to Bechuanaland (1884) and the Sudan (1885). In 1890, establishment of the Royal Engineers' Balloon Section formalised the role of balloons for military use, and in the Boer War (1899–1902) the British deployed them to observe and photograph enemy movements and to transmit signals via semaphore flags and lamps. Shortly after the Boer War ended, tethered man-lifting kites were developed for the same purposes, and the Royal Engineers added these to their responsibilities.

In 1899, Percy Pilcher, university lecturer and former naval officer, was killed at Market Harborough, Leicestershire, when his rudder-controlled 'soaring machine' (glider) crashed. Sir Walter Raleigh, official British air historian of the First World War, speculated that had

Pilcher survived 'it seems not unlikely the he would have been the first man to navigate the air on a power-driven machine.' And the *Daily Mail*'s reference to 'the British Empire' may have been prompted by a belief, until he refuted the rumour 25 years later, that a New Zealand farmer Richard Pearse had beaten the Wrights into the air on 31 March 1903.

Significantly, in 1906 neither Zeppelin's nor the Wrights' feats were universally recognised. LZ (Luftschiff Zeppelin) 1 flew for only eighteen minutes and was followed by less successful trials. Not until 1908 did LZ.3 attract firm German military interest.

During the morning of 17 December 1903, Orville Wright made the first controlled flight in an aeroplane. Above sand dunes on an island off the Atlantic coast of North Carolina close to the settlement of Kitty Hawk, he remained aloft for twelve seconds and travelled 120ft. Between them Orville and his brother Wilbur completed four flights that morning, the last covering 852ft. Wilbur Wright recorded that the brothers 'returned home, knowing that the age of the flying machine had come at last'.

Others were less convinced. Their feats that day are now undisputed, but for some years afterwards considerable doubt existed about the brothers' claims. Sceptics dismissed the Wrights as fanciful 'bicycle mechanics' (a reference to their regular occupation), and in 1906 the Paris edition of the *New York Herald* ran the headline 'Flyers or Liars'. The following year the president of the French Aero-Club denounced the Wright's 'phantom machine' and in 1908 *L'Illustration* declared hazy photographs of a Wright machine in the air a 'fabrication'.

The Wrights did little to discourage such derogatory comments. Only five locals witnessed the historic events that chilly morning, and the brothers from Dayton, Ohio, refused to reveal technical data about either their achievement or their aeroplane. Starved of authentic information, reporters gave full rein to their vivid imaginations. In vain did Wilbur Wright condemn 'a fictitious story incorrect in almost every detail'.

Despite the aura of disbelief, once news leaked out in 1904 that the brothers were conducting more flights near Dayton, two Royal Engineer officers, Lieutenant Colonel (Lt Col) J.E. Capper and Colonel (Col) J.L.B. Templer, travelled to Ohio. They were greeted politely, but the Wrights declined to discuss their work or even to show the two British soldiers their machine. Nevertheless, on returning to England, Capper warned that, if the Wrights were to achieve what they predicted

> ... we may shortly have as accessories of warfare scouting machines which will go at a great pace and be independent of obstacles on the ground, whilst offering from their elevated position unrivalled opportunities of ascertaining what is occurring in the heart of the enemy's country.

In 1905, afraid that others might gain public recognition after copying their technique and deny them financial benefit for their achievement, the Wrights had a major change of heart. They approached their own and foreign governments for a commercial arrangement regarding use of their expertise. In 1906, their hand was legally strengthened when a patent was registered in the United States in respect of the three-control system they had fashioned: elevator to control pitch; rudder for stability; and wing warping for roll or banking. Similar patents were secured in several European countries including Britain. Between 1905 and 1909 either directly, via Capper or through an appointed agent, the Wrights sought to do business with the War Office four times and the Admiralty once. The stumbling block, which other European countries also encountered, was cost. Before the Wrights would even demonstrate their machine, allegedly they required a guaranteed order worth £20,000, plus a further sum to train pilots.

Moreover, quite apart from the Wrights, great strides were undoubtedly being made in France, where pioneers fitted front wheels to their machines instead of skids, allowing them to dispense with the rail along which the brothers launched their aeroplanes. Proud of his nation's advances in aviation, the president of the French Aero Club, Ernest Archdeacon, declared that, 'to the genius of France is reserved the glorious mission of initiating the world into the conquest of the air.' After seeing Brazilian-born Alberto Santos-Dumont fly 80yds (73m) in a biplane powered by a 24hp engine in France in 1906, the British newspaper proprietor Lord Northcliffe concluded: 'England is no longer an island … It means the aerial chariots of a foe descending on British soil if war comes.'

Yet official support for aeronautical research and experiment in Britain, echoing the *Daily Mail's* earlier complacency, remained at best lukewarm. In 1907, the Secretary for War assured his department 'that aeroplanes would *never* fly', and the following year his successor, while conceding that they had, maintained, 'we do not consider that aeroplanes will be of any possible use for war purposes.' Nonetheless, some assistance was already being given to two contrasting figures. A serving officer, Lieutenant (Lt) John Dunne, was encouraged by the War Office to test his embryo aeroplane on a grouse moor in Scotland. In England at Farnborough, near Aldershot in Hampshire, a flamboyant former American circus performer and in 1911 naturalised Briton, Samuel Franklin Cody, was striving to perfect his own aeroplane after working on airships and man-lifting kites. Dunne's efforts ended in failure, but on 16 May 1908 Cody travelled for 50ft an estimated 5–6ins above the grass. Precisely five months later, he made the first recognised aeroplane flight in England over 1,390ft.

Almost immediately, hopes of developing British military aviation were dashed. The year after Cody's flight a committee, 'dominated' according to one critic by 'some of the older Service men … [who] showed an extraordinary lack of imagination', ruled against further War Office investment in aeroplane development. Thus far, German authorities had spent £400,000 on military aeronautics, the French some £50,000, the British £5,000; about half of that on aeroplanes. On 23 July 1909, a press release from Whitehall explained: 'When it is possible to cross the Channel … and to land at a fixed point, the War Office may be able to regard recent experiments seriously'.

Two days later, Louis Blériot did just that by landing his monoplane near Dover Castle. He flew 33½ miles (54km) in 37 minutes and incidentally, pocketed a £1,000 prize. The *Daily Graphic* exclaimed that the aeroplane could no longer be regarded as 'a toy … What M. Blériot can do in 1909 a hundred, nay a thousand, aeroplanes may do in five years time.' The security implications were self-evident. Lord Montagu, a motor car enthusiast impressed by the military possibilities of aviation after watching Wilbur Wright fly in France in 1908, warned that 'aerial machines [are] certain to play an important part in all future warfare'. *The Times'* defence correspondent reinforced Montagu's prediction by stressing the growing size of Germany's air fleet, whilst an exasperated aviation pioneer Claude Grahame-White, who was among several Britons to qualify as pilots in France, toured the country with 'Wake Up England' painted on his biplane's wings. Quoting an unidentified Russian, who insisted that 'it is now clear that future wars will be begun in the air', Graham-White forecast three types of machine: one carrying 'a machine-gun or a gun throwing an explosive shell'; another capable of 'detailed reconnoitring'; the third able to carry out 'swift comprehensive survey work'.

Caution, however, was understandable and military scepticism predictable. Air power protagonists were claiming a revolution in warfare akin to the advent of battlefield artillery in

Samuel Franklin Cody. Flamboyant American circus performer and naturalised Briton. Cody is credited with the first aeroplane flight in the United Kingdom at Farnborough, Hants, on 16 October 1908. He was killed in a flying accident August 1913. Given a military funeral and burial at Aldershot. *(IWM RAE-0789a)*

the fourteenth century and the replacement of sail by steam 500 years later. *Aero* magazine reported that 'an influential officer' attending army manoeuvres had observed: 'It is all very well saying that we should saddle ourselves with a lot of these aeroplanes. But in nine cases out of ten, they would not be a scrap of good.' Cavalry commanders maintained they would go too fast to collect useful information about enemy troop movements and Field Marshal Sir William Nicholson, Chief of the Imperial General Staff (CIGS), deemed aviation 'a useless and expensive fad, advocated by a few individuals whose ideas are unworthy of attention'. The Admiralty agreed; the aeroplane 'would not be of any practical use to the Naval Service'. Tryggve Gran, a future RFC pilot, later reflected:

> Unfortunately, the English State did not take aviation seriously. They [sic] regarded the flying machine and the airship as experiments with great possibilities perhaps half a century in the future. There was no need for haste.

Across the Channel, French aeronautical experiments before and after Blériot's feat were conducted during well-attended demonstrations and international air shows. Advances south of the Alps, especially in military aviation, evolved virtually unnoticed until November 1911, when Italian airmen began dropping bombs (modified hand-grenades) in Tripolitania, North Africa. The previous month they had successfully used aircraft to observe and track Turkish troop movements after the Italian invasion of that territory. *The Times* acidly declared: 'No one could have watched the work of the Italian airships and aeroplanes in Tripoli without being … firmly convinced of the practical value of aviation in war.'

In fact, despite the dismissive comments of senior military officers and lukewarm political opinion, faltering steps had already begun in Britain to acknowledge that reality. An Army Order of 28 February 1911 announced the aim of 'creating a body of expert airmen … the training and instruction of men in handling kites, balloons and aeroplanes and other forms of aircraft'. A month later, the Air Battalion of the Royal Engineers was established and thirteen months afterwards absorbed into the newly-created Royal Flying Corps (RFC). In recommending formation of the RFC, the Under Secretary of State for War, Col J.E.B. Seely, made clear that 'actual warfare in Tripoli' had been persuasive. So were 'foreign manoeuvres', France being the first European power to include aeroplanes in its annual manoeuvres in 1910. In addition to developing long-range airships, Germany too, had begun to pay more attention to aeroplanes in the face of evident French progress. Following a 30km (18½mls) flight by Henri Farman in October 1908, a member of the German General Staff remarked that 'a new epoch of aviation had dawned'.

In January 1912, Seely warned of a serious deficiency in trained military pilots: 'At the present time we have in this country … of actual flying men in the army about eleven and … in the navy eight. France has about 263, so we are what you might call behind.' The Royal Warrant of 13 April 1912, which established the RFC with a Military Wing and a Naval Wing, foresaw the new body comprising 165 officers, 1,264 other ranks, 66 aeroplanes and 95 'mechanised transport vehicles'. Seven aeroplane squadrons, each with twelve machines, and an eighth equipped with airships and man-lifting kites were ultimately planned, of which only the latter (No 1) and two aeroplane squadrons (Nos 2 and 3) were formed by the end of 1912. Maj C.J. Burke, commanding No 2 Squadron (Sqn), warned of the need for effective training: 'An aeroplane will live in any wind and a lifeboat at sea, but they both want good and experienced men at the tiller.'

The recruitment of aircrew for the RFC did not go smoothly. Officers had to seek approval from their superiors and many were deterred on the grounds that transfer or secondment would harm their promotion and long-term career prospects. If they persisted and passed the requisite medical, potential pilots had to qualify for a Royal Aero Club certificate at a personal cost of £75, refunded only when further military training had been successfully completed.

Nevertheless, the RFC slowly took shape. Two of its future commanders, Lt Col F.H. Sykes and Brigadier-General (Brig Gen) David Henderson (aged 49 and reputedly the oldest pilot in the world) learnt to fly in 1911. A third was 39-year-old Maj H.M. Trenchard. In July 1912, he began private flying lessons at Brooklands, near Weybridge, Surrey, where a grass airstrip lay in the centre of the famous motor racing track, with the fearsome warning that inefficient pupils frequently finished nose down in the output of a nearby sewage farm. He avoided that pungent disgrace and over thirteen days completed 1hr 4mins in the air to secure Royal Aero Club flying certificate No 270.

The Aero Club, granted the prefix 'Royal' nine years later, had been formed in 1901 to promote first ballooning then heavier-than-air flight. It rapidly acquired international recognition and the right to certify the competence of pilots, who had mastered basic flying skills. Trenchard's certificate allowed him to attend the RFC's Central Flying School (CFS) for military training, where his 'enviable pluck and perseverance' were noted. However, one instructor remarked that, perched in a Maurice Farman Longhorn biplane, he looked 'as comfortable as a buzzard in a budgerigar's cage'.

Hugh Trenchard was not given preferential treatment; tuition and qualification at this time were rudimentary. Also in 1912, Joubert de la Ferté qualified after 1hr 50mins in the air. On leave at the family home near Weybridge, the young Royal Field Artillery officer was inspired to fly after watching the 'motley collection of stick and string kites, mostly unairworthy, but very exciting affairs' wobble aloft from Brooklands. The following year the founder of the Supermarine aircraft company, Noel Pemberton-Billing, bet aeroplane designer Geoffrey de Havilland £500 that he could learn to fly in a single day. A fascinated spectator recorded: 'We who were watching held our breath at the hair-raising behaviour of his machine as it stalled at every right-hand turn and performed other amazing and unrehearsed feats.' But Pemberton-Billing won the wager.

The CFS opened at Upavon on Salisbury Plain on 19 June 1912. Its airfield astride exposed upland was dubbed 'Siberia' by disenchanted arrivals who found that their living quarters were at the foot of an uninviting, steep slope. The length of the first course, twelve weeks instead of four months, was determined by a shortage of available aeroplanes (just seven), which also meant halving the intended number of participants from the intended sixty. The following year, ninety pilots qualified, the bulk of them going to the Military Wing. The intention of making this particular training establishment smart as well as efficient was signalled by the appointment of a guards officer as its first adjutant.

Lack of aeroplanes for the CFS highlighted a major problem for both wings of the RFC. Britain undoubtedly lagged behind France in aeroplane manufacture and design, so the bulk of machines initially came from across the Channel. Significantly, French words like 'fuselage', 'nacelle' and 'aileron' have become accepted terms for parts of an aeroplane. By 1914, around twenty aviation firms had sprung up in Britain. Several were subsidiaries of large armament companies like Vickers and Armstrong Whitworth, some were grafted on to engineering concerns like J. Samuel White at Cowes, Isle of Wight, or the Coventry Ordnance Works. Many were small enterprises founded by military aviation enthusiasts. Alliott Verdon-Roe, who like Cody designed and flew his own machines, formed A.V. Roe & Co (Avro) with his brother Humphrey. Claude Graham-White, who had qualified to fly in France and sensationally publicised the cause of military aviation, established his firm at Hendon, Middlesex, the Bristol and Colonial Aeroplane was in that city, Supermarine Aviation at Southampton and William Beardmore & Co near Glasgow.

Whatever its size, every aviation business suffered from lack of government backing, and often had to fund the design and construction of its machines in the hope of securing a contract from one of the services. Firms built machines according to designs produced by the Royal Aircraft Factory (RAF) – the former Army Aircraft Factory renamed in 1911 – at Farnborough, like Armstrong Whitworth in the case of the BE2a, or their own staff in a private venture (pv). Orders for three machines at a time proved an exception, and design practices had yet to be refined. Aeroplanes were constructed by hand without standard drawings, so the last machine of a batch might vary substantially from the first. Without the aid of draughtsmen or technical drawings, Tommy Sopwith issued verbal instructions to six mechanics to build his first machine. Fortunately, the Admiralty was impressed, which allowed him to move from a rickety shed, lacking water and lit by paraffin lamps, to more substantial premises at Kingston-upon-Thames, Surrey. Vickers co-operated briefly but unsuccessfully with the Frenchman Robert Esnault-Pelterie before exhibiting its own pv two-seater FB (fighting biplane) 1 at the Olympia Air Show in 1913. Prior to the outbreak of war, Vickers, one of the larger manufacturers, completed just twenty-six aeroplanes. Avro, formed in 1910 and renting a shed at Brooklands, struggled to finance the production of its 504 biplane, which would prove invaluable in training and operational roles during the coming conflict.

At Farnborough, the RAF held a watching brief over all British aeroplane manufacturers. Initially, with a staff of 100 and responsible for aeroplane design, the RAF's role was defined as research and development together with supervision of, and advice to, private firms. Through a legal loophole, officially only authorised to repair damaged aeroplanes, the RAF contrived to transform wrecks into virtually new aeroplanes. In 1911, for example, a Voisin pusher (its engine behind the wing) emerged as a BE (Blériot Experimental) tractor (the engine at the front of the fuselage). On another occasion, a damaged monoplane came out as a biplane. Effectively, the RAF had become another manufacturer by stealth. Its output, however, was not extensive, and overall British aeroplane production remained sparse. A post-war Air Ministry publication recalled these early days: 'When aeroplanes were first put to military use, they could be kept in working order by a motor mechanic, a sail-maker (for the canvas) and a carpenter'. The First Lord of the Admiralty, Winston Churchill, took lessons in one of these dubious constructions:

> I noticed on several occasions defects in the machine in which we had been flying – a broken wire, a singed wing, a cracked strut – which were the subject of mutual congratulation between my pilot and myself once we had safely returned to terra firma.

Despite equipment deficiencies – No 3 Sqn had ten machines of different types and two motor vehicles for transport, one an officer's Mercedes – within months of its formation the RFC began to prove its worth. During army manoeuvres in September 1912, seven machines were allocated to each of the opposing formations, the commanders of which lauded their achievements. The following year, crews managed to identify troop movements from 6,000ft, but over the four day exercise five of the twelve aeroplanes involved either crashed or force-landed.

Apart from this mechanical unreliability, the relay of information posed a major problem. With no air-to-ground communication system, machines had to land at headquarters, which in turn passed on the reconnaissance data to individual units. By the time that process had been completed, the cavalry and often infantry had vanished over the horizon. Attempts to drop messages in weighted bags to forward units had scant success.

Various other ideas were tested. No 3 Sqn used cameras owned by its officers to photograph the defences of the Isle of Wight from 5,000ft. At Hythe, Kent, trials were carried out on the feasibility of arming aeroplanes with machine-guns; weight and an adequate field of fire being primary concerns. On 13 April 1913, the first RFC night flight took place on Salisbury Plain, a perilous undertaking with inadequate instruments. Lighting of petrol flares on the ground to assist night landings together with illumination in the cockpit to show up the compass and tachometer only marginally reduced the danger. In May 1913, Captain (Capt) C.A.H. Longcroft flew 420 miles from Farnborough to Montrose, Scotland, in three stages. Six months afterwards, he managed a 500-mile reverse trip via Portsmouth non-stop, using a long-range tank of his own design.

The War Office soon recognised a need to co-ordinate the efforts to improve a military aeroplane's capability and performance. Royal Engineer Capt Herbert Musgrave witnessed

Workmen fashion wooden propeller blades. *(Peter Jackson)*

Blériot's landing in 1909 and three years afterwards qualified as a pilot at the Bristol Flying School on Salisbury Plain, while on leave. In 1913, he was promoted temporary major in command of an RFC experimental unit at Larkhill. Musgrave's remit was extensive: research connected with balloons, kites, bomb dropping, photography, artillery co-operation and wireless telegraphy. As back-up, Musgrave could call on the National Physical Laboratory for scientific work and squadron commanders for practical trials. On 1 September 1913, Brig Gen David Henderson was appointed head of a new War Office department (the Directorate of Military Aeronautics) signifying recognition of the importance of aviation in warfare. Until then the Master-General of the Ordnance (MGO), as head of the Royal Engineers, had offi-cially retained control of army aviation.

This all seemed promising, but the RFC still had to rely heavily on other countries for aero engines (principally France) and magnetos used for ignition of an internal-combustion engine (Germany). Advances in Britain were further hampered by the effective creation of separate air arms for the two services. In 1909, an air enthusiast Frank McClean, bought a level tract of land at Eastchurch on the Isle of Sheppey, off the north Kent coast, and persuaded the Admiralty to allow four officers to receive flying tuition, which like the aeroplanes they used came free of charge. Henceforth, Eastchurch became the principal training centre for Royal

Navy aviators. During Autumn 1912 an Air Department of the Admiralty was fashioned with Capt Murray Sueter RN as director, responsible 'in regard to all matters connected with the Naval Air Service'. On 1 July 1914, the Admiralty went even further in declaring unilateral independence by renaming the Naval Wing of the RFC the Royal Naval Air Service (RNAS). Apart from complicating strategic co-operation with the Army, this heralded four years of inter-service rivalry and fierce competition for manufacturing resources. However, one area of potential conflict was removed in 1913, when Army airships, their equipment and personnel passed to the Royal Navy, which would henceforth be 'solely responsible for the development of lighter-than-air craft' on the assumption that airships were more suited to fleet support than battlefield activity.

Against this background of bureaucratic manoeuvring and production shortcomings, war became increasingly likely and ultimately inevitable. Britain's convention with Russia to solve their territorial disputes signed in 1907, had effectively divided Europe into two armed camps: the so-called triple Entente (bilateral agreements involving Britain, France and Russia) and the firm treaty commitments of the Triple Alliance (Germany, Austria-Hungary and Italy). A series of disputes in the opening years of the twentieth century, heightened by a dangerous naval race between Germany and Britain revolving round the construction of modern battleships or 'dreadnoughts', had made the political and military atmosphere poisonous. Britain was formally committed neither to France nor Russia should war break out, but from 1839 had been a guarantor of Belgian independence. More recently, staff officers had held exploratory military and naval talks with France. These exchanges were not legally binding, but it would be difficult to remain aloof in the event of hostilities.

Ever since Austria-Hungary's annexation of Bosnia and Herzegovina in 1908, her relations with Serbia had smouldered and not been eased by that country's active involvement in the 1912–13 Balkan Wars with Turkey. The assassination of the Austrian heir, Archduke Franz Ferdinand, and his wife in Sarajevo on 28 June 1914 began a train of ominous reactions. It saw Austria-Hungary issuing a swingeing ultimatum to Serbia on the basis of a shadowy connection with the assassins, Germany mobilising in support of Austria-Hungary, Russia backing Serbia and France honouring her treaty obligations to Russia. On 3 August 1914, Germany invaded Belgium, and the following day Britain entered the First World War.

As the countdown to conflict quickened, even before Sarajevo the Army Estimates for 1914 provided £1 million for the RFC – double that for the previous year and a far cry from the £5,000 set aside by the War Office for military aeronautics five years previously. British firms now received orders for up to a dozen machines at a time. In June Lt Col F.H. Sykes, its commander, gathered the military wing at Netheravon, Wiltshire, for a month's intensive training, and steps were taken to publicise the RFC's proficiency. On 22 June, twelve machines flew past the saluting base at the King's Birthday Parade in Aldershot. Four days later, the Prime Minister reviewed the military wing at RFC headquarters at Netheravon. Five squadrons were on parade, a sixth (No 1) in the process of converting to aeroplanes from airships, and a seventh squadron was being formed at Farnborough. Ready to support the British Expeditionary Force (BEF) across the Channel, the RFC, in essence its Military Wing since the RNAS's defection, formally mobilised on 3 August; a week after the RNAS had been put on a war footing.

When asked by Major-General (Maj Gen) Henry Wilson, Director of Military Operations at the War Office, on 25 July 'Are you ready for war?', Maj Sefton Brancker, a qualified pilot in the Directorate of Military Aeronautics, exclaimed: 'Good God, no!' Hostilities were ten days away.

2

Baptism of Fire, August–October 1914
'A corps of adventurous young men'

Nominally, the RFC possessed 179 aeroplanes, the RNAS (including seaplanes) 93, but many counted on paper had not yet left the factory. An official post-war summary revealed that in reality, the RNAS could muster 'about 50 … usable' machines, the RFC only 90, of which 64 initially went to France, four more having crashed before leaving England.

In August 1914, the French Army possessed 317 front line machines; the German 245. Russia could reputedly field 244 (including four-engine machines designed by Igor Sikorsky). However, France had an extensive eastern frontier abutting Germany to protect. Facing war on two fronts, Germany opposed France and Russia, Russia had to deal with Austria-Hungary as well as Germany. The RFC's role, to provide support for the BEF of four infantry divisions and one cavalry division, was altogether less demanding.

Aware that Germany might encounter opponents to her east and west, Field Marshal Alfred Count von Schlieffen, Chief of the German General Staff, had devised a plan which thereafter bore his name, based on the assumption that Russia would be unable to mobilise for six weeks. By then, German armies would have swept through the Low Countries, descended on Paris and forced France into submission.

Schlieffen died before the outbreak of the First World War, and his successor Helmuth von Moltke, afraid of Germany being cut off from overseas supplies by a naval blockade, excluded The Netherlands from the Schlieffen Plan to leave an 'air hole' for maritime trade. He would advance only through Belgium and Luxembourg. Moreover, Moltke deployed more troops than Schlieffen intended along the French border thus ignoring his predecessor's alleged dying breath: 'Keep the right wing strong.' The French, meanwhile, had not read the script. They crafted their own Plan 17 rapidly to attack eastwards to recover their provinces of Alsace and Lorraine lost to Germany after the Franco-Prussian War (1870–1). Nor did the Russians intend to play ball, being poised to attack Austria-Hungary in Galicia and Germany in East Prussia.

After a declaration of war, the BEF would deploy in support of the French left wing. Traditionally, protection of the national shores was the responsibility of the Royal Navy, with the War Office guarding against invasion and physical occupation of the homeland. The advent of air power blurred these divisions. Although the War Office did not formally surrender its historical role, a *de facto* agreement was reached between the two services. The RFC would support the BEF in the field, the RNAS look after home defence as well as serving the needs of the fleet, taking 'action against Zeppelins' and 'bombing enemy places of military importance'. In August 1914, the RNAS had grenades or 20lb bombs with which to attack hostile airships, together with two aeroplanes and one airship equipped with machine-guns.

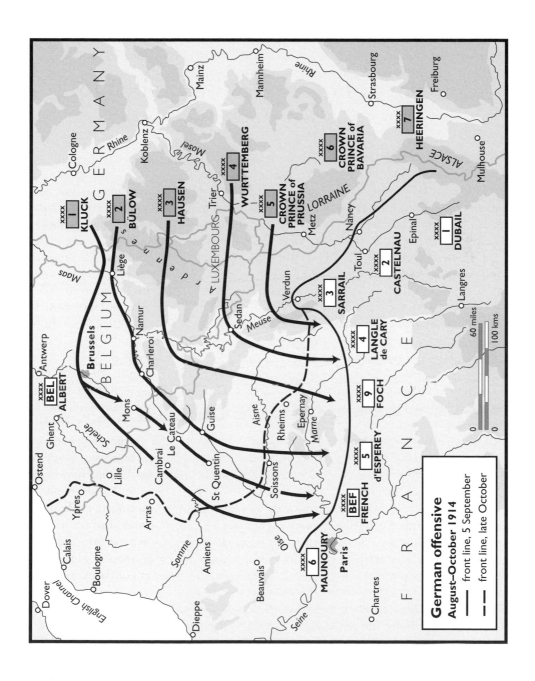

**German offensive
August–October 1914**

front line, 5 September
front line, late October

Anticipating only a reconnaissance role, the RFC had provided its aeroplanes neither with machine-guns nor bombs.

On 9 August the BEF began to cross the Channel, protected by sixteen seaplanes and two airships of the RNAS, prior to deploying in an arc from Maubeuge to Le Cateau in north-east France on the left of French formations. In support, four squadrons of the RFC had been ordered to concentrate at Dover on 7 August and two days later cross the Channel. Their horses, vehicles and ground staff personnel would travel independently to designated embarkation ports. From 'Southampton Docks', two brothers 'Willie and Jim' with No 3 Sqn's non-flying contingent wrote 'just a line to say goodbye' to their mother, adding: 'We leave for somewhere in France, probably tonight'. William Thomas James and James Thomas Byford McCudden were the sons of a retired Royal Engineers' sergeant major and both had joined that Corps as buglers. When living in Sheerness, they were enthralled by the antics of primitive machines from Eastchurch and both transferred to the infant RFC. William qualified as an NCO pilot, but due to a shortage of aeroplanes took charge of the non-flying contingent for the Channel crossing. His younger brother, James, was an Air Mechanic 1st Class and a specialised engine fitter. But he too was intent on flying and had already been aloft as a passenger, sometimes with his brother. In August 1914, though, a glittering career as a decorated pilot appeared highly unlikely.

His brother thought otherwise, making an extraordinary forecast in a letter to his father on 3 August 1914, the day before the declaration of war:

> Jim and myself are very much in it at present, for we form part of the 'expeditionary force' and for the past week we have been busily fixing up everything, aeroplanes, motors, lorries and stores and we have everything ready.

William expected them to go to France on the following Tuesday or Wednesday. He protested that he could not reveal 'much, but I must say that everything had been planned very cleverly. Half of our machines are already at Dover and Eastchurch.' William enclosed £1 for his mother, 'for I hear that food is going up already'. He promised to let his parents know as soon as they moved off, 'and you can bet your boots that the McCudden Syndicate will not be missing when there is something doing'. He predicted: 'I can see Jim coming home with a V.C. or something of the sort.'

In keeping with contemporary optimism, at Montrose in Scotland, No 2 Sqn aircrew locked their rooms and pinned notices on the doors stating that nothing must be touched; they would be back after Christmas. Each squadron decided what would be carried in its aeroplanes. No 2 Sqn opted for revolvers for the crew, binoculars, a spare set of goggles, repair tools, a water bottle filled with boiled water, a small stove, a haversack full of biscuits, cold meat, a piece of chocolate and packet of 'soup-making material'. Setting out over the Channel was a precarious business. In No 3 Sqn Lt Philip Joubert de la Ferté was issued with a motor tyre inner tube to wear round his waist for inflation prior to an emergency descent onto water.

Passage of the squadrons did not go smoothly. Nos 2, 3 and 4 duly converged on Dover; though one No 3 Sqn machine crashed on take-off from Netheravon on Salisbury Plain, killing its crew. At Dover the squadrons were delayed four days beyond their scheduled departure, before which pilots were issued with six miles to one inch maps of France and Belgium in readiness for a dawn take-off. At 0820 on 13 August, Lt Hubert Harvey-Kelly of No 2 Sqn (according to another squadron member, a 'noted individualist' with 'a lighthearted and gay approach') was the first pilot to land a BE2a in France. Shortly after crossing the French coast

Above left: James Thomas Byford McCudden. Joined Royal Engineers as bugler, transferred to RFC as mechanic and went to France in ground crew in August 1914. After qualifying as pilot, he accounted for fifty-four enemy machines and was awarded the VC aged 22 in April 1918. He was killed in an air accident July 1918. *(IWM Q 46099)*

Above right: John Anthony McCudden. Received flying instruction from brother James. Shot down, aged 21, in March 1918 while serving with No 84 Sqn. John McCudden was buried with full military honours by the Germans. *(IWM Q 68559)*

some of No 4 Squadron mistakenly landed in a rough field causing damage to their machines. The fourth squadron, No 5, did not leave Gosport, Hampshire, until 14 August, and three of its machines came down on the way to Dover. Fortunately, their pilots were unharmed and later flew replacement aeroplanes to France. In the words of Duncan Le Geyt Pitcher, an observer at the time and later senior RFC officer, 'a few BE2s and Avros … staggered across the Channel to co-operate with the Army in France'.

The RFC field headquarters (RFC HQ) under Brig Gen Sir David Henderson left Farnborough on 11 August to establish itself at Amiens two days later. On 15 August the Aircraft Park (the RFC's supply and maintenance base in the field) went from Farnborough to its embarkation port, Avonmouth near Bristol, with only four crated Sopwith Tabloids. Of the other sixteen aeroplanes on strength, half had joined the front-line squadrons, the balance being flown directly to Amiens, which the main body reached on 21 August to co-locate with RFC HQ. Not without alarms. Its disembarkation at Boulogne caused army authorities to signal: 'An unnumbered unit without aeroplanes which calls itself an Aircraft Park has arrived, what shall we do with it?' The four operational squadrons had already settled at Maubeuge on 16 August in close contact with the BEF.

Despite the popular belief that the war would be short-lived, positive steps were made to train newcomers for an expanded force in England. On 7 August Maj (temporary Lt Col)

An injured airman is helped by colleagues after returning from a flight. *(Peter Jackson)*

H.M. Trenchard was moved from assistant commandant at the CFS to command the RFC (Military Wing) and depot at Farnborough. He found a sparse assembly of aeroplanes, 'many being taken from the Central Flying School, others being bought from private collectors and makers'. With this unpromising collection, he was expected to build up new squadrons and train recruits, including non-flying personnel. Strenuous efforts were made to persuade 'traded men' in the Army to volunteer for the RFC. An applicant's conditions of service would be modified to permit four years in the colours from the date of transfer. After undergoing a period of special instruction, the recruit would be required 'to perform duties in connection with the management and navigation of all forms of aircraft'.

Non-flying personnel were also obtained via direct entry. One such volunteer was Charles Callender from Stockton-on Tees, who undertook to serve for the duration of the war as a mechanic. Sent to Farnborough for initial training, he had a rude awakening. Standing with other recruits outside the orderly office of the new barracks, he was startled by 'a big, burly sergeant major' bawling: 'Jump to it, you're in the army now … We tame lions here'. Callender recalled that, 'soon we were to find the How, Where and Why'. The recruits were assured by the stentorian NCO that British discipline was 'the finest in the world' and 100 British Serviceman were worth 'a couple of thousand of any other breed'. Intriguingly, Callender added: 'Little did the sergeant major know that he himself would later be caught in the disciplinary machine, buttons cut off his tunic on the barrack square.'

Scarcely had the blood-curdling welcome abated than a corporal appeared clad 'in khaki, breeches, puttees and double breasted tunic'. He wore a cap 'with two brass buttons at the front that shone like diamonds' and marched them off to the Quartermaster's Store, where Callender was allocated a number (4953), 'viciously stamped on the wrist with an indelible stamp and it seared to the heart'. He was issued with his RFC kit and instructed to pack his civvies in a parcel to send home – the last he saw of them for four and a half years. Fourteen days of 'hellish training' followed, 'a man could never forget his training and number as long as he lived'.

As an Air Mechanic 2nd Class, Charles Callender received 2/- (10p) a day. Reveille was at 5am, first parade 5.45, by which time men had to be shaved. Drill continued until 6.30, 'when your head was just like a spinning top, one of the humming variety … Dismiss and you had to run like hell to the dining hall if you wanted a cup of coffee and a biscuit.'

After Farnborough, Callender went to Brooklands, where another RFC training centre had been established. For the first two weeks he was on guard duty day and night, two hours on, four hours off. 'I had often wanted to see the motor racing track at Brooklands, but at this time I was sick of the sight of it.' He had never fired a rifle, but on guard was issued with five rounds in the magazine. The NCOs were 'vicious' and constantly tried to catch

> … us rookies out at the most trivial thing. The language was a little bit alien to me. It seemed that every other word was profane but then I was to learn that this was part of the Serviceman's stock in trade. It gave him height, strength and weight.

Callender was equally unimpressed on seeing in flight a Henri Farman biplane, which appeared 'just a framework of wires, struts and tubes. The pilot sitting in a bucket seat among the bits and pieces liable it seemed to be thrown out at any time'. He added that 'more modern' machines were being built in small factories 'dotted around the aerodrome on the concrete race track'; one being the Martinsyde Scout, which 'would play a very important part in my life in the Service'.

At the Front, the first two RFC reconnaissance flights in France had occurred on 19 August. Capt Philip Joubert de la Ferté and Lt Gilbert Mapplebeck were ordered to identify the positions of Belgian troops in the Nivelle-Genappe area with Mapplebeck additionally required to locate German cavalry believed to be near Gembloux. Shortly after taking off at 9.30am, the two pilots lost contact in cloud. Joubert subsequently landed at Tournai and Courtrai, before returning to Maubeuge eight hours later with absolutely no information about the Belgians. Mapplebeck got lost over Brussels, but did find Gembloux and reported a small body of cavalry heading south-east. The reconnaissance exercise was not, therefore, an unqualified success. But the airmen were over unfamiliar territory equipped only with a map and compass.

Getting lost was not the sole hazard RFC crews faced. Joubert admitted to being 'rather sorry' as he watched British troops arrive in force. 'Up to that moment', airmen had only been fired on by their French allies. Now they were targeted by the British, who were wary of any type of aeroplane, a 'playful habit … [which] did detract somewhat from our expectation of life'. Years afterwards, Joubert wrote that 'to this day I can remember the roar of musketry that greeted two of our machines as they left the aerodrome and crossed the main Maubeuge–Mons road, along which a British column was proceeding'. Cautious aviators painted a Union Flag on the underside of their wings – to little avail. Such hazards were not confined to the RFC. When serving as a cavalryman before joining the air force, Manfred von Richthofen admitted to opening fire on anything that flew: 'I had no idea that German machines bore crosses and the enemy's cockades'.

The French Plan 17 was launched on 14 August; two days later Russian troops crossed the frontier of East Prussia. Both advances would ultimately fail, but in the short term they absorbed German airship and aeroplane resources to the detriment of support for the Schlieffen Plan. Although delayed by strong fortifications at Liège until 17 August, three days later the Germans took Brussels and by 22 August their columns had reached Charleroi in south-east Belgium. That day, the RFC carried out extensive reconnaissance operations. In a Blériot monoplane, Joubert and his observer flew at 2,000ft to the Charleroi region and reported that the French to the east were being driven back. British intelligence officers unfamiliar with aerial reconnaissance refused to believe them. That evening, therefore, British infantry marched towards Mons, unaware that their right flank was now unprotected. Another flight late in the day reported a strong body of enemy troops (General Alexander von Kluck's First Army) advancing westwards out of Brussels. Sir David Henderson was so concerned that he personally took this report to Army GHQ, and it was subsequently decided that the British would hold Mons for another 24 hours to enable French redeployment. Had Joubert's report been believed, the costly rearguard action at Mons on 23 August might have been avoided. But these were early days and the RFC had yet to prove its worth to many soldiers.

During the evening of 22 August, a German machine appeared over Maubeuge and Lt L. da C. Penn-Gaskell persuaded Second Lieutenant (2/Lt) Louis Strange to take his No 5 Sqn Henri Farman up in pursuit. Penn-Gaskell heaved a Vickers machine-gun into the observer's cockpit, which meant that Strange could only reach 3,500ft, well short of the 5,000ft managed by the enemy machine, which serenely completed its reconnaissance. Penn-Gaskell's commanding officer forbade him to take a machine-gun aloft again. The current tactic was to deter aerial incursions by menacing manoeuvres. Height was therefore at a premium, and undoubtedly the extra weight became a liability in this respect.

Having temporarily checked the enemy at Mons, on 24 August the BEF fell back to avoid being cut off and the RFC went with it – not always in an organised fashion given the fluidity of the battlefield. Its HQ, Nos 2–5 Squadrons and the Aircraft Park were frequently out of contact with one another and effectively operated as individual entities for long periods. The Aircraft Park was ordered from Amiens to Le Havre, and amid fears that the coastal area might fall, an alternative base for supplies from Britain was established at St Nazaire in western France.

Between 24 August and 4 September, RFC HQ occupied nine different sites. Staff officer Lt the Hon Maurice Baring recorded the first chaotic halt: 'We slept, and when I say we I mean dozens of pilots, fully dressed in a barn, on the top of, and underneath, an enormous load of straw.' Lack of map-reading skills resulted in transport confusion, and ground staff had often to improvise landing grounds at short notice. Finding somewhere to put down was a constant headache for pilots, they often did not know whether the spot from which they took off would still be in friendly hands on their return.

On the enemy side Oswald Boelcke, with Richthofen destined to be a high-scoring fighter pilot, revelled in the Allies' discomfort. Like the McCudden brothers, fascinated at an early age by the sight of aircraft, Boelcke retained an active interest in aviation after joining the Army. Commissioned into a telegraphic communications unit, 'I never get tired of watching [airships and aeroplanes] and always stare at them with eyes of longing', he informed his parents. Transfer to the air service inevitably followed, but in training he experienced similar frustra-

Above left: Oswald Boelcke. Army commission in 1912, Boelcke qualified as a pilot in August 1914 and immediately saw action in Flanders. He became a celebrated fighter pilot and was awarded the *Pour le Mérite* in January 1916. Commanded Jasta 2 and credited with transforming fighter tactics. Killed in collision with one of own squadron during combat in October 1916, aged 25 and with forty victories. (*Peter Jackson*)

Above right: An Albatros C III. The figure on the left wears a Bavarian pilot's badge below his Iron Cross, and that on the right a Bavarian observer's badge. The pilot is a lieutenant. Observer's rank unknown.

tions to RFC recruits. He disliked the 70hp Taube machine, which he declared a 'brute' unable to get airborne in adverse weather conditions, and experienced 'great misery' waiting for his turn to fly one of the few available aeroplanes. Boelcke therefore had only four solo flights before his first test, which entailed executing figures of eight and landing on a fixed spot. Once hostilities commenced, he fretted that the war would be 'over before I get to the front'.

On 15 August 1914, Boelcke qualified as a pilot. After joining his elder brother's front-line unit, with the Allied retreat now well underway, on 1 September he flew his first reconnaissance operation taking Wilhelm as his observer. While British and French forces continued to pull back, Boelcke's unit moved further forward, but he complained that the Allies were 'bolting so well' that he despaired of ever catching them.

Boelcke would soon discover that, amid the undoubted confusion, the RFC was not idle. Shortly after dawn on 24 August, the day the retreat from Mons began, its machines were aloft and throughout that day reported the worrying progress of Kluck's columns. During a two and a half hour reconnaissance of twelve locations on 26 August, No 3 Sqn observer Maj L.B. Boyd-Moss identified marching troops, motor and horse-drawn transport, and howitzer and artillery activity over a wide area. At one point he recorded 'can make very little progress against wind', a stark reminder of his machine's lack of power. Boyd-Moss saw 'Cambrai in flames and occupied by Germans' after dropping 'bomb into transport' parked south of Blaugies. Then his and his pilot's luck ran out, when their machine was brought down by 'heavy infantry fire'. After burning their aeroplane, Boyd-Moss and Lt G.F. Pretyman (who on 15 September would take the first aerial photos of enemy positions) joined French troops falling back on Arras, before commandeering bicycles to reach Gouzeaucourt where a car took them to the nearest brigade HQ. Having taken off at 11.50am, they rejoined their squadron at St Quentin almost twelve hours later.

The RFC continued to provide vital information to the ground forces. Intelligence reports indicated that on 31 July Kluck's First Army positioned on the German right flank would wheel to the east of Paris, thus putting the BEF at risk. RFC reconnaissance machines confirmed the manoeuvre that day, allowing the BEF to fall back accordingly. Three days later, another critical change of direction was detected, when, flying a BE2a during the evening of 3 September in search of Kluck's cavalry, Joubert came across bivouac fires and horses being watered in streams and ponds. This confirmed that Kluck had moved further east and not south in pursuit of the BEF.

These alterations in the enemy's line of march led to the decisive First Battle of the Marne. Striving to keep pace with the German Second Army on his left, Kluck exposed his own army's right flank to a counter attack from Paris – French reinforcements being famously conveyed to the Front in taxi cabs. The opposing forces clashed on 6 September and for five days the fate of Paris lay in the balance. During that period, the RFC remained the eyes of the BEF and the beginnings of closer co-operation with individual formations was established. Aeroplanes of No 5 and No 3 squadrons reported directly to the commanders of the British I and II corps respectively. Each of these detachments had with it a machine from No 4 Sqn equipped with wireless and capable of communicating with a ground station at RFC HQ.

A major boost to RFC morale occurred when Field Marshal Sir John French paid tribute to the 'admirable work' of the corps in his despatch of 7 September to Lord Kitchener, the Secretary of State for War:

> Their skill, energy and perseverance have been beyond all praise. They have furnished me with the most complete and accurate information which has been of incalculable value in the conduct of operations. Fired at constantly both by friend and foe, and not hesitating to fly in every kind of weather, they have remained undaunted throughout.

Early doubts and suspicions voiced by field commanders had seemingly evaporated.

German retreat from the Marne on 11 September signalled the end of the Schlieffen Plan but initiated a frantic scramble by both sides to secure ground between Luxembourg and the Belgian coast. The so-called 'Race to the Sea' entailed a series of outflanking movements until the front lines stabilised in mid-October.

Oswald Boelcke's tone of triumph turned to despair, as German troops began to straggle past his airfield on 12 September. The following day 'nasty rumours' started to circulate of a massive rebuff for the First and Second Armies, confirmed by orders for the squadron to take off for a rear location in a howling gale. Twice more Boelcke's unit fell back before settling at

Maurice Farman S.11 'Shorthorn'. Pusher biplane with short projecting front skids. Saw action on Western Front as two-seat reconnaissance machine and bomber 1914–15 and later in Mesopotamia. Used extensively for training throughout War. One machine-gun, max speed 68mph at sea level, ceiling 12,500ft. *(IWM Q 55981)*

Pontfaverger 24km (15 mls) north-east of Reims, where Boelcke recorded that several airmen were suffering from 'nerves'. 'If I only knew what sort of things nerves were', he wrote, before moving on to complain that poor weather had restricted flying and made life 'inconsolably dull'. Even when conditions improved, establishment of static front lines removed the excitement of tracking enemy formations on the move. Commenting on the effect of a French aeroplane's attack on Boelcke's airfield, he queried the value of 'this bomb-throwing business'. Boelcke thought that slowing a machine with the extra load was not justified by the minimal damage wrought.

Once the trench-line had crystallised, the RFC looked to extend and refine its operational capability. However, it first had to repair the impact of a violent storm on 12 September, which tore up tents, battered aeroplanes and destroyed equipment. At dawn the following day, from the four operational squadrons only ten aeroplanes were serviceable. A list of urgent requirements was despatched to Sefton Brancker, Deputy-Director General of Military Aeronautics at the War Office, which incidentally revealed both the variety and shortcomings of the aeroplane types in use. RFC HQ did not want more Morane monoplanes, because maintenance crews were 'not trained in their rigging and their spares etc.' Instead, 'standard' BE2c and Avro biplanes were 'wanted very badly'; Reconnaissance Experimental (RE) 5s were 'good' to fill one flight of four, but yet 'not really established'. Maurice Farman Shorthorns were 'only valuable as a gun machine' and moreover, took 'a lot of keeping tuned up in the weather we are having'. Until replacements arrived, the RFC in France could only muster nineteen BE2 and six Avro machines. The remaining twenty-seven of limited ability were RE5s, Blériot monoplanes and Farman biplanes. Apart from the variety of machine, Brig Gen Henderson, commanding the RFC in the field, emphasised their doubtful quality as the intensity of aerial warfare increased. He hoped that 'a catastrophe' would not be caused at the RAF, Farnborough, by adding that single-seat BE2c aeroplanes with 'extra tankage (up to 5 hours at least) would be of considerable value'.

In action, identifying targets for the artillery and reporting on the accuracy of its fire developed into an important function for the RFC. How to convey the necessary information rapidly and accurately in the absence of reliable wireless sets remained a major problem. Capt L.E.O. Charlton, flight commander in No 3 Sqn, pioneered the firing of Very lights above a new enemy gun position. This system was improved by an aeroplane flying at a predetermined height, so that artillery range finders could more accurately locate the hidden battery. On 24 September for half an hour one of the machines carrying a wireless set successfully directed fire onto a German position. The last three messages in the sequence from the aeroplane ran: 'About 50 yards short and to the right … Your last shot in the middle of three batteries in action: search all round within 300 yards of your last shot … I am coming home now'. Three days later, Gen Sir Horace Smith-Dorrien commander of the British II Corps praised the work of an RFC machine directing the fire of 6-inch howitzers: 'It was, at times, smothered with hostile anti-aircraft guns, but, nothing daunted, it continued for hours through a wireless installation to observe the fire and indeed to control the battery with most satisfactory results.'

Combat in the air had now begun in earnest, and on 22 September Gilbert Mapplebeck was wounded during an attack by an Albatros biplane. Enemy anti-aircraft fire did not yet pose a menace to aeroplanes flying out of range of small arms though. Returning from an operation unscathed on 19 September, No 5 Sqn pilot Lt A.E. Borton and his observer Lt A.A.B. Thompson burst into the music hall ditty, 'Archibald, certainly not!' Borton remarked that 'it seemed to sum up our attitude towards the anti-aircraft gun at the time'. The story of this spontaneous aerial serenade spread throughout RFC messes and thereafter the German anti-aircraft guns were universally dubbed 'Archie'.

While the RFC grappled with the German Air Force in France, the RNAS concentrated on home defence and protection of its own warships. The initial threat to British soil was expected from German airships, in reality the rigid-framed Zeppelin and Schütte-Lanz machines the structure of which within an outer fabric envelope contained gas-filled bags to give them lift. Their principal sheds along the Rhine could not be reached from England, so the RNAS established an aeroplane base near Dunkirk. From there it could more easily attack the airship centres, where non-rigid reconnaissance airships with a gas-filled envelope for lift also posed a threat to the fleet at sea. Winston Churchill, as First Lord of the Admiralty, declared that 'passive defence against aircraft is perfectly hopeless and endless. You would have to roof in the world to be safe.' Attack was the best form of defence.

For a short period, Antwerp remained in Allied hands and from there the first raids on the airship sheds were launched. On 22 September, four RNAS machines took off bound for Düsseldorf and Cologne. Only one of the pilots reached his target at Düsseldorf to drop four 20lb Hales bombs (each containing merely 4½lbs of explosive), three of which did not explode with the fourth dropping short. Delayed by poor weather during the afternoon of

8 October, two single-seat Sopwith Tabloids set off for the same targets. One pilot failed to locate the Cologne sheds in thick mist and released his load on the city's main railway station. The other found better weather at Düsseldorf, registered direct hits on his target from 600ft, destroying the roof and a Zeppelin (Z.9) underneath. However, his machine had been severely damaged by ground fire and he force-landed 20 miles (32km) from Antwerp, arriving at the Squadron's airfield just in time to join a hasty evacuation as enemy troops closed in.

After the Race to the Sea ended, British troops occupied a 30-mile (48km) front northwards from Béthune in France into Belgium. There the final sector comprised a salient around the Belgian medieval city of Ypres, which bulged into German-held territory. On 19 October, the first of three major battles in three years began there. It would last for a month.

The RFC's fortunes were mixed during the First Battle of Ypres. No 6 Sqn, hastily trained and sent to the Front, mistook extended patches of tar on a road for troops on the march, the shadows of gravestones for bivouacs. And, despite the Union Flag on its wing, a No 4 Squadron machine was shot down by British infantry. This prompted use of a prominent roundel, based on the French symbol but with blue and red colours interchanged. A more positive note was struck on 21 October when, this time with official blessing, Strange and Penn-Gaskell took up an Avro 504 armed with a Lewis machine-gun and strafed a troop train, although the story was not quite that straightforward. Lt R.O. Abercrombie initially flew in the observer's seat and claimed that the gun, rigged up by Penn-Gaskell to fire over the pilot's head, jammed in action. A furious Penn-Gaskell blamed him, persuaded Strange to go up again, and could find nothing wrong with the weapon. Having failed to locate an enemy machine to attack, he let fly at the train. The Lewis gun was lighter than a Vickers, but weight remained a problem and most crews were still armed with only revolvers, rifles or shotguns. Nevertheless, Penn-Gaskell's achievement held promise for the future.

Of attempts to hit enemy targets with grenades, darts (flechettes) or canisters filled with petrol, Maurice Baring was less optimistic. Referring to an attempt to strike a German airfield in October 1914, he whimsically wrote: 'Theoretically it was a beautiful shot, practically it hit a turnip.' More efficient bombs and better sighting mechanisms were clearly needed.

Apart from such evidence of operational shortcomings, by the end of October 1914, it had become clear that a swift conclusion to the war was no longer possible. Eighteen-year-old Freddie West, son of a British officer killed in the Boer War and a French countess, travelled overland from his Italian home to volunteer in the land of his birth. Questioned later about his motives, he replied: 'Patriotism is a very fine word, but meant nothing to me. I was young and like so many others seeking adventure.'

Those who cut short university studies, left school or abandoned steady jobs and lucrative professions to serve King and Country would have disputed West's cynicism, while identifying with his passion for excitement. Norwegian Tryggve Gran, member of Capt Robert Falcon Scott's ill-fated 1912 polar expedition and himself a volunteer, described the nascent RFC as 'a corps of adventurous young men'. Poet, playwright and wartime staff officer Maurice Baring believed they went to war 'gaily as to a dance', which Sholto Douglas thought struck 'just the right note of the mood in which many of us went off to war'. If so, after three months in battle, the light-hearted dreams of many airmen had already faded.

3

Build-up: The First Winter
'The weather has been atrocious'

In November 1914, wintry weather began to ravage the two lines of trenches now facing one another from the North Sea to the Swiss border. The German airman, Oswald Boelcke, deplored this 'sort of fortress war'. Combined with unfavourable meteorological conditions, which prevented operational flying for days on end, it created 'horrible inactivity and boredom'. His application for transfer to a more active sector was greeted with an assurance that 'this tedious trench warfare was going on along the whole western front'.

The RFC in the field and the RNAS at Dunkirk took the opportunity to consolidate and build up strength for the major land offensive expected in Spring 1915. They did so in an atmosphere of revulsion against alleged German atrocities. The *Daily Mirror* informed its readers that 'the arch-bully Wilhelm is making Europe run with blood to satisfy his overweening ambition and is torturing women and children for a pastime', illustrating the article with photos of human suffering in Belgium and highlighting a woman and her children begging outside their burnt-out house. A *New York Times* correspondent reported from the ruins of Louvain that 'we could read it [suffering] in the fears of women and children being led to concentration camps and of citizens on their way to be shot'.

As the British air forces sought to enhance their operational capacity, strenuous efforts were made to develop an effective British aero engine and reduce reliance on French manufacturers. Not without cost. On 5 November, as the aeroplane designer and pilot Geoffrey de Havilland came in to land late in the afternoon at Farnborough, he saw 2/Lt Edward Busk, who was testing an RAF-designed eight-cylinder engine, crash in a fireball. De Havilland believed that the severity of the accident was increased by the shortcomings in fuel procedures: with no petrol gauges fitted, pilots pumped petrol from the reserve to the main tank until it overflowed. De Havilland himself touched down that day with petrol lapping around his feet. Poignantly, in Busk's belongings were press cuttings about aeroplane fires.

Wireless communication remained frustrating. A 75lb set was bulky for aeroplane use and the ground stations to which this was linked were unwieldy, difficult to dismantle and transport in an emergency. The wireless flight attached to No 4 Sqn had done sterling work in the opening weeks of the war, on 8 December 1914 evolving into No 9 Sqn under Maj Herbert Musgrave, pre-war commander of the Salisbury Plain experimental outfit. The new unit's task was to test and supply wireless equipment to other squadrons and to train men in the use of the radio; a monumental undertaking given that initially Musgrave had only two radio operators to carry out the training and a small group of instrument repairers working under a canvas shelter in a gravel pit. Power to this modest workshop frequently failed and a visiting officer described the entire enterprise as 'primitive'. At least the need

Above the clouds Vickers FB 5 'Gunbus', two-seat fighter-reconnaissance biplane of No 11 Sqn RFC over the front line at Arras in 1916. Operational February 1915, ceiling 9,000ft, speed 70mph at 5,000ft. *(IWM Q 64018)*

for a dedicated training and repair centre 30 miles (48km) behind the lines had been formally recognised.

In Britain, more training facilities were created to cope with rapid expansion of the RFC at Trenchard's instigation, Brooklands being one. By the close of 1914, three reserve squadrons were supplying men and machines to front-line squadrons. On Salisbury Plain, Netheravon was transformed into a flying training centre from which suitable graduates progressed to the CFS at Upavon. Its 'straggling collection of brick-built quarters and sheds' between Tidworth and Tilshead did not impress Algernon Insall and his older brother Gilbert, who discovered that 'Huns' (trainees like themselves thought liable to kill their instructors) were banished to the extremity of the mess situated in a former cavalry barracks.

The Insall brothers reached Netheravon after an adventurous journey. With France already at war, on 4 August 1914 the family left their Paris home to catch a ferry for England and discover mid-Channel the following day, via a chalked message on a blackboard, that Britain had joined the conflict. Algernon and Gilbert enlisted in the 18th Battalion of the Royal Fusiliers, and during training in Surrey, they responded to an appeal for RFC pilots, making imaginative use of ten-minute trips in the air in France and familiarity with Louis Blériot's activities near Paris in their applications. To their delight they were duly chosen 'to join a small band of what most people regarded as pioneers' at Brooklands for flying instruction.

Despite the urgent quest for more men, entry to the RFC was not easy, as the Norwegian former Antarctic explorer Tryggve Gran discovered. An accomplished pilot, nevertheless Gran had his application to join the RFC rejected on 28 July 1914, Britain not then being at war and Gran a foreigner. Returning to England four months later as an officer in the Norwegian Flying Corps he enlisted the help of Capt Edward Evans, Capt Scott's second in command for his polar expedition of 1912, to secure access to RFC stations. Here he built up knowledge and personal contacts, which would prove beneficial when he renewed his application two years later.

Establishment of No 9 Sqn, the wireless unit, at RFC HQ near St Omer was part of a major reorganisation in the field, to ensure closer and more effective co-operation with army formations. Two wings were created: the First (Nos 2 and 3 squadrons) under Lt Col H.M. Trenchard – posted from the depot at Farnborough – to support the Indian Corps and IV Army Corps; the Second (Nos 5 and 6 squadrons) under Lt Col C.J. Burke supporting II and III Army Corps. This system evolved from an unofficial one adopted during the First Battle of Ypres, when squadrons supporting individual corps remained with them rather than return to HQ RFC after operations.

Capt Harold Wyllie, a Boer War veteran seconded from his infantry regiment to the RFC, joined No 4 Sqn as an observer on 1 November 1914. The overland trip to St Omer in France, he wrote:

> … was very much like any other journey of the kind with the exception that every now and then one saw a smashed gun being sent down country for transhipment to England, a bloody bandage dropped from a hospital train, and troops moving in trucks; and there was a truckload of wounded horses but that is another story as Kipling says.

Wyllie found the Squadron's officers

> … billeted in a chateau standing in park-like grounds on the outskirts of the town which among other things boasts a canal, a beautiful ruined abbey, three big churches and on average better looking women than any I have seen in France up to date.

Two days after arriving at St Omer, Wyllie revealed how combat affected behaviour. Attacked by a German Taube, Lt Cyril Murphy 'gave him 24 rounds' and he 'shoved off'. 'Murphy flew about for some time like a terrier with all his bristle up looking for trouble in the shape of more Germans but failed to find a scrap.' Wyllie added: 'He was quite pathetic about it in the Mess that night.' Shortly afterwards a visiting officer hinted that No 4 Sqn was 'having rather an easy time', to which Murphy reacted: 'Be God! It's wiping me nose on the skin of me chest I am, I'm so thin from hard work.'

No doubt with his Boer War experiences in mind, Wyllie observed that 'everything is strange about this war. Motor transport, wireless and flying machines have altered things tremendously.' He soon learnt that while enemy anti-aircraft guns had been called 'Archibald' or 'Archie', the British were known as 'Adolphus'. When not flying, Wyllie sketched aeroplanes and other military scenes on the ground. He also went sight-seeing, recording that on 5 November he had visited two churches: 'One magnificent but the majesty of the design utterly defeated by the taudry [sic] Renaissance altar screen and pictures of with which the building was filled'.

The Squadron was soon on the move to Poperinghe, in the Ypres sector. Travelling by road, Wyllie recorded 'a sickening sight. A horse had been killed by the roadside and someone had been cutting steaks from it without even the preliminary process of skinning … I don't know why it turned my stomach up', he mused.

Once at the new airfield, two of the Squadron 'were loafing around one of the French towns bored to death', when they saw a sign *Femme Sage*. They assumed this meant 'Fortune Teller'. 'The old hag', who answered their knock on the door, 'shook her head, put her hands on her stomach to intimate size and said, "*Non, ici pour les bébés*"' – to the amusement of a crowd curious about what business two British officers had with the local midwife.

On 21 November, No 4 Sqn returned to St Omer and the next day Wyllie recorded that three German aeroplanes had been captured; two forced down by frozen carburettors, the other by fire from an airborne Avro. Soon afterwards, a series of gales struck the area. However, despite particularly strong gusts punctuated by heavy rain, King George V inspected the Squadron on 5 December and spoke to every officer. It was 'a great honour to be asked to touch one's hat to one's King on service', Wyllie wrote.

In between further showers, gales and snowstorms, Wyllie did get some flying; not always with conspicuous success. While striving to gain height after take-off, the engine of a Blériot IX monoplane cut out and the pilot had to glide in to land in a field. His concerned observer noted that, in doing so, 'he missed the top of some hop poles by a few feet'. A flight in a BE8 to test a signalling lamp and another in a Blériot to sketch enemy trenches proved more successful. On 31 December 1914, Wylllie went up in a BE2b on another sketching operation, 'He [the pilot] soared the machine beautifully over Whytschaete in the strong wind that was blowing and I knelt on my seat facing aft and drew in all the trenches visible.'

As No 4 Sqn operated from St Omer, towards the end of November 1914, No 3 Sqn settled at Gonneham, 15 miles (24km) south-west of Armentières, where James McCudden discovered that sugar beet had to be flattened by marching men to make the airfield usable. Now a corporal, he sometimes flew as an observer in reconnaissance machines armed with a rifle. Evidently temporarily despondent, to his 15-year-old sister Kathleen (Kitty) on 15 December he echoed the pessimism of Rudyard Kipling's poem 'Tommy': 'England being against militarism, when the war finishes the soldier will be called no good just because he is a soldier, the same as before the war'.

But this letter from the 'British Expeditionary Force Abroad' revealed an affectionate relationship between brother and sister as well as nostalgia for home and a hint of loneliness. James thanked Kitty for her letter and parcel, handkerchiefs in particular being 'very handy'. He expected that Sheerness 'looks quite crowded with so many soldiers' and seemed surprised that she had been 'several times' on board the warship HMS *Bulwark*. McCudden wondered what she thought of the naval victory over the Germans off the Falkland Islands, where Vice-Admiral Frederick Sturdee annihilated Maximilian Count von Spee's fleet on 8 November 1914. Rather naively he was 'looking forward … with keen anticipation' to a promised flight into enemy territory 'to drop some big bombs'. He had so far enjoyed 'lots of flights' without yet crossing the German lines. McCudden joked that 'you must not get too fat, or you will make my motorbike collapse when I give you your next joyride'.

James McCudden thought Kitty would wait 'a long time' for a Zeppelin raid, 'for as soon as they build them, our naval airmen destroy them in their bomb-dropping "stunts"'. Frivolously he added, 'please remember me to all enquiring maidens', sent his best wishes for a 'Merry Christmas and Happy New Year' and concluded with a plea for her to write soon 'as all letters are very welcome'.

A letter from Kitty's elder brother, signed 'William the Silent', on 10 February 1915 further illustrated family closeness. He expressed surprise 'at you riding on the back of motor-cycles

... and one so young too'. William went on to scold his sister for cavorting with Servicemen in this way, then revealed that he had acquired a 16hp 'Brown two-seater [car] with folding seats at the back for two ... No doubt ... dear Flapper ... you are longing for the fine weather to come again so that you can get off with the boys along the [sea] front'. Like James, he welcomed letters from her and his mother and closed with 'lots of love'.

Approaching the close of 1914, in the far south of the Allied line there was a sharp demonstration of the wider potential of air power, beyond reconnaissance and artillery spotting. In October, four single-seat RNAS Avro 504 biplanes powered by an 80hp Gnome engine were crated, transported via ship from Southampton, then in sealed railway wagons from Le Havre to Belfort in eastern France, where they were concealed in a barn until the morning of 21 November. One machine broke its tail skid in attempting to take off shortly after 9.30am, but the other three (each carrying four 20lb Hales bombs) successfully began their 125-mile (201km) dog-leg route to the target, designed to avoid neutral Switzerland. Flying south of Mulhausen, 25 miles (40km) north-east of Belfort, then parallel to the Rhine over the Black Forest, they turned south-east at Shaffhausen. Avoiding the city of Constance, they crossed the spit of land between two inlets at the north-western of the lake. One of the pilots, Flight Lieutenant (Flt Lt) S.V. Sippe, explained that the three Avros, flying independently, skimmed the water at 10ft hugging the northern shore until 5 miles (8km) from the Zeppelin works, where they climbed to 1,200ft. At 11.55am, 'when half a mile from [the] sheds [I] put machine into dive, and came down to 700ft ... Dropped one bomb in enclosure to put gunners off aim, and, when in correct position, two into works and shed', the fourth bomb failing to release. 'During this time', Sippe wrote, 'very heavy fire, mitrailleuse [machine-gun] and rifle, was being kept up, and shells were being very rapidly fired'. Sippe and Flight Commander J.T. Babbington survived this onslaught to reach Belfort again after a two-hour return flight. The formation leader, Squadron Commander E.F. Briggs, was shot down in the target area and taken prisoner. One Zeppelin in a shed was damaged, the gas-works spectacularly exploded and other buildings were hit. In the context of the time, this constituted a daring, deep-penetration raid with ominous implications for enemy installations far beyond the front line.

Much has been made of the 'Christmas truce' in the trenches, illustrated by the letter home of one soldier: 'Just you think that whilst you were eating your turkey, I was out talking with the very men I had been trying to kill a few days before.' Less has been written about aerial activity in France that day, though precisely what did take place is unclear. One account has the RFC dropping 'a padded, brandy-steeped plum pudding', the Germans responding with a suitably protected bottle of rum. Another contends that Louis Strange deposited a collection of footballs on Lille airfield. These stories, evidently in keeping with the spirit of goodwill, may well be apocryphal.

Undeniably, the RNAS had less friendly intentions on Christmas Day. Seven seaplanes were ferried to the take-off point at sea by converted cross-Channel steamers with the aim of bombing Zeppelin sheds at Cuxhaven, on the estuary of the Elbe river at the base of the Jutland peninsula. Unable to locate their target, the crews settled for a passive overview of the nearby Wilhelmshafen naval base, where three battleships, three battle cruisers and several other warships were sighted. As they did so, the steamers and their protective escort were attacked by German airships and aeroplanes, which failed to cause any damage. On their return the seaplanes were less fortunate. Three landed close enough to be hoisted aboard a steamer, the crews of three more were picked up by a submarine, which had to crash-dive to avoid the bombs of a Zeppelin, and the seventh crew was rescued from the sea by a Dutch trawler. So, although the crews were saved, four aeroplanes out of seven had been lost.

Back home, not all families uttered expressions of goodwill during this festive season. On learning that her son had become attached to the RFC, on 26 December 1914 the mother of Sholto Douglas pithily declared: 'You must be mad'. A classical scholar at Lincoln College, Oxford, he had abandoned his studies for the Royal Field Artillery with which he went to France in August 1914. He later recalled, contrary to doubters like Freddie West, 'at the mention of patriotism, we all felt an instant quickening of the pulse'.

Lt Sholto Douglas' translation to the RFC from the Royal Field Artillery owed much to his distaste for water-filled trenches, the 'exciting' sight of aeroplanes aloft and not least, a somewhat strained relationship with his commanding officer, who considered him 'a self-opinionated young upstart'. Hence, the subaltern's request to become a flying observer was approved with alacrity. On Boxing Day 1914, three days after his 21st birthday and the same day that his mother belatedly penned her disapproval, Douglas rode his horse over to No 2 Sqn at Merville, a large grass airfield between the Lys river and Nieppe forest. He subsequently survived three weeks' probation, during which he learnt Morse perched on a bale of hay in a barn, through the open door of which wafted an unpleasant smell from the adjacent farmyard.

Undeterred by his mother's dismay when he opted for the RFC, Douglas informed his father that 'I am enjoying flying immensely, and I hope to get taken on as a permanent observer.' But he was critical of the 'vague' guidance given to observers, whose duties were varied and onerous. In the absence of wireless in an aeroplane, the observer needed an Aldis lamp to communicate with the artillery or any other ground position by Morse. He needed to be an adept gunner, able to identify and evaluate enemy formations, use a camera or sketch the lay-out of enemy trenches. Yet for none of these tasks did he receive formal training. A comprehensive introductory course was needed, Douglas believed.

Realisation that volunteers were often taken straight from the trenches and sent aloft without guidance, coupled with his own experiences, influenced Douglas's opinion. Shortly after reaching Merville, he was 'casually' informed that he was to go on a reconnaissance operation across the line over Lille. Never having flown before, he had no idea what to look for and returned with a deep feeling of having made 'a complete hash of things'. A sympathetic pilot helped him to fill out his report, and thereafter, Douglas taught himself how to read a map in the air and identify features below 'largely through trial and error'. He made himself proficient in aerial photography, too, even though he had to work in a confined, open cockpit, to change each plate by hand and spoilt several photos due to 'frozen fingers'. Leaving mastery of their operational role to individual observers was both inefficient and dangerous.

In the German ranks, another soldier destined to play an important role on the Western Front volunteered for the German air service in the face of maternal disapproval. Educated at the Dresden Cadet School from which he was commissioned into the 2nd Railway Regiment in April 1911, while attending the Anklam War Academy the following year Max Immelmann enthused about the 'glorious and unique sight' of aeroplanes 'which resembled huge birds, soared into the air and executed daring turns and glides with a truly amazing self-confidence'. Shortly afterwards, he resigned from the Army to attend Dresden Technical High School, where he was prominent in the Aviation Association. Recalled to his regiment in August 1914, he complained to his mother about having to 'play the railwayman's overseer'. However, his application for pilot training was soon accepted, and on 12 November 1914 the 24-year-old was duly posted to Adlershof Recruitment Centre near Berlin before moving to the Johannistal Flying School close by. He acknowledged that his mother disagreed with his choosing 'a life of dangers instead of one with few risks', and sought to reassure her that in the

Max Immelmann. Commissioned in the German Army in 1911, resigned to attend Dresden Technical High School but recalled to service in 1914. Transferred to air service, he gained reputation as a fighter pilot and was dubbed 'The Eagle of Lille'. In January 1916 awarded the *Pour le Mérite*, a decoration thereafter nicknamed 'The Blue Max'. Killed in action, June 1916. *(Peter Jackson)*

Max Immelmann performing as an acrobat in a concert while in cadet training. *(Peter Jackson)*

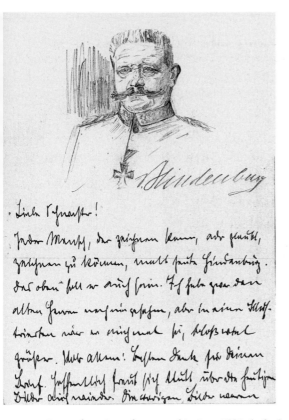

Letter from Immelmann to his sister Elfriede for her 21st birthday in January 1915 in which he assures her that 'I am flying very carefully' and adds a sketch of Hindenburg, whom he believes is unfairly 'usually portrayed as extremely fat'.

air he felt 'at least as safe as in an armchair on the ground and ten times as happy'. Writing to his sister Elfriede, Immelmann included a sketch of the German commander, Field Marshal Paul von Hindenburg, which he maintained was more lifelike than many other portrayals, and he promised her that he was 'taking great care when flying'.

A letter to his mother on 4 January 1915 contained a mixture of naive enthusiasm, reflection, speculation about the future and description of life at the training depot in much the same vein as RFC trainees writing to their parents. He mused about the passing of 'the last traces' of 1914, when figuratively the Christmas forests had been enveloped in darkness. Immelmann was more optimistic for the coming year, forecasting that 'our Fatherland' would once more 'appear in its full glory'. Specifically, he believed that a Luft Verkehrs Gesellschaft (LVG) biplane (LVG C.II with a 160hp engine and a machine-gun in the rear cockpit) about to enter service would bring aerial success. More soberly, he referred to two serious training crashes: the pilot of a monoplane was lucky to escape from his wrecked machine; and that of a biplane, which had failed to level out before plunging into the ground, had been killed although his observer survived. Both accidents clearly shook Immelman, but he completed his basic flying course on 12 February 1915 and moved on to advanced instruction.

As pressure to reinforce the RFC on the Western Front mounted, so the demands of other theatres put additional strain on the embryo British aviation industry. On 27 November 1914, the first aeroplane was despatched to defend the Suez Canal after Turkey had allied herself with Germany and Austria-Hungary. Soon, forces in Palestine, Mesopotamia, East Africa, the Allied enclave at Salonika on the eastern Mediterranean coast and the Dardanelles campaign in Turkey would need support, so the RFC in France would no longer have a monopoly of supplies either of men or machines.

The vulnerability of Britain to hostile air attack continued to cause grave concern. After learning to fly in civilian schools of aviation, the RNAS gave its aeroplane and seaplane pilots military instruction at Eastchurch, those destined for airships at Kingsnorth on the River Medway. Mechanics were trained at Sheerness before posting to an operational unit. Horace Buss had secured Royal Aero Club Certificate No. 409 in 1913 and began his military tuition at Eastchurch on 31 August 1914. Having cleared that hurdle, he found himself flying regular patrols along the Kent coast and occasionally over the Channel from Fort Grange at Gosport. Fear of enemy intruders became reality, when an aeroplane attacked Dover on 24 December 1914. The Germans had formed a *Brieftauben Abteilung* (Carrier Pigeon Detachment) at Ostend equipped with *Taube* (pigeon) biplanes to mount a campaign across the Channel. Pressure to divert aerial resources to defence of the homeland intensified, when during the night of 19/20 January 1915 two Zeppelins raided King's Lynn and Yarmouth dropping high explosive (HE) and incendiary bombs, which killed four and injured sixteen civilians including two children. Neither airship was sighted during 79 sorties (single flights) by defending aeroplanes, eight of which crashed attempting night landings, killing three pilots. RNAS aeroplanes were now deployed to Hendon, and all RFC stations except those west of Farnborough were ordered to have two machines in readiness to oppose a night attack. Additional landing grounds were established in and around London, their illumination made the responsibility of nearby military units. Each would have distinctive lighting to help airborne pilots to fix their position.

On the Western Front, plans were drawn up to expand the forces on the ground to six armies, each of three corps. At the War Office, Maj Sefton Brancker estimated that thirty squadrons would be needed in support: one for each Army HQ, one each for the eighteen corps and six attached to RFC HQ. On 21 December 1914, Field Marshal Lord Kitchener, the Secretary of State for War, scribbled on Brancker's proposal: 'Double this. K'.

As the new year dawned, Harold Wyllie of No 4 Sqn demonstrated the widening scope of RFC activities. On 6 January 1915, he flew on a 'strategical reconnaissance', which entailed penetrating enemy-held territory beyond the battlefield to survey support facilities like ammunition dumps and railway centres. (The adjective 'strategical' or, more commonly 'strategic', was used in the context of a theatre of war like the Western Front; 'tactical' applied to a battlefield such as Ypres). Wyllie also revealed the perils, which awaited airmen not engaged in operations. Lt J.A. Cunningham, a pilot with whom Wyllie had flown, went back to England to collect a new Morane Parasol machine. Returning to France,

> his engine failed over the Channel and picked up again after he had lost 2,000ft. He went on again, climbing, but the engine again failed and seeing a destroyer he made for her. He got to within 40ft of the water and had let go his belt, abandoned the rudder and was standing up in his seat holding the stick, when the engine suddenly picked up. He scrambled back into his seat, got his rudder and got to Calais. He made a good landing, but the aerodrome being under water he ran into a ditch and smashed the machine rather badly … a pretty close call.

Arrival of a Farman Shorthorn (without the prominent, forward-projecting skids of the Farman Longhorn) armed with a machine-gun on 11 January was important enough for Wyllie to note. Towards the end of the month, taking advantage of clear weather and when

Max Immelmann posing with his fur cape. Pour le Mérite at throat. Iron Cross decoration on chest. *(Peter Jackson)*

possible flying twice a day, Wyllie was again aloft sketching enemy trenches at St Eloi and Messines, in the Ypres area. All too often though, he recorded his frustration that cloud prevented flying.

On 5 February, he did get away on a dawn reconnaissance to Wervicq, where 'a battery of guns opened on us ... The shells were humming under, over and on both sides. There seemed to be no way out of it and neither Marsh [the pilot] nor myself thought we should want any breakfast.' However, good fortune favoured them: 'I never believed it possible to be under such fire and survive. The noise was deafening and the air filled with smoke. They fired over 100 rounds.' He reflected, 'this is getting too warm to last – sixth time my bus has been winged.' After Marsh and Wyllie landed, a German aeroplane had the temerity to drop 'a petrol bomb' on the airfield. 'Adolphus' engaged him, 'but the firing was bad'. Wyllie was now due for seven days leave. Between 10 November 1914 and 5 February 1915, he had flown thirty-three reconnaissance or sketching operations for a total of 54hrs 50mins at heights of 2,000–7,000ft.

'The weather has been atrocious' wrote an RFC pilot as the first winter of hostilities drew to a close, a sentiment amply confirmed by entries in Harold Wyllie's diary and by Max Immelmann, who complained to his family of 'terrible weather'. Flying flimsy machines, few of which were protected by shelters when on the ground, the RFC had not only to battle against the gales, snow, rain and biting cold, but come to terms with the stark realisation that this would not be a brief campaign, 'over by Christmas'. On the plus side, Kitchener's commitment to providing sixty squadrons for the Western Front confirmed that the air component had proved its worth in action and become an indispensable part of warfare.

In the short term, though, the Secretary of State's figure comprised little more than a mirage. The harsh reality was that at the beginning of March 1915, exclusive of the Aircraft Park with eighteen machines on charge, the RFC in France comprised just eighty-five aeroplanes divided into three wings. With this limited force, twenty-one more than had initially flown to France in August 1914, it must provide support for the Army's Spring offensive and protect other areas of the front not directly engaged in the main battle.

4

Failed Offensives, 1915
'Ants walking across a billiard table'

On 10 March 1915, the British First Army launched a major attack at Neuve Chapelle, 10 miles (16km) south-west of Lille, to eliminate a German salient and capture Aubers Ridge. A 'hurricane' bombardment of 35 minutes preceded the infantry advance, which an RFC observer described as being like 'ants walking across a billiard table'. By 13 March, when forward movement ceased, the British had captured Neuve Chapelle but not Aubers Ridge, incurred 12,892 casualties and suffered the first of many costly setbacks in 1915.

Prior to the attack, the German trench system opposite the British First Army had been photographed and sketched by RFC crews to a depth of 1,500yds (1,372m). The results were then analysed and traced onto a large scale map of the area, copies of which were distributed to all units involved in the ground operation. Once the battle began, the First Wing carried out reconnaissance in the fighting zone; Second and Third wing machines hit 'strategic' targets beyond the immediate battlefield.

On 10 March, Capt G.I. Carmichael of No 5 Sqn, flying a single-seat Martinsyde Scout armed with one 100lbs (60lbs explosive) light case bomb, set out to attack a railway junction north of Menin in the enemy rear. After successfully negotiating 'archie', he picked up the railway line and switched off his engine in the hope of gliding undetected, only for his dreams to be swiftly shattered by a stream of machine-gun bullets. Opening up his engine, he reasoned that as the target lay beyond Menin, to adjust for forward momentum he must release his bomb just after passing the station buildings – a prime example of the inexact fashion of contemporary bomb-aiming. Looking back, he saw the bomb explode short of the junction. As Carmichael turned away, he was met with a dense hail of rifle and machine-gun fire, where the previous night's briefing had not identified a troop concentration. After heaving rifle-grenades onto his opponents, as he pulled out of a dive, his engine began to splutter. Carmichael found the joy stick sluggish, the ailerons unresponsive, and vibrating violently, his machine chugged back at 200ft. On landing the whole structure collapsed, 'tired out and forlorn' according to its pilot, who was given a day off to recover.

Further afield, Douai, Lille and Don were attacked by six aeroplanes on 11 and 12 March with scant success. Three RFC machines were shot down, though one observer managed to escape to neutral Holland and eventually tramp back to his unit. On 12 March a disaster occurred on the ground when a mechanic tried to fix a modified artillery shell (used as a bomb) to the wing of a No 3 Sqn Morane-Saulnier Parasol. The safety mechanism proved inadequate when he dropped the shell and the subsequent explosion killed twelve men. Not all of the load went up, but the Squadron commander forbade anybody to clear the undamaged shells and during the night, Maj J.M. Salmond (later to command the RFC in the field)

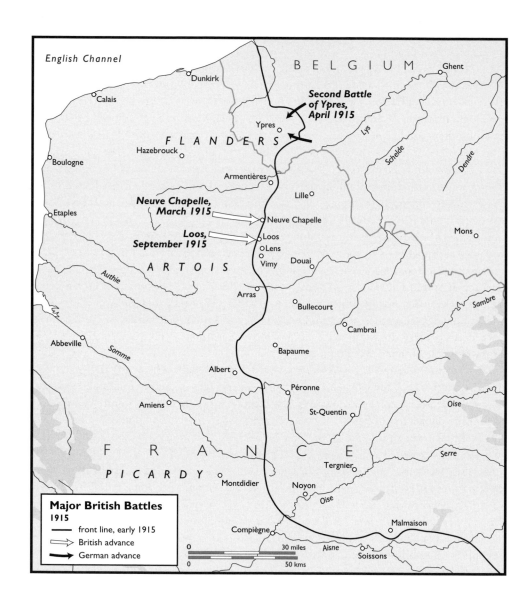

English Channel

BELGIUM

Ghent

Dunkirk

Calais

**Second Battle
of Ypres,
April 1915**

Ypres

FLANDERS

Lys

Schelde

Dendre

Hazebrouck

Boulogne

Armentières

Lille

Neuve Chapelle,
March 1915

Neuve Chapelle

Mons

Etaples

Loos,
September 1915

Loos

Lens

ARTOIS

Vimy

Douai

Arras

Bullecourt

Sambre

Cambrai

Abbeville

Authie

Somme

Bapaume

Albert

Péronne

Oise

Amiens

St-Quentin

Serre

FRANCE

Tergnier

PICARDY

Montdidier

Noyon

Oise

Malmaison

Compiègne

Aisne

Soissons

did so himself. In his diary Harold Wyllie provided some light relief, describing the application of a young officer for an interpreter's post. He translated '*L'Anglais avec son sang froid naturel*' as 'the Englishman with his usual bloody cold', and, Wyllie dryly recorded, 'was not taken on'.

HQ RFC established an advanced base at Hazebrouck to oversee direction of the air effort in the Battle of Neuve Chapelle. Required to provide close support to the troops, First Wing commanded by Lt Col H.M. Trenchard had its advanced HQ at Merville. To fulfil his formation's allotted tasks, Trenchard organised thirty-six aeroplanes into six groups. Five would co-operate with specified army formations: two Royal Artillery groups; IV Corps; First Army HQ; and together, I Corps and the Indian Corps. The sixth would carry out 'bombing duties'. For communication with the ground, eight of the aeroplanes were equipped with wireless sets; ten others used signal lamps. The infantry were to lay out strips of cloth to indicate progress and their capture of intermediate objectives for the airmen to see and report. In practice, these arrangements were less than satisfactory. Clearly, each RFC Wing must have its own wireless machines and ultimately, each squadron its own wireless flight with, overall, a more effective training system created. No 9 Sqn was therefore disbanded and subsequently reappeared as the RFC's wireless school at Brooklands.

Activity gathered pace at the Front as the weather improved, but ability to fire forward through the propeller of an engine still proved elusive. A French pilot, Capt Roland Garros, fixed metal plates to the wooden blades of his propeller to deflect bullets from the vulnerable mechanism, and in sixteen days he brought down five enemy machines. During a bombing raid against Courtrai marshalling yards on 19 April 1915, his engine cut out, and after a forced landing, Garros was captured before he could burn his Morane-Saulnier L machine. The Germans discovered the firing device, dismantled the aeroplane and transported it to Berlin for the designer Anthony Fokker to examine. Fokker did so out of curiosity, as he was already working on an interrupter gear to allow forward firing. Capture of Garros' machine did not initiate the process. When Oswald Boelcke began to fly one of Fokker's modified machines, he explained 'quite a simple business' to his younger brother Max. Attached to the fuselage in front of the pilot, a machine-gun had a safety catch connected to the engine by a rod, which activated whenever a propeller blade went in front of the barrel and automatically released once the blade passed clear.

During March 1915, a major reorganisation occurred in the German forces. The air service was separated from other communications bodies, like the railways, with which it had hitherto been associated. A Head of Military Aviation was appointed to control and equip all army airship and aeroplane units. Flying sections at the front remained under the orders of generals commanding the corps or armies to which they were attached, but in each of these formations an aviation staff officer now co-ordinated air operations. At the same time, the Army High Command established direct control over a bomber unit of thirty-six machines at Ostend and a smaller one at Metz for long-range operations as and when required, similar to the Independent Force of bombers created by the British three years later.

On 22 April German troops launched the Second Battle of Ypres, which would last a month and end with the Allied salient squeezed even tighter around the town. On the lookout after a prisoner had revealed plans for its use, Capt Louis Strange saw a yellowish green fog drifting from the enemy trenches towards French units on the British left: poisonous chlorine gas released from 500 cylinders prior to an infantry assault. Swiftly a four-mile gap was torn in the Allied line and only desperate defending by Canadian troops stemmed the tide, though a tactical withdrawal took place later, when RFC units also fell back. Harold

Note the overall slung over the fuselage, indicating an off-duty shot. *(Peter Jackson)*

Close up view of a FB 5 'Gun Bus' pusher, developed by Vickers as a private venture. Saw action in opening phase of the war before being used extensively for training. One MMG in front cockpit. Ceiling 9,000ft, top speed 70 mph. *(Peter Jackson)*

Wyllie recorded that on Saturday 24 April, No 6 Sqn's airfield was shelled 'by a high velocity gun of about 6-inch calibre. One had to walk up and down quarterdeck fashion and pretend to be amused in case the men got a bit unsteady.' However, it was 'soon plain' that the station had become untenable and the Squadron withdrew to Abeele, 10 miles (16km) west of Ypres.

On the German side of the line, Max Immelmann began his operational career as a pilot south of Ypres shortly before the second battle commenced. In a letter of 1 March, Immelmann, like Sholto Douglas having faced maternal disapproval at his transfer to the air service, described his first crash when landing on rough ground. 'The machine got a nasty jolt from a heap of manure, which bounced it up again' before turning over and trapping him underneath. He crawled out to find his aeroplane a complete write-off, but cheerfully added that he had previously completed 130 smooth landings, so he had no qualms about remaining a pilot. In mid-March Immelmann was posted to Rethel, 150km (94 mls) from Paris and 35km (22 mls) north-east of Reims, to fly a reconnaissance two-seater LVG. Writing to his mother from there on 14 March, he complained about lack of fresh vegetables, so 'kind gifts' of tinned fruit and beans and spinach would be 'heartily welcome'. He revealed that poor weather had prevented flying that day, the highlights of which had been his dog (Tyras) falling backwards over a sofa and the slaughter of a pig on the adjacent farm. Immelmann gently disputed his mother's contention that Germany was fighting for peace, not victory. History proved that military triumph ensured a much longer peace than negotiated settlement: on average, forty rather than seven years. On 31 March, Immelmann passed his final test to conclude almost five months of pilot training.

Max Immelman with his dog Tyras.
(Peter Jackson)

He remained at Rethel, where on 6 April he reported 'snow, rain, hail, wind and sunshine alternately'. There was one piece of good news. The crew of a French Caudron biplane had mistaken the Oise for the Marne river and landed thinking they were at the friendly aerodrome of Châlons. Moving to Vraz a week later, Immelmann began spotting for the artillery, observing the fall of shells and correcting the range and line by communicating with the gunners 'by means of signal lights which burn so brightly that they are visible by daylight'. He further explained that from 2,000m (6,500ft) individual trenches and shell holes could be clearly identified. His LVG machine had been strengthened for battle by installation of metal sheets under the tank and the two crew seats, and 'other gadgets' – such as racks for bombs – had also been added. During April, Immelmann moved to Döberitz, near Berlin, to join newly-formed Flying Section 62 which included Oswald Boelcke, who would have a considerable influence on him. Immelmann had flown forty-two reconnaissance or artillery co-operation flights in Flanders before the close of 1914, but chafed at lack of fighting opportunities until he joined Flying Section 62.

In May 1915 another German officer destined to become a celebrated fighter pilot transferred to the air service. Manfred Count von Richthofen, son of a Prussian officer, had followed his father into the cavalry. After service on the Eastern and Western fronts, like many British airmen he became disillusioned with 'boring' life in the trenches to which his unit had been consigned. He was further irritated by his appointment as assistant adjutant to an infantry brigade, complaining that he had not gone to war 'to gather cheese and eggs'.

At the flying training school in Grossenhain, Saxony, Richthofen opted for observer training, fearing that the war would be over before the three-month pilots' course could be completed. Sitting in the front cockpit of a pusher trainer, he found 'miserable', communication with the pilot impossible: 'If I took out a piece of paper it disappeared' in the wind, a fate likely for his scarf too unless tightly wound. Transferred to the Western Front after serving in the east, Richthofen was assigned to a bomber unit in which he flew as an observer/bomb-aimer in an AEG (Allgemeine Elektrikitäts Gesellschaft) GII machine, initially from Ostend. A chance meeting with Boelcke on a troop train in September 1915 encouraged Richthofen to become a pilot, the war after all not heading for a swift conclusion. Richthofen approached Boelcke, already applauded in the German press for his aerial victories, and asked him how he achieved success. Boelcke replied, disarmingly, that he simply flew up close and shot straight. However, in further conversations, often during a game of cards, Boelcke discussed flying in greater depth. On reaching his destination, Rethel, Richthofen began unofficial flying lessons, on 10 October 1915 making his initial solo flight.

In the meantime, by April 1915 RFC squadrons were frequently ranging beyond the battlefield. The Germans used airships for reconnaissance purposes as well as long-distance bombing, and Harold Wyllie wrote about the 'most gallant act' of a pilot sent to locate the shed of a Zeppelin engaged in this type of operation. On approaching it, he saw a captive (anchored) balloon with a German manning a machine-gun attached to it.

> He proceeded to execute some split arse spirals round the balloon and heave grenades at it. After which, he dropped two bombs on the shed. Unfortunately, one fell behind and the other missed by about 10ft. By that time everything in the neighbourhood that would go bang was firing at him, but he got off with 20 hits. Good lad. The Colonel is still wondering how he can best describe the term 'split arse spirals' in his official report.

The pilot concerned was Lanoe Hawker, the German aerodrome Gontrode near Ghent on 25 April 1915 and for his exploit, Hawker was awarded the Distinguished Service Order (DSO).

Active service. RFC Squadron at Treizennes airfield showing hangars, administrative buildings and motor vehicles (top right). *(IWM Doc 765)*

The following day, No 2 Sqn based at Merville attacked Courtrai railway complex east of Ypres through which enemy reinforcements were pouring. Twenty-seven-year-old 2/Lt William Rhodes-Moorhouse was one of the BE2a pilots, who were obliged to leave behind a protective gunner so that his machine could carry a 100lb bomb to the target. After graduating from Cambridge, Rhodes-Moorhouse became actively involved in monoplane experiments, gained his pilot's certificate in 1911 and the following year became the first man to cross the Channel with two passengers, one his wife. He joined the RFC in August 1914 and found himself in charge of the workshops at Farnborough until 20 March 1915, when he joined No 2 Sqn in the field. Rhodes-Moorhouse took off for Courtrai alone on 26 April, and like other pilots engaged in the raid, was told to use his discretion as to the height he bombed from.

Closing on the target, he glided down to 300ft, where the blast from his bomb rocked the machine violently. Regaining full control, his problems were far from over. As he struggled to gain height, according to an eyewitness, 'he was subject to a tornado of fire from thousands of rifles, machine-guns and shell fire'. Severely wounded in the thigh and rapidly losing blood, Rhodes-Moorhouse refused to land in enemy territory, making his way back 35 miles (56km) at 100ft to Merville. There 'he executed a perfect landing and made his report', which confirmed that Courtrai Junction had been devastated. Rhodes-Moorhouse died of his wounds the next day.

The Times held that 'the story is too simple and too splendidly complete in itself to need any artifice or narrative or comment; it speaks to us all.' The First Wing commander, Trenchard, wrote to Rhodes-Moorhouse's widow concerning 'the death of your gallant husband … I fear that he will not be able to be replaced. The only consolation that I can offer is that he died a very gallant death, fighting to the last.' William Rhodes-Moorhouse was posthumously promoted lieutenant and awarded the VC, the first such honour for the RFC. His body was transported for burial to the family home, Parnham House, Beaminster, in Dorset.

The limited carrying capacity of RFC machines in mid-1915 was demonstrated in another way. Charles Frederick Algernon Portal (known as Peter, a family nickname) graduated from Christ Church College, Oxford, intending to practise Law. Instead, on 6 August 1914 he enlisted in the motorcycle section of the Royal Engineers. In France, Cpl Portal survived a crash with Sir Douglas Haig's staff car, after reputedly falling asleep on his machine, to be commissioned and subsequently volunteer for the RFC. In July 1915, Portal became an observer in a two-seater Morane-Saulnier Parasol. He found that No 3 Sqn's machines were fitted with bomb racks, an elementary release gear and primitive bomb sight. The main task, however, remained reconnaissance. Theoretically, the Parasol could carry a machine-gun, but in practice Portal discovered that weight determined it could not carry an observer as well. So he opted for a rifle and 100 rounds of ammunition.

Even while the Second Battle of Ypres was in progress, another attempt to capture Aubers Ridge beyond Neuve Chapelle began. Such was the importance of aerial support that poor weather prompted a delay until 9 May. Infantry were to lay out white cloth as they advanced and three Maurice Farman machines equipped with wireless were to report their progress. However, enemy resistance was so strong that not even intermediate objectives were reached. The line of attack was adjusted towards Festubert, but by 24 May fighting petered out with the British having gained just 600yds over a 4-mile (6.5km) front. The loss of an aeroplane to anti-aircraft fire during artillery spotting underscored the increasing danger of this type of operation.

During May a McCudden family tragedy demonstrated once more that losses could happen far from the battlefield. Still a maintenance NCO, James was promoted sergeant on 1 April 1915 and later that month his pilot brother went as an instructor to Fort Grange airfield, Gosport. On 1 May, William wrote to his mother about 'great excitement' the previous night at being ordered to stand by 'to frustrate the endeavours on the part of the Zepps [sic] to disturb the lethargic calm that prevails over Portsmouth', the nearby naval base. He expressed 'disgust' that nothing positive had come of the alert. Shortly after posting this letter, William McCudden took up an American RFC volunteer, Lt Norman H. Read, for an instructional flight in a Blériot machine. The engine failed just after take-off and the American was thrown clear of the crash, but, strapped in, McCudden perished. Before the end of the month, another personal disaster would strike the family, when Mary (Cis to her brothers) lost her naval husband in an explosion at Sheerness naval base.

James McCudden burst into tears on hearing the news of William's death, but his enthusiasm for flying was not curbed. On 8 June, after months of unauthorised trips, he officially flew an hour-long reconnaissance operation in the Lens area. He complained to Kitty, though, that life was 'very monotonous ... the same day after day', mischievously adding a reprise of a previous letter: 'Please remember me to any fair maidens I know.'

By June 1915 the Vickers FB 5 'Gunbus', which carried thirty gallons of petrol and allowed up to three-hour flights, had become a valuable acquisition at the front. The pilot's aids comprised an air-speed indicator, engine revolutions (revs) counter, compass, altimeter and fuel-level gauge. A pusher, which had the observer in the front cockpit with a clear field of fire for his Lewis gun and a 47-round replaceable drum whose spent cartridges fell into a canvas bag, it acquired an early reputation for mechanical unreliability. During April 1915 one pilot reputedly flew thirty times, on twenty-two occasions having to force land. Mechanics

William Thomas James
McCudden. Eldest of four
brothers serving in RFC,
killed in flying accident on
take-off at Gosport May
1915. Passenger, American
Lt Norman Read, survived.
(IWM Q 68558)

were unfamiliar with the 100hp Gnome Monsoupape engine, but once they mastered the servicing techniques, reliability markedly improved. There was, too, an encouraging example of the fighter's aerial ability. On 10 May during the Second Battle of Ypres, patrolling the salient, a No 5 Sqn Gunbus noticed an enemy machine 3–4 miles away flying higher. Climbing steadily to 10,000ft, Lt W.H.D. Acland gave chase undetected and from a range of 45m (147ft) his observer raked the German aeroplane. As the enemy machine dived Acland followed him down, the German observer firing a pistol, which prompted another stream of machine-gun bullets before the enemy aeroplane crashed.

Meanwhile, at home the frequency of airship raids and the inability of the defences to deter them, was causing mounting alarm. Hugh Chance, an old Etonian, had been commissioned into The Worcestershire Regiment in March 1915 and soon afterwards found himself at Maldon, Essex, guarding against possible invasion. One evening he was watching a film in

Above: Chilly flight. German biplane clears snow-covered peak. *(Peter Jackson)*

Left: This picture shows the German summer uniform worn in the Middle East. Many British airmen served both in this theatre and on the Western Front. *(Peter Jackson)*

Ground crew of the German Naval Air Service. *(Peter Jackson)*

the local cinema, when 'a great roaring' caused the audience to rush into the street where 'a huge Zeppelin airship flying very low overhead' could be clearly seen. Unopposed, it deposited bombs and incendiaries on ironworks near the Blackwater river, and a light shining in Chance's battalion headquarters 'brought another shower which fortunately did no damage apart from destroying a wooden carpenter's shop and killing a blackbird.'

Not long afterwards the battalion moved to Epping Forest under canvas and another low-flying Zeppelin appeared. Chance presumed that 'the bomb-dropper' had been so surprised at such a juicy target that he forgot to arm his bombs. They buried themselves in the ground close by and failed to go off. Chance reflected that the only coastal anti-aircraft defences at this time were two Rolls Royce cars each armed with one small pom pom gun. Neither they nor patrolling aeroplanes seemed much of a deterrent, he reflected.

In Britain RFC training establishments were continuing to turn out increasing numbers of qualified personnel. One intrepid graduate was Robert Smith-Barry, later to become a formidable figure in the training system. On 18 August 1914, he crashed at the front. His observer was killed, and he suffered two broken legs and a smashed knee cap. Reputedly, he persuaded a nurse at the hospital in Péronne to call a horse drawn cab, which took him to St Quentin. From there he travelled in the guard's van of a train to Rouen and ultimately secured a passage across the Channel to a military hospital. There his wounds healed, although he would thereafter walk with a limp and need a stick. Despite these disadvantages, he determined to fly again and in March 1915 manoeuvred himself onto a training course at Northolt, Middlesex. Smith-Barry had difficulty in working the rudder bar, but persevered to pass successfully. In due course, he would command an operational squadron in France.

Patrick Huskinson illustrated the rudimentary nature of training in early 1915 and incidentally, the prejudice against the RFC still demonstrated by some regiments. Passing out from the Royal Military College Sandhurst, he intended to join the 60th Rifles only to find flying regarded by it 'as an odd and somewhat vulgar activity'; adding, 'an attitude of mind which was by no means uncommon'. He therefore joined the more sympathetic Sherwood Foresters and progressed to the RFC, where he found flying rather uncomfortable. 'In those days', he recalled, 'you sat behind a tiny windscreen literally *on* the aircraft and not, as now, snugly within it. A chilly business on the warmest day.' To his dismay, he found that the 50hp engines of training machines were prone to catch fire, and he admitted that he did not immediately attain a high standard of navigational skills. On one exercise, he flew from Lincoln to Dover brandishing a copy of Bradshaw's railway guide, constantly diving on stations to get his bearings, only to find that most were named 'OXO' – a prominent advertisement for that popular beverage. When he eventually reached an operational squadron in France in April 1916, he would have completed only fourteen hours solo.

Ranald Macfarlane Reid also joined the RFC from a regiment, in his case after active service. He enlisted in the Army on 4 August 1914 and ten days later was commissioned into The Argyll & Sutherland Highlanders. In January 1915, he went to France with The Black Watch, where during the Battle of Neuve Chapelle, a sniper's bullet went 'through my balmoral bonnet and just grazing my head'. Nor was everyday life pleasant:

> The trenches were pretty grim and waterlogged in places … rotting duckboards. Dead bodies were numerous, sometimes in the parapets or lying between the lines … After the grim experience of the battlefields, I determined … to get above the mud and murder.

His parents pulled strings through a family friend, 'so I was winkled out of the infantry, despite their strong opposition to any such transfer'.

Reid underwent flying training at Montrose in a Maurice Farman Longhorn, on which he went solo. But he was soon 'confronted' with an American-built Curtiss biplane. Reid did not realise that in this machine he must push the joystick well forward to get the tail up. 'So this first Curtiss flight was a disaster, ending with a mighty cartwheel and crash upside down'. He survived to 'take my ticket' in a Longhorn, the test including figures of eight, landings and a timed cross-country flight.

For more advanced training, he progressed to the Maurice Farman Shorthorn, which 'for experience' he was ordered to fly from the south of England back to Montrose. The weather proved 'grim' and he made several forced landings en route. The engine was so unreliable that he 'learnt to look out for convenient fields' in case of emergency. Towards the end of the year, still in training, he moved to Thetford, Norfolk, on FE (Farman Experimental) 2b machines, 'delightful, friendly old warriors, pretty easy to fly, no vices, strong as horses. But … they were very slow'.

Transferred to Dover in April 1915, after a 'not very happy time' at Brooklands, Air Mechanic Charles Callender was not impressed with the operational capability of available aeroplanes either. At the airfield above the Channel port, brick-built hangars housed different types of aeroplane, though mainly the Avro 'with its long skid sticking out in front to stop it from tipping on its nose'. Callender's first job was to hold down the tail of a machine about to take off, and one day a pilot asked him if he would like to go up with him. Delighted at the opportunity to fly, Callender got into the Avro's rear seat and pulled his hat down over his ears, while the pilot circled Dover for twenty minutes. It proved a 'very bumpy' ride.

When the machine 'passed over a newly ploughed field with the sun shining on it, a series of air pockets was caused making the plane more difficult to handle'. As the pilot came in to land, Callender was afraid the aeroplane would strike the clock tower of the Duke of York's College. When they were down safely, the pilot shook Callender's hand and revealed that this was his first flight with a passenger. Callender admitted to being relieved not to have known that before take-off, adding: 'Poor fellow he killed himself next day in a crash.' On another occasion, Callender and other ground staff were ordered to push all unserviceable aeroplanes out onto Swingate Downs 'to fool the snoopers. Everything we had was made to look a lot.'

Callender witnessed several air raids while at Dover. Soon after he arrived two enemy aeroplanes appeared at noon one Sunday and dropped bombs on a brewery. Neither the suddenness nor the extent of the attack particularly concerned Callender and his fellows: 'We were anxious to know if our beer supplies would be interrupted.' Days later, around midnight a Zeppelin came over, causing the guns of Dover Castle to open up: 'It was a lovely sight and quite new to us. About every other shell was a tracer, so as to allow the gunners to see where the shells were travelling.' But the German airship moved out of range and slowly disappeared inland. 'Guns mounted on aeroplanes at this time were a very medieval affair', Callender reflected, pilots 'quite thrilled' when he devised a 'mounting with swivel attachment'. He observed that successfully crossing to France by air still rated as 'an achievement'. One day, six machines left Dover for St Omer, but only two arrived, the rest ditching in the Channel. All eight airmen from the floating machines were saved by patrolling vessels, though one testy Scotsman 'played hell' because the Royal Navy fished him out of the water with a boat hook.

At the Front, during June Max Immelmann had moved to Douai with Flying Section 62 in response to the Allied Spring offensive. He explained to his mother that he shared a small villa with Boelcke and Lt von Teubern, finding Boelcke a 'quiet fellow with sensible views'. Boelcke revealed that he deplored the lack of ambition among contemporary fighter pilots, who went 'for pleasant excursions round our lines and never got a shot at the enemy'. Boelcke was more ambitious, savouring 'the joy of having a good clout' at Allied machines beyond the line: 'One must not wait till they come across, but seek them out and hunt them down.'

Boelcke painted a picture of relaxed confidence in Douai, despite Allied ground attacks merely 20km (12.4 mls) away. Shops and hotels were open, 'civilians [were] going for walks, the boys returning from swimming and the girls from tennis', he wrote to his parents. Like Immelmann, Boelcke received parcels from behind the lines, in his case from an unusual source. While stationed at Trier (Trèves) in August 1914, he had been billeted with Frau Kunz and her two young daughters, who treated him as part of the family. When Boelcke admitted to being short of reading material, Frau Kunz sent him 'a whole bookshop'.

Immelmann's correspondence from Douai revealed that his main work involved photographic reconnaissance. He was confident that the British and French would not break through on the ground and saw 'no harm in Italy coming in' against Germany as this would open up new battle areas preventing the Allies from reinforcing the Western Front. On 3 June 1915, Immelmann thanked his mother for a long letter and revealed that he had run into trouble for the first time. The previous day, ordered with Teubern as his observer to photograph enemy positions, he had evaded an enemy machine to cross the line near Lens. But another harassed him in the target area, which led to a 'wonderful game' of manoeuvring without either aeroplane opening fire. After completing their task, Immelmann and Teubern flew back unmolested.

They were not so lucky on 3 June. As Teubern was busy taking shots of a British position, Immelmann saw a Farman biplane approaching 300m (almost 1,000ft) higher. The machine

Fokker Triplane in flight. *(Peter Jackson)*

came closer and closer until it was directly above Immelmann, whose view was blocked by the wings of his own biplane. Then he heard 'the familiar "tack, tack, tack, tack"' of machine-gun fire, and small holes began to appear in his right wing. Immelmann had to cope with his attacker, while Teubern continued to photograph. Immelmann wrote that 'it is a dreadful feeling to wait without being able to open fire until perhaps you are hit'. Teubern completed his work, but on landing Immelmann discovered that they had been extremely fortunate: 'The lower part of the cowling, which cover the engine looks like a strainer'; damage, he claimed, caused by 'dum-dum' soft-nosed expanding bullets. This detailed account of a narrow escape, like many relayed by Allied airmen, could scarcely have cheered his mother. For completing this operation, Immelmann was awarded the Iron Cross Second Class, and he soon moved from reconnaissance aeroplanes to fighters.

Towards the end of June 1915, Oswald Boelcke enthused about the arrival of new wireless apparatus with which to direct 'our artillery fire instead of the coloured lights formerly used'. He was even more excited about the advent of a 150hp two-seater machine in which he scored his first victory on 6 July, though to his parents he condemned the dramatic manner in which the press had written up a straightforward encounter. Shortly after his initial success, Boelcke forsook the two-seater for a single-seat Fokker E.III with which he stalked Allied artillery spotters silhouetted by the evening sun.

On the Allied side of the line on 26 May 1915, precisely five months after beginning life in the RFC, Sholto Douglas, not content with an observer's role, commenced pilot training in France. He took to the air in a 80hp Caudron, which he considered 'somewhat weird and primitive … [with] the gliding angle of a brick'. Nevertheless, in little over a week he gained Royal Aero Club certificate No. 1301. Reporting to Shoreham-on-Sea, Sussex, for military aviation training, he mastered the 'antediluvian … large, clumsy' Shorthorn before moving to

Hounslow and then the CFS for his final test. At Upavon, he duly acquired his pilot's wings, 'one of the proudest moments I have known in my life'.

Harold Harrington Balfour, like Douglas, forsook the front line for the air. Gazetted 2/Lt in the Special Reserve of the King's Royal Rifle Corps on his seventeenth birthday, 1 November 1914, he had watched airmen aloft as a youth while recovering from bronchitis in France, and revived his fascination during regimental manoeuvres on Salisbury Plain, admiring 'the god-like RFC pilots'. Now thoroughly hooked, he borrowed money from his father for flying lessons at Hendon on elderly Grahame White box-kites from whose precarious structure a pilot peered through his legs into space. Two even more dubious Beatty-Wright machines with twin propellers run on bicycle chains from a small Gnome engine were also available. For these 'there were no instruments of any kind and the only engine control was for an electric-light switch with a piece of piping fixed to it as a lever'.

Despite these tribulations, on 5 July 1915 Balfour secured Royal Aero Club Certificate No 1399. He could therefore fly, but without specialist training could not join the RFC. He returned to his regiment and still under eighteen years of age, went with it to France. Life in squelching trenches poorly protected with parapets of canvas sandbags and the distressing sight of unrecovered bodies lying in No Man's Land, prompted him to respond to a call for volunteers to join the RFC. With his basic flying qualification, he resisted attempts to make him an observer and returned to England for instruction as a potential RFC pilot. Unfortunately, almost at once he succumbed to diphtheria. After recovery, he spent the rest of 1915 in depots like Farnborough drilling recruits.

Unlike Sholto Douglas, Harold Balfour or Ranald Reid, Robin Rowell had not served at the front, when he transferred from the Royal Engineers to the RFC in June 1915, admitting that during his military service 'all the time I had a longing for the RFC'. Suspecting that his commanding officer would refuse to forward his application as he had done with other officers, Rowell resorted to subterfuge. He wrote to Col Sefton Brancker at the War Office and was asked to call on him. Rowell applied for a day off on the grounds that his 21st birthday was imminent and armed with a letter of introduction from a family friend, after travelling to London on the night train he spent the whole of the following day in the War Office. Brancker seemed only interested in his height and weight (5ft 9ins and 9 stone stripped) and whether he could ski. Satisfied, he told Rowell to apply via his commanding officer, who dare not veto this application.

On 22 June, Rowell reported to Farnborough for pilot training. There he met an old friend, Gordon Richardson, 'at this new game for eleven days' and seemingly 'a veteran and expert' as he knew the parts of an aeroplane. Richardson further impressed by showing him a training machine in a hangar. 'So much sailcloth, wire and sticks', Rowell thought and asked how the pilot stopped it. 'You can't stop it; you can only switch off the engine and let it stop itself' came the unpromising reply. No brakes were fitted to aeroplanes at this time, only a tail skid to slow momentum on landing.

An opportunity soon arose for Rowell to make his first flight in the early evening when the wind had died down sufficiently for 'novices' to go up. His instructor told him to 'jump into' a Maurice Farman Longhorn. On learning that Rowell had never flown before, he opted to take him 'down the Straights', which entailed flying along a line between the RAF airstrip and Laffan's Plain and back (3-mile/5km return flight).

Once the mechanics had started the engine and the chocks were removed from under the wheels, 'off we went, bumping down the aerodrome as we gathered speed, touching the ground more lightly and less frequently as we went, until eventually we were off the ground

… It was a strange feeling, and I hung on to the two struts at each side as hard as I could.' As the Longhorn passed over trees, 'the old engine began spitting fire behind me' and Rowell began to wonder how the machine could turn to go back, when 'suddenly the machine heeled over to 45 degs.' Rowell thought it was going completely over and clung on even more tightly. Looking over the left-hand side of the aeroplane he could see the ground and the canal, which caused him frantically to lean to the right. The machine righted itself and was again facing the RAF. After he landed, Richardson asked how he had liked the experience. '"Great fun", I said, with a sense of guilt', recalled Rowell more shaken than he cared to admit and worried about being able to execute such elementary turns himself.

When not flying, Rowell studied the theory of flight, how aeroplanes were rigged, the maintenance and care of engines. Pilots had to learn the Morse code and how to fire a Lewis gun, which was 'just beginning to be used in the air'. There were, Rowell discovered, two ways of instructing a pupil in the art of flying. Each 'novice' could be put into a machine whose wings had been clipped so that he could only fly 10–15ft at a time; in effect, a series of hops.

> You can easily picture a school of thirty would-be birdmen charging ten at a time round the aerodrome knocking off their wheels, colliding, and standing on their noses. It may be right to crawl before you can walk in learning many things, but not so much so in flying.

Farnborough favoured a less perilous form of instruction and the one more generally adopted in other training establishments. By mid-1915, most of its machines had dual controls.

> For the first two or three flights you would be told to watch the movement of the levers in front of you; you would then be told to take hold of them and follow them with your hands; and after half-a-dozen trips you would be allowed to control the machine in a mild way, once you were up off the ground.

The instructor would show the pupil how to land, adding breezily that 'putting the machine on the ground is as easy as falling off a log. At your first attempt, you would probably make a beautiful landing', only to hear the instructor's discouraging voice: 'Yes, but the ground is twenty feet off', as he took over and glided in to land.

The training flights were normally short and one day, when Rowell had a total of two and a half hours in the air, his instructor declared it was time for his first solo. 'What an awful moment!' Rowell wrote.

> This indubitably is the worst flight a pilot ever makes. He is never competent to fly a machine alone; but by some extraordinary guarding of providence he will make a successful flight, and then the ice is broken and he makes good headway afterwards.

For his initiation, Rowell climbed into 'the old Maurice Farman'. 'Go ahead, then' were the only words of encouragement. Once aloft, Rowell used the forward outrigger as his guide, his eyes fixed on it 'intently, keeping it in line and level with the horizon'. Rowell was concerned that he might be climbing too steeply, but lacked the courage to take his eyes off the outrigger to glance at the airspeed indicator. But he realised that this was 'imperative … and so keeping my head perfectly still, I swivelled my eyes on to the instrument board, only to get another fright'. He was flying at over 40mph, 'a speed at which Longhorns are not supposed to lift, much less have any grip of the air with their controlling surfaces'. Instantly, Rowell pushed the controls forward 'and as luck was with me they answered; up went the tail, and in a second or two I was charging down hill with the engine full throttle, nearly jumping out of the frame … So I went on, alternately stalling and diving as I went round'.

Time to turn for home. 'I put on a little left rudder and no bank – I was afraid to bank – and the machine turned gradually, slipping outwards as hard as it could go, making a terrific draught on the right side of my head.' As he prepared to land, Rowell recalled that 'the perspiration was now rolling off me and my knees were so weak that I could barely press the rudder controls'. He switched off the engine and started to glide, but suddenly panicked that he was too close to the ground, pulled up before starting another glide with the result that the Longhorn 'bounded like a kangaroo'. But he did get down feeling pleased with himself: 'What a joy it was all over'. He had been round Farnborough safely without wrecking the aeroplane. His elation lasted until his disgruntled instructor materialised. The landing was 'disgusting' and he wondered how Rowell 'didn't fold up the whole outfit … Keep your controls still until the last moment, instead of pulling them backwards and forwards as if you are drawing beer in a bar', he roared.

Eventually, Robin Rowell could successfully ascend to 1,000ft, execute three figures of eight over a designated ground marker, and managed twice to land from 1,000ft without using his engine, to finish within 10 yards of another marker. He now had his Royal Aero Club certificate.

A week before Rowell began his RFC training at Farnborough, writing from France on 15 June to his sister Kitty, James McCudden asked whether she had 'had a visit from the Zeps [sic] yet?' Unknown to him, the growing Zeppelin threat to London had resulted in a swift increase in defensive arrangements, with six RFC machines being put on permanent alert, two each at Joyce Green, Hainault Farm and Sutton's Farm to the east of the capital. In addition, a ring of 13-pdr anti-aircraft guns was established to protect the approach to the capital from the north-east. During a Zeppelin night raid on 31 May, the first bombs fell on London causing forty-two casualties and £18,596 of damage. An inquest on two of the people killed recorded a verdict of 'murder by some agent of a hostile force'. Then, on 7 June, encouraging news came from across the Channel. In the early hours Flight Sub Lieutenant (FSL) J.S. Mills, an RNAS pilot stationed at Dunkirk, resisted fierce ground fire to release four 20lb Cooper bombs on the airship base at Evère from 5,000ft, which utterly destroyed LZ.38 in its hangar.

Another RNAS pilot from Dunkirk registered an even more spectacular triumph that day. In drifting fog close to Ostend, 22-year-old FSL Reginald Warneford glimpsed the silhouette of an airship moving inland from a training cruise over the North Sea. Closing with it near Bruges, Warneford's Morane-Saulnier L monoplane came under vigorous machine-gun fire from LZ.37's gondolas, as its commander dropped ballast to gain height. Although his machine climbed more slowly Warneford kept up the pursuit, and seized his chance when the German airship began to descend towards its base near Ghent. This allowed Warneford to get higher than his enemy. Released 550ft above the envelope, five of his 20lb bombs fell harmlessly through, the sixth ignited a gas bag. The violent explosion tore the airship apart but also threw the Morane upside down into an uncontrolled dive, which Warneford fought successfully to correct. 'There were pieces of something burning in the air all the way down', he recorded. As he levelled out, the blazing remains of the Zeppelin hit the ground. Discovering that his machine's tanks were almost empty, Warneford landed in enemy territory and keeping a wary eye for hostile troops, refilled them from the spare petrol cans he carried. As he finished his task and took off, rifle fire sped him on his way, but he escaped unharmed, the first Briton to destroy a Zeppelin in the air.

Reginald Alexander John Warneford. Merchant seaman before joining RNAS. Awarded the VC for chasing and bringing down a German airship near Ghent by bombing from above on 7 June 1915. Ten days later he was killed in an air crash at Buc aerodrome near Paris. *(IWM Q 64212)*

Within 36 hours, he had a telegram from the King awarding him the VC, gazetted on 15 June. In Paris to receive the Knight's Cross of the Legion of Honour in recognition of his feat, two days later Warneford was dead. Both he and his passenger, an American journalist Henry Needham, on a short flight above Buc aerodrome were not strapped in and fell from the open cockpits as their machine suffered mechanical failure coming in to land killing both men. The previous day Warneford had been given some roses in a restaurant with the comment that his mother would be proud of him. Inexplicably, many of the petals dropped off and Warneford said, 'I feel I shall die before I return home.' He was buried in Brompton Cemetery, and George V wrote to Warneford's mother expressing not only condolences but regret that he would not have 'the pride of personally conferring upon him the Victoria Cross, the greatest of all naval distinctions'.

A month later came another major boost to morale, with the award of the VC to a third pilot. Twenty-four-year-old Capt Lanoe Hawker had transferred to the RFC from the Royal Engineers in October 1914, and already gained the DSO for his daring at Gontrode Zeppelin base on 25 April. During the evening of 25 July, patrolling alone over the Ypres salient he attacked three German machines in a single-seat Bristol Scout C, according to Cecil Lewis, another pilot and author of *Sagittarius Rising*, 'so small that even an average man had to be eased in with a shoehorn'. Hawker's machine had a Lewis gun mounted on the left side of the cockpit, set at an angle to fire downwards beneath the lower wing of his biplane. Thus any attack had to be launched from the starboard rear of an opponent, making Hawker vulnerable to a gunner positioned behind his pilot. Although raked and damaged, the first German machine escaped, but the engine of the second was disabled and the pilot forced to land. Over Hooge, at 10,000ft Hawker spotted a third machine, an Albatros directing artillery fire. Skilfully manoeuvring, with the sun behind him Hawker achieved complete surprise. The enemy machine crashed in flames behind the Allied lines killing its crew of two. A bonus in the wreckage was a marked map showing a German gun position hitherto undetected. Hawker's VC citation read: 'The personal bravery shown by this officer was of the very highest order, as the enemy's aircraft were armed with machine guns, and all carried a passenger as well as the pilot.' Sadly, like so many other airmen, Hawker would not survive the war.

Within a week the RFC was celebrating yet another triumph. Twenty-six-year-old Capt John Liddell, an Oxford First Class honours graduate in Zoology and member of the British Astronomical Association, had qualified as a pilot at Brooklands pre-war but went with The Argyll & Sutherland Highlanders to France in August 1914. Mentioned in Despatches and awarded the Military Cross (MC) before being invalided home, he recovered to become attached to the RFC in May 1915, and on 31 July gain a VC. On patrol in the Ostend-Ghent area, his machine was severely damaged in aerial combat and his right thigh bone broken. The aeroplane fell 3,000ft before the wounded pilot regained consciousness and control though still under fire. After half and hour he managed to land the aeroplane back at his station, 'notwithstanding his collapsed state'. The citation stated that

> … the difficulties experienced by this officer in saving his machine and the life of his observer cannot be readily expressed, as the control wheel and throttle control were smashed, and also one of the under-carriage struts. It would seem incredible that he could have accomplished his task.

Although Liddell appeared likely to recover in hospital, his condition deteriorated. After his leg was amputated, blood poisoning took hold and he died on 31 August 1915, the Feast of

St Aidan – Liddell's second Christian name. Liddell's Commanding Officer in The Argyll & Sutherland Highlanders wrote: 'We were very proud of our VC and he will always be affectionately remembered, not only for the honour he has gained for us, but also for his great abilities and delightful disposition.'

Col H.M. Trenchard assumed command of the RFC in France on 19 August in place of Maj Gen Sir David Henderson, who returned to London as overall head of the Corps. He now controlled 12 squadrons and 161 aeroplanes, which he aimed to deploy aggressively. Trenchard quickly realised, however, that the RFC had too many aeroplanes inferior to German machines, such as the Fokker monoplane in which Immelmann gained an Iron Cross 1st Class on 1 August for shooting down a British two-seater. Increasing the operational number of machines was not enough; quality was crucial and specialisation of roles advisable. The day before Trenchard took post, Lt Sholto Douglas joined No 8 Sqn at Marieux, a 'busy airfield' with canvas hangars in a row in front of the wooden huts in the trees of forest which stood along two sides of it, and indirectly supported Trenchard's conclusion. He noted that the BE2c pusher was superior to earlier models but still took an hour to climb to 6,000ft. As a pilot, he felt distinctly uncomfortable 'to have a Lewis gun yammering away only a few inches above my head' when his observer in the front cockpit fired backwards.

In his quest for more positive action, Trenchard was also faced with a sobering set of statistics. An analysis of longer range, 'strategical' bombing beyond the battlefield between 1 March and 20 June 1915 showed that only three attacks out of the 141 carried out could be deemed successful. He also came to realise that not all those on the ground appreciated his efforts, when rebuked by an artillery officer: 'Don't you see … that I'm far too busy to have time to play with your toys in the air.'

The autumn assault in the Artois and Champagne regions launched by British and French divisions on 25 September would further test the RFC. In Champagne, the French briefly held Vimy Ridge but after promising early progress, failed to achieve the anticipated breakthrough. Further north at Loos, 10 miles (16km) from Arras, the British suffered the same fate. Swift initial advances raised unreasonable hopes. A junior officer later recalled that 'most of us who reached the crest of Hill 70 and survived were firmly convinced that we had broken through that Sunday, 25 September 1915'. The suburbs of Lens seemed open ahead, 'but alas neither ammunition nor reinforcements were immediately available, and the great opportunity passed'. As another participant wrote: 'How heavily we had suffered could be gauged by the bleeding mass of men that lay in the shelter of the roadside'. When the attack finally came to a halt on 16 October, the British had suffered 50,380 casualties (including some 15,800 dead or missing).

After Loos and other less publicised clashes in 1915, Field Marshal Sir John French paid tribute to the RFC's 'plucky work in co-operation with the artillery, in photography and the bomb attacks on the enemy railways … [which] were of great value in interrupting his communications'. Between 23 and 28 September, 82 100lb and 163 20lb HE plus 26 incendiary bombs were dropped. Railway tracks were reported to have been hit in fifteen different places, five trains damaged and installations such as signal boxes destroyed. On 26 September, separate attacks on Valenciennes from 5,000–6,000ft struck locomotive sheds with spectacular results, an ammunition train. French's praise was followed by promotion of the RFC's commander, Trenchard, to brigadier-general.

Away from the front, on another continent, Canadian-born Douglas Joy discovered that transfer to the RFC could still be tricky. Commissioned into a cavalry regiment seventeen days after the outbreak of war, on 2 February 1915 he applied to join the Canadian Aviation

Corps. At his interview, it emerged that he had never even seen an aeroplane but was keen to fly and had a sound theoretical grasp of aeronautics. So, because RFC entrants must be certified aviators, he was sent to the Curtiss Flying School on 10 May. The School charged for a course of instruction, which with all other training costs, including living expenses, must be met by the fledgling pilot. He would receive a gratuity of £75 on qualification but only if accepted into the air arm. Joy took the gamble.

Half the course was on Curtiss F-type flying boats from Toronto harbour; the rest in the Curtiss JN-3 tractor aeroplane from Long Beach airfield, west of Toronto. On 20 July 1915, Joy received British Empire Aviation Certificate No. 1525 after performing two figure of eight manoeuvres round a pair of markers 500m (1,650ft) apart, then landing with the engine off close to a prescribed marker, and a third test requiring him to cut his engine, glide and land successfully after a straightforward flight. Joy's final tests, which varied from those applied elsewhere, showed that there was no universal agreement about assessing a pilot's ability. When he qualified, Joy had flown a total of eleven hours.

On 16 August, after travelling to England, Joy was gazetted probationary 2/Lt in the RFC backdated to 22 July and sent to Shoreham-on-Sea for military training. To his dismay, he discovered that the promised £75 would not be forthcoming until he had gained his wings in England. He was soon fuming in a letter to his mother that his treatment was 'most insulting', the 'incompetent' instructor 'telling me that I allowed the machine to flop all over the place', which made Joy 'very angry'.

In a letter on 26 August, he confessed to being 'fed up'. Addicted to flying, he had been forced to undertake a course of lectures 'to which nobody dreams of paying much attention and if you do attempt to pay any attention you find that the lecturers are sort of hopeless and inefficient'. In an early test, he gained twenty-six marks out of a possible eighty, which placed him near the top of the group. Evidently, Joy was unimpressed with his fellow pupils and their instructors. He did not think any better of the aeroplanes: 'Frankly I was fearfully funky about flying shortly after I came here. The machines are like bird cages, so many wires, with a bunch of squib firecrackers inside them' and inferior to the Curtiss biplanes which he had flown in Canada. A Henri Farman biplane, in particular, he deemed 'a cow' to fly.

Joy remained far from the action in which Max Immelmann was closely involved, though like him still thoughtful of his family. On 11 October, Immelmann apologised for not getting home for his mother's birthday, but hoped that the next year would fulfil her wish 'to see peace in the world again'. On 28 October he noted his fifth victory two days previously, for which Duke Ernst Henrich of Saxony telephoned his congratulations and an engraved silver goblet was fashioned. Practically, he sent money to his mother to subscribe to the War Loan appeal; something which Oswald Boelcke also did frequently. Since news of Immelmann's successes had been publicised, his mail had markedly increased though he could not see that he had achieved 'anything particular'. He was wary of unscrupulous people getting hold of his correspondence and warned his mother that she would earn his 'eternal' displeasure 'if anything of mine is published'.

Immelmann acknowledged his debt to Boelcke, who devoted considerable time to studying Allied tactics. Faced with formations of fighters protecting observation machines, he looked to German aeroplanes operating in pairs. In this mini-formation, he often flew with Immelmann who nevertheless was not averse to raising doubts about Boelcke's victory claims. Immelmann only counted machines which 'crash or land' on the German side of the line, whereas Boelcke included any seen to come down in Allied territory. If Immelmann applied this criterion, his total in October 1915 would be seven. This seems to have been a passing irritation and the two pilots continued their friendship and practical co-operation until Boelcke was posted further south.

In mid-September, Boelcke moved to Metz, where he carried out escort duties with one of the bombing units controlled directly by the Army High Command. His victory tally continued to rise, but to his parents he deplored exaggerated press accounts of his achievements and like Immelmann, implored them not to make photos available to newspapers or magazines. Nevertheless, he continued to send them detailed descriptions of his exploits, explaining that this would prevent them from imagining combat worse than it actually was. 'My fast, nimble Fokker makes a fight in the air hardly more dangerous than a motor trip.' There was no need for them to worry.

In Britain, there was much to worry about, with a sharp reminder that the homeland remained vulnerable to enemy attack. During the late afternoon of 13 October, six Zeppelins were detected approaching London and aeroplanes on stand-by brought to immediate readiness. Lt John Slessor was on duty at Sutton's Farm, Essex, and ordered to patrol in his BE2c at 10,000ft. He caught sight of an airship over London, but was himself spotted. As Slessor manoeuvred to attack from above, the Zeppelin released ballast, opened up its engines and climbed out of range. Frustrated, Slessor picked up the Thames and patrolled in the Chingford-Tilbury area until his fuel ran low. As he prepared to land in the dark, fog partly obscured the flare path. An attempt by a searchlight crew to aid illumination only made visibility worse and Slessor severely damaged his machine on landing. He walked away unscathed. The inescapable reality was that of the defending aeroplanes to go up, his was the only one even to spot a Zeppelin. Both of John Cotesworth Slessor's legs had been affected by polio in childhood and an army medical board had ruled him 'totally unfit for any form of military service'. However, a family friend secured his direct entry to the RFC in which he was commissioned on his eighteenth birthday, four months before his Zeppelin quest.

The year 1915 had not been a good one for the British ground forces, in which the costly major offensives had been peaks in a pattern of continuous probes, attacks and counter-attacks along the whole front. By 9 December, in Flanders and France 404,459 casualties had been incurred for precious little territorial gain. Tryggve Gran wrote that 'the casualty lists showed that the air war too was taking a sacrificial toll', singling out for criticism the expensive practice of making 'quite unprotected' machines bomb at low level. Gran's claim of 'a sacrificial toll' at first glance looks absurd. Up to 9 December the RFC had incurred 174 casualties (dead, wounded and missing), in reality a high proportion of available manpower on the Western Front in 1915.

Like the Army, the RFC was painfully coming to terms with a new type of warfare. With the onset of the second winter of the war, it was poised for another period of consolidation, reorganisation and renewed hope.

5

New Look: The Second Winter
'Three cheers for old Lloyd George'

On 6 December 1915 at Chantilly, 25 miles (40km) north of Paris, British, French, Russian and Italian representatives (Italy having joined the Allies on 26 April 1915) met to finalise operations for the coming year. Agreement was reached to attack on three fronts: Britain and France in the west, Russia in the east, Italy from the south.

Thirteen days later, a significant change in command occurred, when Gen Sir Douglas Haig replaced Field Marshal Sir John French at the head of British troops on the Western Front. From the outset, Sir John had been generous in his appreciation of the RFC, but Haig and Trenchard had enjoyed a close working relationship ever since Trenchard took charge of the First Wing in Flanders when Haig led the British I Corps.

Preparation of the two British air forces for the new year were based on an analysis of events in 1915 and their own anticipated capability for 1916. The Lewis gun firing .303in bullets fed from a revolving drum had been generally adopted, although there was still a disturbing tendency for the mechanism to jam. In two-seater machines, whether pusher or tractor, the observer had freedom to manipulate and reload. However, in a single-seater, the pilot faced greater difficulty. He must stand up to fire and reload his machine-gun fixed on the upper wing, while still flying his aeroplane. In November 1915, the Director of Military Aeronautics at the War Office invited the Vickers Aircraft Company to examine this problem. A month later its chief designer, G.H. Challenger, came up with a modified system involving less frequent drum changes and a more flexible field of fire. Development of a bomb-sight at the CFS, which allowed pilots to gauge speed over the ground rather than the less accurate air speed, was another important advance in 1915.

Tactical innovations had also proved beneficial. Identification of targets simply by map references was refined into a system of squares on a map coupled with evolution of a clock code. A spot on a transparency had twelve radial lines (numbered 1–12) emanating from it and eight concentric circles (each with a letter of the alphabet A–F, Y–Z) representing distances 10–500yds. An airborne observer would place the spot over a target on his map and signal the fall of shot to a battery using the same lay-out: A2, for example. The squared map and clock system would remain in use throughout the war. By November 1915, better daylight visual communication had evolved between ground and air, signal lamps and strips of cloth being supplemented by the use of coloured smoke flares.

Notwithstanding the competition for manufacturing sources between the RFC and RNAS, a solution to which had prompted Maj Gen Sir David Henderson's return to the War Office, during 1915 vast strides were made to improve the design and provision of aeroplanes. To some extent, in the short run design would remain simpler than construction, with manufacturers still geared to limited production runs. Vickers, according to its official historian, at this time represented a good example of 'this small and still amateurish British aircraft industry'. At its Crayford works, five types of aeroplane were under construction. Four were variations of the RAF's BE design, the fifth Vickers' own 'Gunbus'. Only the BE2c and Gunbus would exceed 100 machines. With relaxation of the RAF's monopoly, during 1915 Vickers opened a new works with bigger production capacity at Weybridge, adjacent to the Brooklands racing track. By June, the BE2c was being turned out there, and in October 1915 a conference at the RAF further widened design opportunities for civilian companies. The following month, Henderson reiterated the need for such a development, when he complained that machines were 'still in the stage of experiment and speculation'.

The fruits of the October 1915 manufacturing and design initiatives would be felt in the future. The present, especially on the home front, brought more acute problems. On 8 September 1915 a Zeppelin raid on London killed thirteen and wounded 87; on 13 October the casualties were 71 killed and 128 injured. Mounting attacks against the capital caused Lord Kitchener to reproach Henderson: 'What are you doing about these airship raids?' he demanded. The Secretary of State for War brushed aside Henderson's protest that the RNAS exercised responsibility for home defence. 'I do not care who has the responsibility', Kitchener replied. 'If there are any more Zeppelin raids and the Royal Flying Corps do not interfere with them, I shall hold you responsible.' It may have been entirely coincidental that shortly afterwards the RFC determined to increase the night training of pilots for anti-Zeppelin patrols and ringed London with ten airfields ready to intercept hostile airships.

Despite passing references in early letters, the McCudden family correspondence contained no details of airship raids. Their exchanges were more personal and domestic. Writing on 12 November to his younger sister, James McCudden gave a glimpse of life at the front and a yearning for news from home. Thanking Kitty for her 'welcome' letter, he noted that the weather was 'positively awful'. However, he had managed eighty minutes over the enemy lines 'yesterday' armed with a machine-gun. He saw only one 'Hun', which was too far away to engage. A bonus was that 'at 7,000ft [he] could see the Straits of Dover over 60 miles away'. McCudden hoped that his mother had received a letter in which he asked her to send him some gramophone records 'as soon as possible … Mother can use a box and make up a parcel of the needles and what she wishes to send, and records well packed all together'. McCudden had, to his regret, not heard from 'one of the "S" girls' for some time, asked his sister for her latest photo and whether she was still learning French. He hoped to get leave for Christmas and ended with an optimistic comment: 'We have now got the upper hand of the Hun's artillery and we now put over three shells to their one. So three cheers for old Lloyd George', the Minister of Munitions.

Another fillip to morale occurred with the gaining of a further RFC VC. Patrolling in a Vickers Gun Bus on 7 November 1915, with Air Mechanic T.H. Donald as gunner, according to the citation 2/Lt Gilbert Insall 'sighted, pursued and attacked' a German machine, which led the British aeroplane over an artillery concentration. Undeterred, Insall closed on the enemy so that Donald could empty a drum into him and stop his engine. The German sought refuge in a cloud but Insall did not give up, diving through, locating him below and again opening fire. The enemy aeroplane landed in a ploughed field and its crew scrambled out continuing to shoot at their tormentor. Insall therefore went down to 500ft, allowing Donald to fire again as the enemy made their way off on foot. By now, hostile ground positions had opened up, though this did not prevent Insall from dropping an incendiary on the German machine, which went up in smoke.

He turned for home, from 2,000ft diving over the enemy front line as Donald sprayed the trenches. Insall then realised that his petrol tank had been holed, but contrived to land behind the cover of a wood 500yds inside the British line, where enemy small arms fire was found to have perforated the fuselage. Overnight, screened from the enemy, repairs were carried out and the following day Insall and Donald flew back to their own station.

Five weeks later, on 14 December, Insall and newly-promoted Cpl Donald encountered and pursued another enemy machine over the German lines. This time they were not so fortunate. Donald was hit in the leg and the petrol tank holed far from home. Insall set off back only for an anti-aircraft shell to explode beneath the Gun Bus and a piece of shrapnel lodge at the base of his spine. After temporarily losing consciousness, Insall managed to land the damaged aeroplane but was immediately captured. Incredibly, one of the stretcher bearers who tended the pilot had played hockey against Gilbert and his brother Algernon Insall pre-war, when the brothers visited Hannover with the University of Paris team. Insall's family, now back in Paris, had no news of his fate until a pencil-written post card from him noting briefly that he was alive, wounded and a prisoner arrived via the Red Cross.

His war, though, was not over. Following a successful operation and convalescence, Insall found himself in a prison camp at Heidelberg, where he and two companions took six months to tunnel out and enjoy just five days freedom before recapture. After a stretch of 'solitary' as punishment, Insall was moved to Krefeld, where this time he made off in a cart during daylight, to be retaken after an energetic pursuit across fields, which resulted in fifteen days solitary confinement. On to another camp, near Hannover, from which he and two more companions walked 150 miles (240km) to the neutral Netherlands in August 1917. Promoted captain, Insall would finish the war as a flight commander in a night-flying squadron defending London.

While Insall was recovering in captivity, James McCudden wrote a long letter to his mother on 20 December. Since the beginning of November, he had been flying regularly as observer with the Officer Commanding (OC) No 3 Sqn, Maj E.R. Ludlow-Hewitt, in the rear cockpit of a Morane-Saulnier P monoplane, whose parasol wing placed on struts high above the fuselage allowed McCudden's Lewis machine-gun a wide arc of fire. On a reconnaissance to Valenciennes the previous morning, Ludlow-Hewitt evaded a Fokker, piloted McCudden believed by Immelmann, and two two-seat machines due to the Morane's superior speed. 'Reads like a fairy tale, don't it?' he wrote. 'Archie' proved more troublesome on the way back: a shell burst 'under our tail ... nearly knocked me out of my seat'.

During a second flight that afternoon, McCudden was busy marking enemy trenches on a map, when he glanced up to see 'that beast Immelmann' about to dive on the Morane's tail: 'I do not believe I ever moved so quickly in all my life'. Swiftly dropping his maps, he grabbed the machine-gun as Ludlow-Hewitt jinked the machine before diving sharply to the left and away. 'I was very pleased with my work yesterday – 4hrs 40mins in the air and two fights with the famous Immelmann', concluding his account with 'I think I have given you enough thrills for the present'. He assured his mother that he anticipated 'a good time' in the Mess at Christmas, adding a domestic plea: could she send as soon as possible two pairs of 'cycling stockings for use with my flying boots ... it is jolly cold I may mention'. Crews often suffered from frostbite in their open cockpits, despite donning heavy leather clothes and fleece-lined boots. Sometimes airmen used whale oil or Vaseline to protect their skin, not always successfully.

Ludlow-Hewitt confirmed that he, too, thought they had twice encountered Immelmann on 19 December 1915 and recalled McCudden banging on the fuselage and shouting to him to straighten out so that he could get a clear shot at their attacker. The pilot opted instead to break away 'very much to my relief and to McCudden's disgust'. Independently,

McCudden illustrated the importance of mutual confidence in air crews. He had so much faith in Ludlow-Hewitt 'that if he had said "come to Berlin", I should have gone like a shot'. On 19 January 1916, as they were in the throes of combat with an Albatros, McCudden's machine-gun jammed and he resorted to using his rifle against the enemy. His days as an observer were numbered, though. On 31 January 1916, James McCudden left No 3 Sqn for pilot training, the following day being promoted flight sergeant (F/Sgt).

Trapped within the confines of the domestic training process that winter, Douglas Joy continued to stew at Dover. Writing to his mother, who was helping in a Canadian Officers' Convalescent Home in Dieppe, on 6 December 1915 he complained about 'a poisonous place, mud, rain, fog and wind. A rotten mess, no flying and nothing for me to do at present'.

In another letter to her on 21 January 1916, Joy perked up. The machine-gun course he was attending at Hythe he thought 'very good'. The German Fokker, he explained, was 'not very new to us' though increasing in numbers. It was 'a little faster' than the Morane-Saulnier, which it resembled, but if he went to the front with his present squadron, he would have 'a much faster machine' than the Fokker. He further revealed that 'while taking this course about machine-guns, I have heard of some devilishly ingenious scheme of fighting in the air which we propose to use. I hope that the Germans don't think of the same things.' Three days later, he told Jean Joy that he had flown a 'very fast' new machine, with which he was delighted but details of which he could not reveal; it was a Martinsyde Scout. Shortly afterwards, he expressed more mixed feelings. Delighted that the machine could climb 1,000ft a minute, nonetheless he found the Martinsyde 'very heavy … with tremendous momentum on landing'. This made it 'run a long way on the ground, rather bad for forced landings'.

At the end of 1915, eighteen reserve squadrons were working up in England and eight operational squadrons engaged in flying training in addition to the CFS at Upavon and its satellite establishment at Netheravon. The need for a vigorous and productive training system was underlined in the final months of 1915. On 11 November one reconnaissance machine was lost and two others shot down on a bombing raid to Bellenglise; three days later a BE2c had to abandon its reconnaissance when the pilot was wounded. Worryingly, another BE2c was shot down well behind the British lines at Ypres on 14 December and five days later yet another BE2c perished near Oostcamp, while a further reconnaissance machine crashed on landing. Many of the aeroplanes engaged in reconnaissance operations that day were damaged. The inferiority of this slow pusher type had been foreseen, but more advanced machines were not yet available. Apart from its shortcomings in combat, they still found it difficult to make progress into the prevailing westerly wind. Returning from a bombing raid in a BE2c, Sholto Douglas 'beat back against a strong wind', found himself way off course and had to land at a convenient French airfield.

Max Immelmann was one of the German pilots inflicting losses on the RFC. He had achieved his sixth victory on 7 November and a week later in commemoration received a large Meissen plate personally from the King of Saxony, depicting a Taube machine in combat with a British biplane. In a letter to his mother describing this, he included a request for food to be sent 'at any time', once more underlining his dismay at the scarcity of supplies at the Front. By now Immelmann's aerial successes had thoroughly irritated the RFC. On 13 November a formal letter was concocted suggesting that a British pilot should meet him 'in a fair fight' above the trenches at a designated place and time. Should the challenge be accepted, anti-aircraft guns on both sides were to remain silent. The aerial version of a medieval joust never took place; according to the British the message not dropped, curiously the Germans claimed it was.

Having each achieved eight victories, on 13 January 1916 Boelcke and Immelmann were awarded the *Pour le Mérite*, a medieval order renamed by Frederick the Great of Prussia in 1740, when French was the court language. Due to the deep blue colour of its cross and the name of one of the first two airmen recipients, the decoration became informally known as 'The Blue Max'. To commemorate his award, the officers of Flying Section 62 presented Immelmann with an inscribed silver goblet, the King of Bavaria invited him to dinner, congratulatory telegrams arrived from the King of Saxony, Crown Prince of Prussia and Chief of War Aviation among many others. Tryggve Gran, the Norwegian aviator, ascribed Immelmann's success to development of a distinctive manoeuvre, which caught 'unsuspecting machines' by surprise and was dubbed 'The Immelmann Turn'. In this, he attacked an aeroplane from below, then executed a distinctly dangerous stall turn as he climbed above to attack from a different direction masked by his opponent's wings. However, Immelmann claimed to his mother that he did 'not employ any tricks when I attack', and post-war the experienced RFC observer, Algernon Insall, insisted that a British pilot, Capt C.G. Bell, devised the 'up-and-over change of direction' later ascribed to the German.

Immelmann complained on 5 February of inclement weather, which prevented flying, but assured his mother that it was not cold enough for him to wear his fur coat, though he thanked her for sending him boots and slippers. He explained that he had no need to visit Lille for entertainment, because Douai boasted its own theatre, cinema and circus. Immelmann did not feel justified in taking leave, as he was fit and well, and was sorry that this made his sister Elfriede 'sad'. He declared himself delighted with the Fokker E.III equipped with twin Spandau MG 08 machine-guns and the news that debates in the British Parliament had confirmed that German squadrons now exercised air supremacy on the Western Front.

De Havilland (DH) 2. Single-seat, pusher fighter known as 'spinning incinerator' due to early crashes. Single machine-gun, front line action 1916–17. Ceiling 14,000ft, 93mph at sea level, 2¾ hours endurance. *(IWM Q 67534)*

Back at Douai since December 1915, Oswald Boelcke had enjoyed a wide range of cultural, sporting and social pursuits pre-war and he too wrote to his parents about formal dinners and theatre visits. Like his attempt to calm their fears about the dangers of aerial combat, this may have been a further attempt to create an impression of normality. Shortly after the award of the *Pour le Mérite*, in a letter he described an encounter near Bapaume which he had to break off through lack of fuel. To his brother, he admitted being economical with the truth. The main tank had been 'shot … to pieces' and very little remained in his emergency tank. His machine had sustained several hits and bullets had passed through his jacket sleeves. Breezily, he urged Wilhelm not to worry, as 'I'm looking after myself all right'. Nevertheless, when Boelcke moved to the Verdun Front prior to the great German offensive, he found himself in hospital before the end of February with a high temperature and 'some silly intestinal trouble'. He insisted that this was not stress-induced: 'If only mother would stop worrying about my nerves', he wrote, 'I have none so I cannot suffer from them'.

Despite Trenchard's reservations about the quality of the RFC machines, when he took over command in August 1915, manufacturing backlogs meant that new types arriving in France remained inferior to German machines. Neither the pusher two-seat FE2b nor single-seat DH2, which went into frontline service in 1916, had been designed to cope with the Fokker. The DH2 had the added disadvantage of proving unstable in high winds, earning it the unenviable tag of 'spinning incinerator'. In February 1916 No 20 Sqn equipped with the FE2b reached the front, followed shortly afterwards by No 25 Sqn.

Ranald Reid, who had served in the infantry at the battle of Neuve Chapelle, took off in a FE2b of No 25 Sqn from Lympne, Kent, on 21 February 1916. Both his parents had travelled from Scotland to see him away on 'the great day'. All the Squadron's machines reached St Omer unharmed on completion of what was 'quite an adventure in those days'. The airfield at St Omer was snow-covered and Reid was not the first airman to discover with dismay that an open cockpit was 'icy, despite leather flying clothes and huge furry boots'. His first patrol proved traumatic, too:

> I felt unaccountably sick and ghastly, but did not dare beg off. It was freezing cold up aloft, with strange black monoplanes looming in sight and nosing around and other quite unrecognizable flying machines all about: Friend or Foe? But I landed safely and the bright yellow jaundice all over me startled the ground crew and I was glad to know my malaise had not been funk.

Air Mechanic Charles Callender and Canadian-born pilot Douglas Joy were with No 27 Sqn, which was also ordered to France in February. Callender had broken his 'monotonous' existence by securing the last ground staff vacancy in the newly-formed squadron and soon found himself crossing the Channel from Southampton. He was unimpressed with the ship, which 'bumped about all over the place' as it slowly made its way beyond the Isle of Wight. It was 'an eerie business' passing through 'a line of British destroyers', along the French coast and upriver to Rouen, where a shock awaited Callender. 'We were paraded stark naked on the railway platform there and inspected by three or four doctors with the French public gawping through the railings'. Having survived this ordeal, the ground staff were transported by lorry some 80 miles (128km) to the village of Treseings, where they camped in a field, the adjoining one being commandeered as the aerodrome. Eight men were allocated to a tent, which on 13 February was pitched on ground covered in snow.

FE 2b in flight. Two-seat pusher fighter reached Western Front in February 1916, but finished the war as a night bomber. Armed with two Lewis machine-guns, it carried up to eight 20lb bombs for day bombing, one 230lb bomb, two 112lb bombs or equivalent at night. *(IWM Doc 761)*

Callender reflected that it was 'a tricky business … setting down … on practically No Man's Land' facilities for some 300 officers and men plus their operational needs. The Martinsyde Scout would prove a sturdy fighter and bomber during 1916, but the 'majority' of these machines delivered from the factory were 'not up to standard'. 'Many modifications and attachments' would in due course be fashioned in the Squadron blacksmith's shop, including gun mountings, gun sights, bomb sights, camera fittings and central section petrol tanks. In the meantime, work to establish the new aerodrome went ahead in uninviting wintry conditions.

The snow proved the downfall of one unfortunate. Leaving his tent one night, he decided not to make a chilly trek to the distant latrines but relieve himself at a closer, more convenient spot. He 'left a telltale orange coloured trickle mark in the snow'. His aberration earned him eighty-four days of 1st Field Punishment. During this period he was guarded day and night, spent fours hours daily marching at the double carrying a 56lb pack and rifle, digging trenches and washing kitchen utensils, with two spells of one hour per day tied to a gate. His pay was stopped as well. Callender wrote that this draconian punishment for such a minor offence left its mark on the Squadron and in the ensuing two years nobody else received such a sentence.

While Callender and other ground crew settled in France, aircrew and their machines remained at Dover. To his married sister Nina, Joy explained that the ground crew had left on 5 February, the aeroplanes would follow them in a day or two. Joy outlined the organisation of the Squadron of three flights, each comprising a captain and three lieutenants; the Squadron being commanded by a non-flying major. Fortunately, the wind which prevented them from taking off kept the Zeppelins away; during their last visit seven airmen had been killed 'but you will never see anything about that in the papers'.

On 20 February, writing to his mother from 'RFC Swingate Downs', Joy grumbled that they were still 'not off', delayed now by a lack of machine-gun mountings. A week later he declared it 'unbearable' that they remained in Dover. The previous day he had been required to patrol from Broadstairs to Dungeness for two hours at 7,000ft, above the cloud where the sun shone brightly, but he could not see the ground on occasions for ten to fifteen minutes and descending to 1,500ft proved 'quite bumpy'. In his letter of 27 February, he recorded 'great excitement' because a 'large liner struck a mine just off here and went down in four minutes': the P&O liner *Maloja* in which 155 passengers were lost. Almost as an afterthought, Joy added that 'one of the RNAS men killed himself in a Bristol Scout this morning'. Thus, as February closed, No 27 Sqn remained split: ground personnel in France, aircrew and their machines at Dover.

At the front, aware of the growing enemy airborne menace, on 14 January 1916 Brig Gen Trenchard declared a mandatory change of tactics:

> Until the RFC are [sic] in possession of a machine as good as the German Fokker ... It must be laid down as a hard and fast rule that a machine on reconnaissance must be escorted by at least three other fighting machines ... This should apply to both short and distant reconnaissances.

The escorts were to fly in close formation and if any were detached the operation must be immediately aborted. Effectively this reduced the capability of the RFC by detailing four machines for a single reconnaissance, but the exposure of British aeroplanes to the Fokker monoplane gave Trenchard no option. 'Flying in close formation must be practised by all pilots', he enjoined.

An unidentified friend serving with No 4 Sqn underlined his personal qualms about the Fokker threat on 13 January 1916 to Harold Wyllie in England:

> I tell you Wyllie poking your nose over the Deutcher [sic] lines these days is no light hearted amusement, but quite 'split arse' and hot as Hell ... Come and join us for our own benefit, but if you have any ties or inclination to live to a ripe old age stay in our tight little island, as you have done your share twice over. 'Archie' is no better or no worse since you left, which is to say that it is quite bloody awful – curiously enough I don't think I funk him more than I did before. What I do funk is the Fokker – I was attacked by one single handed and he had me served up hot as my gun was fixed for low in front [firing] and he just did anything he liked – my sole weapon was two fingers pointed heavenwards.

The enemy machine did not get close enough for the kill. Nevertheless, its bullets were 'on and around me all the time and I thought I was done for' until close to the trenches Wyllie's correspondent safely managed 'a vol pique [dive] with the oil coming out of the breathers and got in'.

The anonymous pilot revealed that even before Trenchard's order about escorts, 'long reconnaissances' had been protected by three or four Vickers Gunbus fighters or four BEs 'close together' if no Vickers were available. 'Some great big raids' had been carried out 'combined with the French'. 'The last show' had been in close formation 'like a flight of ducks and the escort of fighters all around'. At times the force had to 'grope through a fog of Archie' and the density of the formation made it 'a picnic' for the German gunners: 'One hit left a draughty hole in my top plane just above my head'.

The letter did end on an upbeat note. On Christmas Day 1915 he, 'went and dropped greetings to the old Hun and he had the cheek to send four Archies [sic] with evil intent – however

I spoilt his aim by looping to each shot and cheered up the men in the trenches who sent in a message of thanks to the Wing.' No carols, football matches nor truces over this Festive Season.

Back in England, on 15 February 1916, a Joint War Air Committee (JWAC), chaired by Lord Derby, was created to resolve the manufacturing muddle, which Lloyd George had condemned as involving 'haphazard, leisurely, go-as-you-please methods'. Grandiosely, and quite unrealistically given its inability to force through reforms, the JWAC was 'to ensure that the manufacture, supply and distribution of materiel required is in accordance with the policy of aerial warfare laid down by His Majesty's Government'. The statistics made sorry reading. In August 1914, only ten contractors were involved in building airframes; by 31 May 1915 that figure was thirty-one. But lack of aero-engine production presented a serious drawback to the whole manufacturing process. At the end of May 1915, 2,953 were 'on order' in Britain of which just 141 had been delivered. The competition for resources between the RFC and RNAS, in particular, required urgent attention. In January 1916, Henderson emphasised the 'grave possibility of duplication and consequent waste', highlighting a recent Admiralty invitation to fourteen manufacturers to compete for contracts, three of which were already committed to the War Office: 'Competition of this kind is bound to delay our progress seriously'. The JWAC, with representatives of both services as members, thus faced a difficult task round the conference table. It duly descended into acrimony and ended in failure after just six weeks.

As threats from Zeppelins further inland and shorter-range aeroplanes in coastal areas multiplied, efforts continued to improve aerial defence in England. While waiting to go to France, Douglas Joy emphasised once more the inability of defenders to catch attackers even in daylight. On 24 January 1916, he explained to his mother that recently two raiders had caused casualties in the port area. As duty pilot he had taken off, but been far too late to intercept. The very next day, a similar raid took place and 'in a very short time two hornets' nests … [were] buzzing hard', as both the RFC and RNAS aerodromes put up machines – to no avail.

At the Channel port, as had already been apparent in London, there was little or no co-ordination of effort between the two air arms, something which clearly needed to be tackled. On 18 June 1915 the Admiralty had requested the War Office (and thus the RFC) to assume full responsibility for the aerial defence of Britain. At the end of the year, nothing had been resolved, which perhaps explains Kitchener's irritation with Henderson. Not until 16 February 1916 did Field Marshal Lord French, now C-in-C Home Forces, accept responsibility for London and soon afterwards for the rest of the country. Inevitably, this placed an added burden on the RFC at the very time it was coming under renewed pressure in the field. A Home Defence wing was separated from the Training Brigade comprising seven squadrons equipped with BE pushers, armed with Lewis guns, 20lb Hales bombs and Ranken darts (an incendiary device invented by a naval officer) with which to attack Zeppelins.

In France, the RFC formed into brigades (of two wings) with their own dedicated Aircraft Park, each to support an army. The first came into being on 30 January 1916, the second on 10 February, ready to participate in Allied plans to wear down enemy reserve formations once the weather improved. On 21 February those hopes were painfully and severely dashed. That day the Germans launched a major assault on Verdun, which would pin back the French for eleven months.

As Spring 1916 approached, with its new set-up the RFC therefore had to cope not only with the growing aerial threat from the Fokker, but a major change in Allied strategy which would involve British commitment to actions hitherto unforeseen and designed to relieve the pressure at Verdun. However, whatever the clashes in the corridors of Whitehall and the boardrooms of manufacturers, the two British air arms were set to co-operate more closely in France.

6

Hope and Despair, 1916
'Chivalry had to take a back seat'

With the approach of Spring 1916 rising losses in the air caused intensification of the political furore in Britain already mentioned by Max Immelmann. In vain, the Under Secretary of State for War (H.J. Tennant) claimed that 'we have machines quite equal in efficiency and speed to the Fokker aeroplanes'.

Noel Pemberton-Billing was one persistent critic, who addressed several of the mass meetings packed with anxious citizens, which took place in London and throughout the country. 'Tall, monocled and debonair', he had founded the Supermarine Aircraft Company and been winner of the bet with Geoffrey de Havilland that he would learn to fly in a day. Pemberton-Billing had resigned his commission in the RNAS, during which he was involved in planning the raid on the Friedrichshafen Zeppelin works, to enter the House of Commons and castigate the Government for its perceived neglect of aerial needs. With characteristic lack of modesty, in his maiden speech on 14 March 1916 he claimed to be the only MP qualified to speak with authority on air subjects.

Eight days later Pemberton-Billing was on his feet once more, this time to devastating effect. Focusing on 'inertia' and 'blunders' concerning aeroplane construction, he condemned 'the hundreds, nay thousands' of machines ordered 'which have been referred to by our pilots at the front as "Fokker fodder" … I do not wish to touch a dramatic note, but if I do, I would suggest that quite a number of our gallant officers in the Royal Flying Corps had been murdered rather than killed'.

Of the long catalogue of mishaps, which Pemberton-Billing attributed to faulty design and construction, at least some were caused by poor weather or pilot error. However, in an effort to quell the political and public unrest stirred up by Pemberton-Billing's allegations, the Government established a body chaired by Mr Justice Bailhache 'to enquire into the administration and command of the RFC with particular reference to the charges made in Parliament and elsewhere'. The Bailhache Committee would not report for another ten months.

Meanwhile, to help counter the enemy's aerial menace, early in March No 25 Sqn flying the FE2b had moved from St Omer to Auchel, 30 miles (48km) south-west of German-held Lille, and Ranald Reid, the former Argyll & Sutherland Highlanders' officer, went with it. On the new station, he found that 'uniforms were motley. County regiments, Scottish regiments and many "maternity jackets", that is double breasted – indicating direct entry to the RFC'. A sweepstake was organised for the first pilot to shoot down a Fokker, which was allegedly claimed by Lt Lord F.D. Doune of the Scottish Horse Yeomanry even though his victim was rumoured to be a German nobleman with a wooden leg.

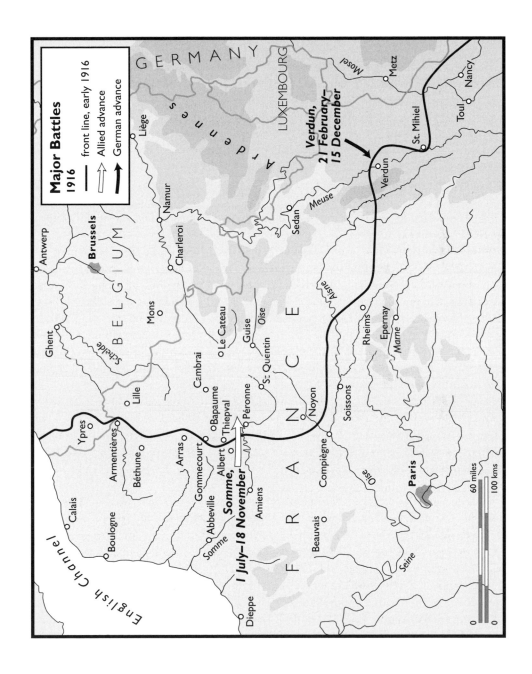

Major Battles
1916

— front line, early 1916
⇨ Allied advance
⮕ German advance

GERMANY

LUXEMBOURG

Ardennes

Liège

Antwerp

Brussels

BELGIUM

Namur

Charleroi

Mons

Le Cateau

Guise

Oise

S$_t$ Quentin

Sedan

Meuse

Verdun, 21 February– 15 December

Moser

Metz

Nancy

Toul

St. Mihiel

Verdun

Aisne

Rheims

Epernay

Marne

Ghent

Scheldt

Lille

Cambrai

Ypres

Armentières

Béthune

Arras

Gommecourt

Bapaume

Thiepval

Albert

Péronne

Noyon

Soissons

Compiègne

Oise

Paris

F R A N C E

Calais

Boulogne

Abbeville

Somme

Somme, 1 July–18 November

Amiens

Beauvais

Seine

Dieppe

English Channel

60 miles
100 kms

Reid disliked dawn patrols against Fokkers intent on 'seriously interfering' with artillery-spotting British machines. Flying a fighter gave

> … a strange, other-worldly feeling. There, high above the battle front, perhaps a lovely, cold spring morning, peaceful and sunny, and away on the distant ground, marvellously clear trails of smoke from the trains. Then far below, one spots a light grey shape moving between the clouds: an Albatros or Taube glides across the green-brown earth. One dives to strafe it; the Boche pilot is alerted and dives away earthwards. But suddenly there is an unpleasant crackling behind: the Albatros had been a decoy, or is being escorted, and two or three nasty spitting little monoplanes come whizzing in to attack: a fierce turn or two but the odds are too great. Despite the known danger of diving away, one plunges earthwards like a stone, to luckily live and fight again. Or it may be a single combat with a lone Fokker on the prowl.

Another duty, Reid discovered, was 'guard pilot', on stand-by to get airborne in a Bristol Scout:

> This was a tricky little biplane and in my hurry to take off one day, I swung slightly off the star-shaped runway, breaking the prop and crashing upside down over the ten-foot drop at the end of the runway. Not amusing, but we had had no proper instruction on Scouts.

After some time mainly carrying out reconnaissance and 'light bombing raids', Reid found himself appointed flight commander to a squadron flying the DH2, 'a nasty little rotary-engine "pusher"'; a posting he managed to talk his way out of.

As Reid settled in at Auchel, on 16 March Harold Wyllie returned to France with No 23 Sqn. The first flight left Dover at 11am. All machines flew at 7,000ft to land safely at St Omer, the following day advancing to their operational station at Le Hameaux, 35 miles (56km) north-east of Amiens. Until 28 March, the Squadron experienced 'extraordinarily bad weather', with 'hard gales, snow and rain', but on 29 March some pilots did manage a 'tactical reconnaissance' with unpleasant consequences. In the process, one machine was 'much damaged, two main spars shot through and the fuselage pierced just in front of the observer'. Wyllie's aeroplane was hit in the left elevator and wing, and the cold was so 'intense' that in several machines the compass froze.

The following day, Wyllie went up again. 'My face feels like one big bruise after the cold yesterday', and on 30 March another pilot was 'rather badly frost bitten'. In the first week of April, low cloud frustrated attempts to take photographs, and a newly-arrived commanding officer was distinctly unsympathetic. 'He has', Wyllie wrote, 'the worst eye for weather I have ever come across. He cannot tell whether clouds are at 500ft or 120ft', and he would criticise crews for not taking photographs 'in foul weather'.

Wyllie added his voice to those who condemned inadequate pilot training. On 4 May, an 'area reconnaissance' had to be abandoned 'because the formation was bad … One of the BE pilots had not the foggiest notion of finding his way. It is a disgrace that young pilots should be sent out on service absolutely ignorant of the most elementary precautions to be taken on cross-country flying.'

After the irritating delay during February, on 1 March No 27 Sqn aeroplanes finally left Dover to reinforce the RFC. Shortly after his arrival in France, Douglas Joy wrote to his mother:

> Cross Channel flying is most exciting. It was a cloudy day but the sun was shining through the clouds and the clouds were in a series of layers with clear spaces between them. I came

over at 7,000ft and for a part of the time had the 'wind up' most horribly as I could not see the sea. As a matter of fact I was only out of sight of any landmark for about fifteen minutes, but that means a long distance in an aeroplane. Arriving at Calais, I thought I was quite happy but as I continued I found that the country was a mass of canals and ditches and little ditches and little baby ditches. When I arrived at Headquarters I was so glad to see a real aerodrome that I forgot our machines required a lot of care and skill to land so I crashed the undercarriage.

From the Squadron's complement of twelve, two had crashed on take-off, and now Joy watched the other nine fly on to the Squadron's operational station while he waited for his machine to be repaired.

When Joy rejoined the Squadron, he found that its Martinsyde G100 Scouts, each with a single 100hp Rhône engine and nicknamed 'The Elephant', were part of Lt Col Hugh Dowding's Ninth Wing attached to RFC HQ. He decided that 'elephant' was 'an extremely good suggestion'. The Martinsyde had also been compared to a locomotive, because after flying the pilot found himself 'smothered in soot'. Joy was thinking of fitting his machine with 'a dummy chimney in front and a stoking door in the rear'. When in the air, 'I had my right elbow over the side and my head poked out to the right to see where I am going.'

Joy was orderly officer on 12 March with the task of squadron censor. To his mother, he wrote that it was 'rather tragic reading all these men's letters to their families and sweethearts. It brings war very close to you to realise the huge numbers of families that have been separated, and widely so'. He also had his eyes opened in another way – to human frailty. 'A number of men are awful liars. From their letters you would imagine that they were in imminent danger of being killed day and night', which was 'ridiculously ludicrous'. Only the sound of distant guns, which sometimes shook the buildings, could be heard and occasionally a German aeroplane would drop bombs 'around us … [in] rather an absurd performance'.

Albert Ball, destined to attain lasting fame in the ensuing year, also reached the front early in 1916, although his arrival at No 13 Sqn during February was hardly auspicious. Keen to be an engineer, he left Trent College, Staffordshire, according to his head master 'an undistinguished pupil'. At the outbreak of war, he joined The Sherwood Foresters and was quickly commissioned, then became interested in flying and determined to be a pilot. Ball was so keen that he would motorcycle from Luton to Hendon to take lessons early in the morning at his own expense before his unit's first parade of the day. He was seconded to the RFC on 29 January 1916, exactly one week after qualifying as a pilot. Unimpressed by his lukewarm training reports, his commanding officer in France, Maj A.C.E. Marsh, effectively put him on probation by threatening to send him back for further training.

Ball soon overcame Marsh's doubts. On a reconnaissance flight in a BE2c, he was in a group attacked by enemy aeroplanes including three Fokkers. After escaping their attentions, on the way back a troublesome engine forced him to land prematurely. Overnight, he carried out repairs, took off but was again obliged to land in a snowstorm. When it cleared, Ball got airborne once more and eventually reached Marieux airfield the day after setting out. Marsh was suitably impressed.

Not content with reconnaissance duties, Ball relished aerial combat which proved difficult in a slow two-seater, so he persuaded Marsh to let him fly one of the Squadron's two single-seat machines; though only after he had proved his ability to cope with a similar aeroplane at St Omer. Ball would make his name as a fighter pilot. Without his determination in those first two months in France he would not have been given the opportunity.

A fellow pilot remarked that he 'used to spend most of his time when on the ground looking after his machine or his gun … by no means an exceptionally good pilot at first, but he
was always practising and improving himself'. There remained something of the adolescent
about this modest God-fearing man, who wrote: 'I always sing when up in the clouds; it is
very nice … It makes me laugh when you say it is dangerous to fly. I felt just ripping.' On
another occasion, he recalled that he and his opponent ran out of ammunition after a lengthy
dog fight. So 'we flew side by side, laughing at one each other for a few seconds, and then
waved adieu to each other and went off. He was a real sport, was that Hun.' By nature withdrawn and quiet, on the ground Ball could often be found munching slices of his mother's
homemade cake.

On 7 May, Ball transferred to No 11 Squadron, which had two single-seat Bristol Scouts
and one single-seat Nieuport to protect its Vickers Gun Bus two-seaters on operations, with
a prophetic recommendation from Maj Marsh: 'He is a conscientious and keen young man
and should do well.' Eight days after arrival, flying a single-seater at 12,000ft over the German
lines, Ball spotted an Albatros well below him. He dived, caught the enemy completely by
surprise and fired 120 rounds into him at close range until, in Ball's words, he 'turned over
and was completely done in'; the first of many victims. Ball was one of a new breed of fighter
pilots produced by the single-seat machine, who began to hunt independently when not
assigned to escort duties.

On the ground, Ball opted for a tent on the aerodrome, rather than accommodation in the
nearby village, so that he could respond rapidly in an emergency. He surrounded his canvas
haven with a small vegetable and floral garden, a practice he continued when he went to No
56 Sqn. There he wrote home for seeds to plant in the garden he was cultivating: 'You will
think this idea strange, but, you see, it will be a good thing to take my mind off my work; also
I shall like it'. As Ball showed promise at the Front, another pilot who would have a more
lasting impact on British military aviation was qualifying at the CFS. Not content with an
observer's role, Charles Portal had returned to England for pilot training and on 27 April 1916
graduated with twenty-nine hours dual and solo time in his log-book. In May, Portal went to
No 60 Sqn at Vert Galand in France, where he flew a single-seat Morane Saulnier N monoplane fighter with metal deflectors fitted to its wooden propeller and nicknamed 'The Bullet'.

Ewart Garland was still in training, when Portal joined No 60 Sqn in May 1916. Born in
Canada of an Irish father and English mother, he went with them to Melbourne, Australia,
where his father became chairman and managing director of the Dunlop Rubber Co. Ltd.
The family, which comprised three other boys and a girl, owned a large 'Victorian Colonial
Style' house with living-in servants. Garland's father had 'two or three motor cars', each of his
boys rode motorbikes 'and a horse or two'.

Garland's elder brother fought at Mons in 1914 about which he wrote 'vividly and poignantly'. Charles described how 'lighthearted young boys thirsting for heroic adventure and
comprehending only victory were the next morning shocked, tired, desperate and frightened
old men – that is those who miraculously survived.' It was scarcely a ringing call to battle, and
Ewart did not immediately respond.

After leaving school, he went to a sheep station as 'general dogsbody' for a year. There he
'got bitten with the wish to fly aeroplanes', thanks to a school friend who had joined a flying
school at Melbourne. Visiting him, Garland found 'one solitary machine, a sort of box kite
with an engine'. Soon his friend had left for England to join the RFC, and in September
1915 Garland followed him, encouraged by his father, who paid for his passage and gave him
twenty gold sovereigns as a nest egg.

Staying with relatives of family friends in London, Garland joined the Inns of Court Officers' Training Corps (OTC) and applied for a commission in the RFC. He duly reported to Christ Church College, Oxford, on 16 April 1916 for a three-week introductory course. Shortly afterwards, he informed his parents that he was 'intensely happy' and enclosed the Inns of Court badge 'as a remnant of the six weeks I spent in it'.

On 3 May, Garland went for flying training to Shoreham, where he appears to have had an energetic instructor. On 18 May, after performing aerobatics over Brighton, they landed on the beach and had tea at the Metropole hotel only to notice that the tide had turned. They just got back to the machine before it was swamped and took off. Two days later, Garland completed his first solo flight after another seaside excursion. The instructor had gone up with him 'and did a few "stunts" over Worthing … and landed on wet sand. We stayed there 20mins while he talked to his girl', as the crowd gazed on the three of them and the machine 'with awe'. Minus the girl, officer and pupil returned to Shoreham and landed. The instructor 'got out and after a few advices [sic], I started alone'.

As in other letters, Garland described his flight and added asides about danger and crashes presumably not thinking about the effect on his anxious parents thousands of miles away.

> I wasn't even thrilled or excited or anything. You open the engine out until she is doing about 50mph over the ground and then lift her slightly and she soars up about 80–100ft. Then you have to stop climbing so quick and take her gradually up to 500 or 1000. The engine of course makes a deafening row but is very comforting because you are dependent on it. After circling round a few times I got in direction to land and when about 1/2ml from aerodrome cut off engine to make her glide down. This is rather dangerous but is of course the only way to land. Then when a few feet off the ground you feather her a bit until she touches. It sounds easy but, by Jove, it's not too easy.

Coming to earth at 50–55mph, he wrote, 'it is very, very easy to land too heavily and smash up. I only hope I'll have good luck all through.'

Garland explained that before going solo, he had three hours 'actual instruction' in the air and about an hour and a quarter 'purely as a passenger'. Because the weather had been fine, all of this had been completed in seventeen days; during a spell of poor weather it could take up to six months. He must now fly another six hours solo before more advanced training. Garland wished his parents could be there to see him fly, and also that he had 'a girl hereabouts', though 'decent [sic] girls are hard to find'.

On 22 June, Garland wrote from Dover about an 'interesting' flight. He had often wondered what it would be like to enter cloud. 'Now I know', he observed. 'As you climb up you find yourself in a very slight fleeting mist. Then all of a sudden you see a white wall and the next moment you are enveloped in what you might compare to a thick mist in which you can see nothing but the machine. No ground, no sky. Nothing!' Then he was through the cloud 'with a rush of cold'. The sun was shining and 'below it looks like billowing snow. You want to get out and play on it.' Garland wished he could paint the scene. Suddenly, through 'a rift' in the cloud, he saw 'the beautiful green and white coast of Dover 2–3,000ft below'. After a 'two days' graduation examination at Reading, on 6 July Garland gained his wings, which allowed him to dispense with the unwieldy German-like helmet forced on trainees. He could now don 'a simple close-fitting helmet'.

In France during Spring 1916, at Douai Max Immelmann's unit continued to support the German Sixth Army. Aviation Section 62 completed its first year of service on 5 May,

Aerial photography. German observer demonstrates use of his camera equipment. *(Peter Jackson)*

A recovery vehicle in France holding an unknown aeroplane. *(Peter Jackson)*

having accounted for twenty-five hostile machines for the loss of just two of its own. But Immelmann complained of a current absence of activity in his area. Although suffering from sunburn, he informed his mother that he was in good health and thanked her profusely for 'the Easter eggs, chocolate hares and gingerbreads'. He deplored 'imbecile' members of the Reichstag for considering peace moves at a time 'when we must put all our strength into the war'. Despite his complaints about lack of action, in a letter of 18 May Immelmann could describe his fifteenth victory against a Bristol fighter whose pilot was so intent on shooting down a German biplane that he forgot to keep an eye on his tail. This success brought a card with the simple message, 'God be with you', from the Duchess of Saxony. Nine days later, thanking his mother for her amusing letter, he assured her that he always carried her lucky clover leaf with him.

Poor weather restricted flying at the beginning of June, and Immelmann spent much of the time discussing tactics and future plans with Maj Stempel, staff officer with the Sixth Army. Stempel later wrote that summaries of Immelmann's practical experience accompanied by illustrative diagrams were circulated among the Army's pilots. Partly as a result of their discussions, it was decided to create squadrons of single-seat fighters responsible to Sixth Army headquarters. Immelmann was selected to form the first of these and after Aviation Section 62 left for the Eastern Front on 13 June, busied himself with its creation. He was aware that the new British fighters could out climb the Fokker and was therefore putting his faith in the forthcoming Halberstadt and Albatros biplanes.

F/Sgt James McCudden would soon be joining this contest. After five months training, on 5 July 1916 he reached the Pilots' Pool at St Omer. His Royal Aero Club 'aviator's certificate', issued on 16 April for 'having fulfilled the conditions stipulated by the FAI [*Fédération Aéronautique Internationale*]', had a quaint pre-war air. It began: 'We the undersigned recognised by the FAI as the sporting authority of the British Empire certify that …' Three days after arriving at St Omer, McCudden moved to No 20 Sqn at nearby Clairmarais, where he found the FE2d pusher armed with a forward-firing machine-gun for the pilot and two machine-guns for the observer. He stayed under a month at Clairmarais before transferring to the Ypres sector where No 29 Sqn re-equipped with the single-seat 'spinning incinerator' DH2 pusher, which could reach 10,000ft in thirty minutes and maintain 80mph at that altitude. On 6 September, McCudden's first combat victory was confirmed by Anzac troops, who reported his opponent's crash. A perfectionist, McCudden constantly analysed his own performance, on 21 October deploring his failure to shoot down a Rumpler biplane. 'Had I sighted in front of him instead of at him, I think I should have got him. Experience teaches', he wrote. After another inconclusive clash, he blamed his own 'too hasty' aim.

Having at last completed his prolonged training and reached the Front, Douglas Joy wrote enthusiastically to his mother on 25 March 1916 about 'more gadgets on my machine, camera mounting and lighting for night flying'. His squadron was billeted in a chateau with sheets on the bed and 'real American bathrooms'. The aeroplanes, which No 27 Sqn had, were 'very much faster than any other machine I have yet met in the air'. They were also more sturdy. One pilot flew 'slap bang' into a 15,000 volt high-tension wire with ¼in cable and then 'through a telegraph line with forty wires'. His machine was 'absolutely wrecked', but the pilot had only 'a few scratches and a bad shaking up'.

To his brother Ernst (Ernie) he wrote that 'for the moment it does not seem at all like war here'. The 'very modern chateau [was] beautifully furnished, electric lights, decent American bathrooms: in fact more luxurious than we have at home'. A nine-hole golf course was in the grounds, a tennis court on the lawn and in one of the aerodrome hangars, a racquets court. Joy

27-2-16.   R.A.P.
                         Farnboro.
Dear Addie
        Very sorry not to have
written to you before.
    I am now at Farnboro
learning to fly.
    I have been in England
since the end of January.
I expect to go out to France
again in about 3 months time
as an aeroplane pilot.
    I am learning to fly on a
80 horse-power Avro biplane.
It does about 80 miles an hour
and is a splendid machine.
We have several captured
German machines here,
which we are using.
Since I came home I have seen
"Now's the Time," "Betty, Bric-a-
Brac," and "Tina "3 times, and
they all are good, with the
exception of "Now's the time"
which I did not care for
much. Trusting you will write
soon.   Yours Sincerely
                   Jim.

Left: Letter from James McCudden to Miss Addie Meaken of Plumstead, dated 27 February 1916, in which he points out that the British are using a number of captured German machines. McCudden's family complained that his letters were always short.

Below: Friend or Foe? A total wreck shows the flimsy nature of First World War aeroplanes. *(Peter Jackson)*

A Bristol F2A Fighter, forerunner of the highly successful F2B Fighter. A3346 was one of the first examples built, and it is seen here in France with No 48 Sqn, Royal Flying Corps, in early 1917. *(Peter Jackson)*

vastly preferred this location to Dover, where 'our grub was rotten, the place was swamped in mist, and we had far more work of a most disagreeable and tedious kind to do.'

He informed his brother that he had flown 'a long way' behind enemy lines taking photographs. '"Archie" is too damn good these days', he added. 'He makes a rotten noise, smells rotten and makes a rotten lump and flash in the air'. So far he had been lucky, 'although several times he has made me chase my own tail to make him puzzled'. Joy explained that his biplane was a fast single-seat scout with a powerful water-cooled engine. He usually flew on half throttle, which allowed him 'to make rings round any other type of machine I have yet met in the air'. It could climb quickly, and Joy had often been up to 3 miles (almost 16,000ft) 'where your heart begins to pump'. However, the Martinsyde Scout was 'very hard to land', normally requiring three to four attempts. Joy admitted to his brother that he had 'crashed several undercarriages'. But, he concluded, 'aviation is most fascinating and I could go on writing about it all night'.

While Joy achieved his ambition to fly operationally, Stuart Keep's persistence at length brought him success. When 'the country was flooded with recruitment posters' in 1914, he had wanted to join the RFC. Like other aspiring pilots, however, he discovered the need for a Royal Aero Club Certificate, the cost of which had risen to £100. This sum would be refunded when he qualified, but 'in those days it was a big IF'. He 'reluctantly came down to earth' and in May 1915 was commissioned into The Royal Warwickshire Regiment. After 'mud wallowing' in France, he was sent home with blood poisoning in May 1916. In hospital, a fellow patient gave him 'several tips' on how to get into the RFC; so he decided to try again.

Joy 'hobbled up' to the War Office to be severely ticked off for not having gone through the usual channels but did secure an interview with a staff officer. 'I proceeded to put my case before him in as rosy a light as possible to show him that I was the one man the RFC had been waiting for.' However, nothing positive could be done until Keep regained full mobility. At a rehabilitation centre, he persuaded the medical officer to pass him fit and Keep put together 'a fine imposing package', which this time he did forward through official channels: 'I already had visions of soaring into the clouds.' To his dismay, he learnt that instead he was to be posted to the infantry depot at Rouen. Forsaking fourteen days' embarkation leave, Keep badgered the local military authorities and the RFC at Adastral House in London. At length, the infantry posting was cancelled and in August Keep went to No 24 Reserve Sqn at Netheravon for practical and theoretical instruction. Unlike the Insall brothers, he found Netheravon 'fascinating, right out in the country surrounded by undulating downs covered with short, green turf, the living quarters built in red and white, and beyond the long line of hangars and behind them the workshops'.

Stuart Keep explained that 'the pupils donned great leather helmets rather like pudding basins with heavy padding round the edge as crashes were frequent and the helmets helped to save cracked skulls.' This was the headgear so disliked by Ewart Garland. Keep's first flight involved a wide circuit of the aerodrome with an instructor: 'Altogether it had only lasted about five minutes, but it was the most wonderful five minutes that I've ever spent in my life.' In due course, he went solo and moved on to a more advanced training centre at Rendcomb, Gloucestershire, 'By this time I was beginning to consider myself quite an aviator but my pride was soon to receive a fall.'

During the evening of 12 September, although it was 'a bit windy' he took up 'an old BE8A affectionately known as the "bloater" from its fishy appearance'. The rotary engine had a habit of 'liberally' spraying the pilot with castor oil, but, more worryingly, the machine had 'a strong inclination' to turn to the left. 'This was popularly supposed to be due to the fact that the old thing was used to doing left-hand circuits round and round the aerodrome like the donkeys on the sea shore and resented any attempt to make it leave its usual course.'

Keep took off without difficulty, but at 200ft 'the engine went on strike'. The next he knew was that

> … we were rapidly making for earth sideways. Then there was a horrid bump and a sound of much splintering of wood and a cloud of dust and I was crawling out from the shattered remains of the poor old bloater. Except for a few grazes on my hand, I was unhurt but the bloater's days were done – probably owing to my treatment as I had no experience of rotary engines.

Keep 'retired from aviation for a few days', then successfully took up another BE8A which restored his confidence. After passing the requisite tests, Stuart Keep gained his wings on 26 October 1916.

Like Keep, the doggedness of another soldier, John Jeyes, took him into the RFC. As a schoolboy at Oundle, Jeyes was fascinated by 'the early vintage aircraft flown by Gustav Hamel' and by watching aeroplanes taking part in a London–Liverpool race. 'My schoolboy hopes were that perhaps one day I could have an opportunity to take to the skies. Flying seemed to be so elusive and almost intangible.' After leaving Oundle, Jeyes worked in the family business, while he decided which branch of the services he would join. He preferred the RFC 'but I was not sure that I would be able to cope with the demands and challenges involved'. On the other hand, he was not keen on the infantry: 'I was really upset by the tales and experiences which we had heard about trench life in France.'

So, when he reported to Northampton Barracks, he intended to apply for the RFC. However, 'somehow I was caught up with the RSM', who enlisted him and told him he would go to Colchester the following day: 'I went home wondering how I found myself being posted to an army unit.' Jeyes had planned to see the recruiting officer, Maj A.E. Ray, before the RSM secured 5/- (25p) for enlisting him. Early next morning, Jeyes went to the barracks, avoided the RSM and waited half an hour to see Maj Ray. Jeyes reminded him that he had seen him on 11 May 1916, when 'under eighteen years old' and Ray had told him to come back in a month, Jeyes having been born on 3 June 1898.

As he was explaining the position to Ray, the RSM appeared and said that Jeyes had been attested and was due to go to Colchester. To Jeyes' relief, Ray 'took the law into his own hands', secured the papers from the RSM and said that he would deal with the matter. The result was that Jeyes did not go to Essex, was given two months to confirm his choice of the RFC and the RSM failed to pocket 5/-. In August, Jeyes thus found himself at Denham Cadet Camp near Uxbridge earning 1/- (5p) a day at the beginning of his RFC career.

At the front, Harold Wyllie revealed the mounting strain of the life to which John Jeyes aspired. On 13 June, he got up at 2am for a dawn reconnaissance, but to his irritation poor weather caused its cancellation. Then he learnt that 'I am to go over the lines with two pilots who have put in one reconnaissance and one patrol between them. No experience in formation flying or fighting. Sometimes I feel that I simply cannot carry on any more under present conditions.'

He recorded on 20 June that 'a spy' reported one of the Squadron's pilots had been shot down by an Allied aeroplane. Then one of his pilots 'completely lost his nerve and told me to-day that he could not go on flying'; so he was sent back to England. Wyllie was informed by the squadron commander that he had been recommended for an MC, but to his disappointment the award would not be confirmed. On 15 July, Wyllie heard that he was to go home on promotion. Two days before he had taken the opportunity to visit his brother Bill at a nearby infantry position. 'This was the last time I saw my brother,' who was killed shortly afterwards, and before the Armistice Harold Wyllie would lose another brother in action.

The summer of 1916 proved an active period for ground forces and the RFC, as the Germans continued to make serious inroads at Verdun. On 28 June, Sir Douglas Haig explained that the forthcoming offensive on the Somme, supported by French troops on the British right, would be conducted 'with such vigour as will force the enemy to abandon his attacks on Verdun'.

In the run-up to this battle, the RFC had several encouraging signs; in particular, as Immelmann sensed, that the Fokker might no longer be quite so menacing. Late on the evening of 18 June, two patrolling FE2b machines of No 25 Sqn came across three of the German aeroplanes and with the advantage of height, attacked. One immediately made off, the other two flew towards Lens with the British in pursuit. As they did so one of the Fokkers suddenly climbed and shot down the leading FE2b, whereupon the second British machine opened fire. As this FE2b manoeuvred to attack, the German fell away steeply and crashed. Later 2/Lt G.R. McCubbin would discover that his observer (Cpl J.H. Waller) had accounted for Max Immelmann, who that day was flying a 100hp machine because his more powerful type was unavailable. At the time, No 25 Sqn merely noted that McCubbin had 'fought and crashed a Fokker'.

While agreeing that Immelmann was dead, for he had crashed on their side of the line, the Germans ascribed his end to structural failure of his machine, which was seen to break in two in mid-air. His brother Franz maintained that eyewitness reports confirmed the fatal sequence of events were similar to structural failure suffered by another machine flown by Max on 31 May; an incident which he was lucky to survive. Oswald Boelcke believed that malfunction of the interrupter gear led to Immelmann shooting off his own propeller, arguing further that a piece of the fractured propeller had torn through the bracing wires to the fuselage, which disintegrated. Whatever the reason, there was no doubt that one of only three airman holders of the *Pour le Mérite* at the time had been removed from the fray. Immelmann's mother recorded how moved the family was by 'the hundreds of telegrams, letters and poems which poured in daily for a period of many weeks', including messages of sympathy from the Kaiser and King of Saxony. Thousands lined the streets of Dresden as Immelmann's funeral cortège passed, but the fact remained that like so many other mothers in other nations, his must cope with grief for a son lost in action. In operational terms the RFC had achieved a major coup.

Immelmann died a fortnight before the Battle of the Somme, in preparation for which Trenchard established an advanced HQ at Fienvillers, where the Ninth Wing had three squadrons and two flights. Attached to each of the four British armies was an RFC Brigade with its own Aircraft Park. In total, twenty-seven squadrons were deployed with 421 aeroplanes exclusive of a further 216 at the depots; a substantial increase over the twelve squadrons available in October 1915. In his post-war reflections on this period, Maj Gen Sir Sefton Brancker claimed that one No 15 Sqn BE2c of IV Brigade had been fitted with armour plating for the pilot 'to some purpose'. Indeed, a 'bullet proof seat' had been available earlier, but the 'general practice' was to discard it even if installed on the grounds that the added weight adversely affected speed and manoeuvrability.

The principal role in the British infantry attack on the Somme would fall to Gen Henry Rawlinson's Fourth Army, comprising five corps to which 110 aeroplanes were allocated in direct support. The Fourth Army was to advance on a 14-mile (22km) front and initially penetrate 1.5 miles (3km), allowing the Reserve Army to exploit the gap created, take Bapaume and swing north towards Arras. The preliminary bombardment made the ground shake violently at Bertangles, 40 miles (64km) behind the front line, where Algernon Insall who had travelled from Paris with his brother Gilbert and future VC winner to volunteer for the RFC had been appointed adjutant to the 3rd (Corps) Wing. When a lull occurred on the appointed day, he knew that the troops were about to go over the top. 'It was a moving experience,' Insall reflected.

The Battle of the Somme, which would in its various phases continue for four and a half months, began on 1 July and on that opening day claimed 57,470 British casualties, approximately one-third of them killed. Newspaper headlines the following day were fanciful: 'The Big Advance', 'All Goes Well for England and France'. Readers learnt that 'the nation was thrilled [that] the great British offensive' had commenced so well with 'our gallant soldiers' overrunning sixteen miles of enemy trenches.

On the opening day and throughout the bitter struggle in the ensuing months, the RFC played the pivotal role that Trenchard intended. During the course of the battle, he reiterated his aim of exploiting 'the moral effect of the aeroplane on the enemy, but not to let him

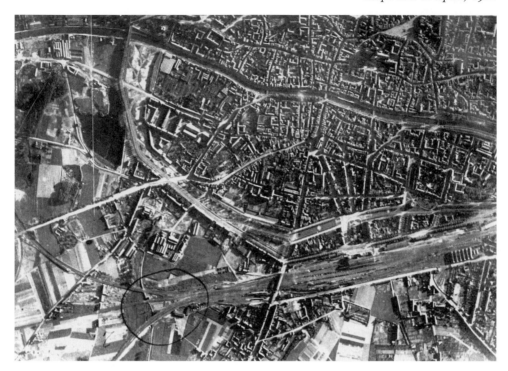

Bombing Target. Railway lines, stations and good yards were prime targets in a bid to disrupt enemy communications. Railway junctions proved most profitable. Here one is highlighted on a target photo. *(IWM Doc 762)*

exploit it on ourselves. Now that can only be done by attacking and continuing to attack.' Close support, aggressive patrolling, the bombing of enemy rear areas, such as ammunition dumps and railway junctions, were all prominent. Enemy troops likened low-level attackers, which 'cruised ceaselessly and almost at ground level above our trenches and shell holes', to 'buzzards who had fixed on their prey'. During the afternoon of 1 July, bombers hit St Quentin station, causing a massive ammunition explosion and 180 troop casualties. 'The men were panic-stricken and fled in every direction,' a German report admitted.

Hugh Chance, who had found himself under Zeppelin attack in Epping Forest the previous year as an infantry officer, joined No 27 Sqn at Fienvillers, 10 miles (16km) west of Albert and approximately 15 miles (24km) behind the front line in July 1916 and during the Somme battle found his Martinsyde Scout detailed for bombing raids. The machine had no proper bomb sight, 'only a wire contraption fixed to the right side of the cockpit'. Chance got his rigger to make a hole in the floor of the cockpit through which he could pick out the target. Even then, unless flying low and therefore subject to dangerous small arms fire, he found it difficult to identify a specific target. 'Many of our bombs must have fallen ineffectively,' he concluded.

Further to discomfort the enemy, Chance revealed, HE bombs were supplemented by rolls of toilet paper and 'as many china articles as could be found'. He recalled how over one target, the lavatory accessories unravelled as they fell earthwards 'followed by a "jerry", which we fondly hoped would fall on the head of an unsuspecting enemy gazing up at our paper streamers'. Broken gramophone records, empty soda water bottles and 'other rubbish' swelled the unofficial bomb load.

Canadian-born Ewart Garland, who lived in Australia, reached No 10 Sqn at the front in July 1916 to discover 'very funny' wintry weather. Flying on a familiarisation reconnaissance with 'an experienced observer', he remarked that the trenches looked 'like ugly jagged cuts', flashes and puffs of smoke were 'all over the place'. When off duty, he swam in a convenient canal and as there were 'a few horses on the Squadron for our use' had managed 'a couple of gallops'. In his letters, he portrayed a casual mixture of operations and social activity. On 26 July, he flew a patrol in the morning and played tennis in the afternoon. He recorded that, at first, in his quiet sector he 'enjoyed a Battle of Waterloo sort of life, active flying being interspersed with riding, tennis, visits to Béthune for teas, dinners, drinking etc.' The Mess, too, had

> … a Waterloo flavour … meals of several courses, correct wines including port circulated in a correct and proper manner. Liqueurs with coffee were *de rigeur*. This 'officer-gentleman' kind of life did not last long, and before many weeks had passed war conditions set in and life became much less pleasant with a growing fear of death seldom far off.

On 13 August after tennis and a two-hour artillery observation stint, Garland and some others attended the men's concert. The following day, the highlight of his diary read: 'Got roller for tennis court from local hospital'. That day's appended comment was more sober: it was 'quite usual' to drop 20lb bombs from 6,500ft on a random target 'with minimum accuracy'. On one occasion he merely offloaded his two bombs 'on the large city of Lille, regardless of where they actually fell'. This troubled Garland:

> I shudder to think of the innocent French civilians which must have been hit during the war as it was an accepted thing throughout the Flying Corps to bomb in this casual way. I do not recall that complaints ever reached us from French Command.

On another occasion, he reflected that towns were full of troops and frequent raids were 'meant to upset enemy morale, quite as much as to cause material damage'.

It was not all work: 'Higher Authority discreetly encouraged occasional binges, which were often pretty wild, ending in such rough stuff as rugger scrums and schoolboy horseplay.' Garland observed that these parties were 'a release valve from both boredom and war nerves i.e. fear of being shot down in flames'. One such dinner followed by a party until after midnight occurred on 16 August, ending with singing in which Garland took part. As a result he was nicknamed Harry Piller after 'a star of light musicals'; and 'Harry' became his name for the duration of the war. RFC HQ staff officer Maurice Baring would visit the Mess 'from time to time … to perform various parlour tricks such as balancing a liqueur glass on his bald pate while relating doggerel verse'. Sholto Douglas, the former Royal Field Artillery officer, independently paid tribute to Baring's morale-boosting visits, when his entertaining antics were interspersed with community singing of raucous ditties in which he enthusiastically took part. 'A plumpish, bald-headed, middle-aged man of the intellectual type', Baring had 'an endearing manner of his own … One of the great characters of the RFC', Douglas declared.

Douglas Joy, too, became involved at the Somme. He escorted photographic operations or machines attacking 'the Hun sausage balloons', took part in bombing railway targets and troop positions. A 'special mission' occurred on 28 July to bomb Mons railway station from 2,000–3,000ft, a location where 'a great deal of danger' existed. He wrote to his sister Nina the next day:

Thank heaven it is all over. While it lasted it was exciting and interesting and we did what we set out to do, a bombing show at a very famous place, a long way over the lines. We had an ideal day for the job … huge mountainous masses of woolly clouds with large gaps between them through which we dodged about and through which we came over very low, quite unusually low.

He flew regularly, sometimes leading operations, until he went on a fortnight's leave to England on 18 August.

Albert Ball, who often took off before dawn and landed for the final time at dusk, need not have fought on the Somme. Awarded the MC in June, he had been offered the opportunity to remain in England as an instructor, but as he explained to his mother, he had volunteered to 'go out again and have another smack'. It was not that he particularly wanted to go, 'but every boy who has loving people and a good home should go out and stand up for it'. He continued: 'I shall fight for you and come home for you, and God always looks after me and makes me strong; may He look after you also.' Ball did reveal reservations, however. 'Oh I do get tired of always living to kill. I am beginning to feel like a murderer. I shall be pleased when I have finished … I hate this game, but it is the only thing one must do just now.' By the end of the Somme battle, in addition to his MC, Ball would have gained the DSO and two bars for his exploits.

During the four and a half months of confrontation along the Somme, reinforced from Dunkirk by No 8 Sqn RNAS flying single-seat Nieuport 17 and Sopwith Pup fighters, the RFC recorded 298 bombing raids 'with definite targets'. Specifically, 17,600 bombs were dropped, 19,000 photographs taken, 8,612 artillery targets registered following air observation, 164 enemy machines destroyed and another 205 'driven down damaged'. Buoyed by the success of the fighter patrols, Sir Douglas Haig optimistically demanded twenty extra fighter squadrons.

Not all aerial activity was confined to the Somme. Elsewhere, fighting continued in the air and on the ground, and the RFC gained another VC. Thirty-two-year-old Capt Lionel Rees from Carnarvon, a regular officer in the Royal Garrison Artillery, at his own expense while on leave took lessons at the Bristol Flying School at Larkhill on Salisbury Plain to gain Royal Aero Club Certificate No. 392 on 7 January 1913. He became attached to the RFC on 10 August 1914, served as an instructor at the CFS and on 25 July 1915 landed at Amiens in command of No 11 Sqn. He had flown ahead of his pilots, who were astonished on arrival to see their commanding officer in overalls repairing his machine, damaged in combat the previous day. In the ensuing three months, Rees shot down three enemy aeroplanes, damaged several others, was mentioned in despatches and then awarded the MC for completing a photographic operation while under aerial attack.

Back in England, he commanded the CFS as a temporary major before returning to France in charge of No 32 Sqn. Contrary to normal practice, Rees continued to fly operationally. On 1 July 1916, patrolling alone in a DH2 with its single Lewis machine-gun, he mistook a group of aeroplanes for friendly bombers returning from a raid, only to discover on getting closer that he had stumbled across ten of the enemy. He immediately dealt with one which attacked him, sending it back over its own line belching smoke. Five more opened fire at long range, but dispersed when he flew towards them. Rees severely damaged two and gave chase to two others, which broke away. As he caught them, he was hit in the thigh (a wound that would leave him with a permanent limp) and temporarily lost control of his machine. He soon recovered to resume the chase and fire all his ammunition at his quarries before setting off

Lionel Wilmot Brabazon Rees. Pre-war Royal Artillery officer attached to RFC in August 1914. He was awarded the VC August 1916, when commanding No 32 Sqn, for an action which left him with a permanent limp. Post-war assistant commandant RAF Cranwell, before commanding the RAF in Palestine and Transjordan. Retired from RAF in 1931. *(IWM Q 68027)*

home. The VC citation referred to his 'conspicuous gallantry and devotion to duty' in turning his own error to such devastating advantage.

Arthur William Tedder was yet another infantry officer to reach the RFC via the trenches. After graduating from Magdalene College, Cambridge, a gifted pianist and landscape artist, Tedder was destined for a diplomatic career. Instead he joined the Army, in January 1915 being commissioned into The Dorsetshire Regiment. Six months later, he married Wilhelmina Rosaline Foster to whom he wrote daily from the Front. When a knee injury threatened his military future, Tedder determined to transfer to the RFC, which he did in January 1916 after regaining mobility. Within four months he had learned to fly and been promoted captain. His life in the air was certainly not without incident: on 21 June 1916, in a letter to his wife, he described how anti-aircraft fire had 'put a shrapnel bullet through the nacelle of my aircraft, in one side and out of the other, cutting one of the petrol pipes and passing down between my legs. Petrol came pouring out in a continuous stream.' No fire occurred, but Rosaline Tedder must have been concerned that on another occasion her husband would not be so lucky.

In August 1916, appointed a flight commander with No 25 Sqn, Capt A.W. Tedder painted his two-seater FE2b in Cambridge blue. On patrol during the evening of 8 September, he came across a Roland biplane 1,500ft below him above Mericourt Wood being attacked by a FE2b and FE8. Tedder dived to follow the German machine as it made off towards Douai, caught up and allowed his observer to fire one and a half drums into it from 500ft. Tedder then spotted two Fokker monoplanes to the east and closed on them. One 'sheered off', the other flew aggressively towards Tedder. Before he could attack, Lt G. Nelson in the front cockpit of the British pusher opened fire at 200yds, causing the Fokker to dive and make off towards the east. Tedder remained on his tail long enough for Nelson to drill one and a half drums into the enemy aeroplane, where hits were seen on the wings and fuselage before he flew out of range. Such an encounter illustrated the daily work of aerial patrols, which were an integral part of the fighting on the Somme.

Harold Taylor also flew with No 25 Sqn on the Somme. Born at Clapham in 1896, he had a strict Anglican upbringing and joined the Boy Scouts, where 'we got a very good grounding to be patriotic'. When war broke out, he wrote: 'I and many others were no doubt fervent patriots through the medium of the Scout movement and writers such as Rudyard Kipling.' In August 1914, he and three of his friends enlisted 'to fight for God, King and Country', initially in The East Surrey Regiment.

Almost two years later, June 1916, Taylor found himself in The Machine-Gun Corps bound for the Somme, delighted to play an active role in 'the War to end all Wars'. Later he mused: 'I wonder whether we would have been so confident had we known that we would soon be in a Hell which it would be impossible for any human being to describe.' Once in the line, his youthful enthusiasm faded fast, 'As if death, stench and rats were not enough in a few days I discovered that lice had taken possession of me, my clothes were housing hundreds upon hundreds, the whole earth was full of them. There was nothing we could do about it.' Caustically, he added: 'Some gentleman invented … "Harrison's Pomade" for killing lice. Fortunes must have been made with this, but it made very little difference, when applied, in fact they seemed to thrive on it.'

Taylor was highly critical of newspaper censorship, too:

> The people at home were told about the Somme offensive but no photos of its horrors ever reached the press. Photos of a few tommies with steel helmets on were shown going over the top, no dead men were around and most of the pictures were taken behind the lines.

Correspondents, he maintained, were not allowed 'to report the full horrors of this battle where many men were drowned and not mortally wounded by shell or bullet'. When his unit came out of the line, in the rest area the Commanding Officer spoke about the RFC's 'urgent need' for gunner/observers. Taylor volunteered and was interviewed at RFC HQ, being told that he would be informed in due course if he had been successful. In the meantime he must go back to his unit, which was again in the front line.

In September 1916, Taylor learned that he had been accepted for the RFC and found himself posted to No 25 Sqn at Auchel. There he met Sgt Jimmie Green, 'one of the finest pilots I ever flew with', who arranged a complete change of clothing and new kit: 'After a bath … I felt a new man.' Following the discomfort of the trenches, Taylor particularly appreciated the sleeping quarters and meals, 'although for many days I could not lose the stench from my nostrils, I gradually became a normal being once more'. In the front line, death was faced every minute, he mused, but in the RFC at least between operations he could feel safe.

Taylor's first flight in an FE2b pusher was with Capt Oscar Grieg. Clambering into his cockpit, he saw an empty petrol can and wondered about its purpose. 'I found the adventure very exhilarating,' he wrote, taking peeps over the side and without any preliminary instruction, not giving much heed to the route or the countryside below: 'I was quite content to enjoy the thrill of the first flight.' He had a shock on landing, when Grieg told him to write a report of the terrain over which they had flown. Fortunately, Green overheard, told Taylor not to worry because he knew the route, took him into an office and dictated a report which included prominent landmarks in the vicinity of the station. Taylor wrote out this report in his own hand and gave it to Grieg, who declared it 'bloody marvellous'.

Taylor flew frequently with Green, who explained that the mysterious petrol can was for the observer to sit on once clear of enemy territory on the way home. For Taylor discovered that he was expected to stand in the 3ft deep front cockpit, which was made out of 'a few wooden pieces covered in doped [varnished] canvas'. The machine had two Lewis guns each controlled manually by the observer. The rear gun was mounted to fire over the top of the aeroplane, but in level flight 'your angles of fire were not numerous'. The front gun was on a mounting fixed to the floor of the nacelle, with a clip on the right and left into which it could be pressed and swivelled. Each gun fired drums of 95rnds of .303 ammunition. For quick sighting, every fifth round was tracer. When firing the front gun, Taylor learnt to press his knees apart against the mounting, otherwise the recoil would throw the gun out of the clip.

Squadron aeroplanes engaged in a bombing raid, Taylor revealed, adopted a V-formation. The leader had ribbons streaming from each of his rear wing tips; his observer carried white, red and green Very lights. The flying altitude would be announced in the briefing room. After take-off, the machines circled the aerodrome until the leader was satisfied with the formation's height, when his observer fired a green light. If enemy machines were manoeuvring to attack, the leader would fire a red light indicating adoption of close formation to provide better mutual defence. A white light, not usually fired until across friendly lines, meant the end of an operation, time to go home and permission to break formation.

Taylor remembered clearly his first aerial combat against a German pilot of roughly his own age:

> His parents, my parents and ourselves no doubt worshipped the same God. We made supplications to Him to give us victory, and I could not help thinking what a tragedy it was that men could not settle their differences without war, destroying millions of lives.

One method of training pilots was to start them off in machines with clipped wings so they could get used to handling an aircraft without getting off the ground. *(Peter Jackson)*

Taylor's machine had to break away when two other enemy aeroplanes appeared, otherwise he felt certain that he would have registered a kill.

On landing, Taylor 'gave great thought to the happenings of the day'. He decided that he might kill or be killed in aerial combat, and in most fights in the air there were casualties. 'Killing was my duty', he asserted, 'It was far from being a pleasant thought, but this was war.' He concluded: 'One must not forget that this was total war and the order was to kill or be killed, and then chivalry had to take a back seat.' This represented a steep learning curve for Taylor; a sharp contrast to his feeling when he first flew at the Front. Then, he often saw German scouts patrolling their own side of the line, not venturing over British territory. If two machines passed one another on their respective sides, 'on these occasions I invariably gave one passing a salute,' which was usually returned.

During the fighting at Verdun, the Germans had organised small groups of fighters to challenge large French formations. In this initiative, the forerunner of fighter squadrons, Oswald Boelcke led six single-seat fighters from Sivry. Following Immelman's death in June 1916, he had been sent on a tour in the Balkans and Turkey to avoid loss of another German hero, but his rest proved short-lived. Grave concern about British aerial successes in the opening phase of the Somme battle meant that on 11 August he received orders to return to the Western Front, raise and command a new fighter unit, Jagdstaffel (Jasta) 2. Boelcke took almost two months to work up his command. He ensured that his pilots were tactically aware through familiarity with the lay-out and vulnerability of captured Allied machines, while becoming thoroughly conversant with the construction and fighting capability of their own. Through experience, he found that lurking at 5,000m (16,400ft) with the sun behind him he could

Captured Fe2b pusher. *(Peter Jackson)*

profitably dive on unsuspecting opponents below; the origin of the 'Hun in the sun' concept. He drew up basic guidelines for his pilots, which emphasised this tactic, but also urged them to attack at close range, preferably from the rear and never be put off by 'ruses' or other distractions: once committed to an attack, it must be carried through.

On 2 September over the Somme battlefield, Boelcke secured his nineteenth victory. Fifteen days later, his squadron went into action for the first time, accounting for six British machines. Manfred von Richthofen, one of the pilots, wrote of the fourteen BE2a and six FE2b machines encountered, 'of course Boelcke was the first to see them, for he saw more than most men.' By the end of the month, Jasta 2 had flown 186 sorties and scored 25 victories for the loss of three of its own aeroplanes. Boelcke wrote to his parents that the number of men killed was not counted, only 'the machines we have brought down ... We have nothing against the individual; we only fight to prevent him flying against us.' For some days during September, Boelcke was officially laid low with asthma, though like the mysterious stomach ailment in February may rather have been evidence of stress, the 'nerves' which he so strenuously denied. Three weeks after his latest illness, he again sought to quell parental concern: 'Mother need not paint such a ghastly picture of the circumstances and dangers in which I live.' Rather she should recognise that his combat experience and 'technical advantages' through improved equipment gave him a protective edge in the air.

Even before emergence of the German fighter squadrons, there was no disguising the rising number of RFC casualties. On 26 August five BE12s from No 19 Sqn were lost returning from a target. Five days later four No 27 Sqn bombers were shot down, and writing in September, Hugh Chance of that Squadron noted 'at present we are rather short of pilots, as we have lost five in the past week or two.' The volatile and persistent Robert

Smith-Barry, having passed his training course following his severe leg injuries, returned to France in command of No 60 Sqn in time for the Somme clashes. He was appalled at the lack of training among newly arrived pilots, refusing to send them over enemy lines until they had more flying hours. Smith-Barry complained to his wing commander, Lt Col Hugh Dowding: 'They've only seven flying hours to their credit, sir. It's bloody murder.' Sholto Douglas agreed that at this time it had been 'sheer murder' to send pilots into action 'grossly short of training'.

John MacKenzie was not exposed to this uninviting environment due to the determination of his mother; Douglas Joy's future mother-in-law. She had arrived in England in June 1916, knowing that her sons Gordon and Cortlandt had already been killed in action. Two months later, Kathleen learnt that John, her only remaining son, serving in the Army had been ordered to the Front with his regiment. She immediately set out to find the Commanding General, taking a taxi from the Imperial Hotel, Hythe, to the Arlington Hotel at Folkestone. There, Lieutenant-General (Lt Gen) E.A.H. Alderson, Inspector of Infantry and former Canadian commander in France, advised her to see Maj Gen J.C. MacDougall, currently commanding Canadian troops in Britain. In 'thick fog and gathering gloom', the taxi dropped her at the wrong place. She managed to find MacDougall's house, but the General was out. 'Not to be outdone', Kathleen joined a crowd at a nearby corner and asked a soldier if the General was there. On being told he had gone home, she retraced her steps, and 'so we found them'. MacDougall asked Kathleen to write down the details. He then went away and, after a time, returned. 'It will be seen to at once,' he said. 'So we started home all through the mist and dark feeling rejuvenated … we [had] saved John … God be thanked'. However, this was merely the overture to a similar struggle, when John transferred to the RFC.

Mrs Margaret Douglas was not so fortunate. In October 1916 her eldest son, Maj Sholto Douglas MC, returned to France with No 70 Sqn. He took with him a worrying family problem: his brother Archibald (Archie), to whom he had given his first flight and who like Sholto had transferred from the Royal Artillery, had been reported missing. His distraught mother charged Sholto with discovering Archie's fate. Visiting No 42 Sqn, Sholto Douglas learnt that the machine of his observer brother and the pilot, with whom Sholto and Archie had been at Tonbridge School, had disintegrated in mid-air under anti-aircraft fire. The Douglas brothers had been 'unusually close' and Sholto admitted to missing deeply 'the warmth of the relationship'. He had also to endure the wrath of his mother, who blamed him for influencing Archie to join the RFC, a transfer which she maintained cost him his life; 'the illogicality of a distressed mother', Sholto remarked.

On the Western Front, the RNAS had begun operations that would transform its role there. Arguably, by its long-range raids against Zeppelin sheds along the Rhine and the Zeppelin works at Friedrichshafen in the opening weeks of the war, the RNAS had pioneered what became known as 'strategic bombing' involving targets beyond the battlefield. Trenchard would later insist that attacks on 'strategic' targets was initiated by the RFC at the Battle of Neuve Chapelle. To some extent the debate is academic for, indisputably, 'strategic bombing' has come to mean an assault on an enemy's war industries – destroying battlefield weapons in their factories before they could reach the front line. In the summer of 1916, the RNAS launched such a campaign from eastern France.

In April, *The Times* revealed that the range of bombing operations had increased from 230 miles (368km) in May 1915 to 350 miles (560km). One aeroplane that contributed to this enhanced capability was the single-engine, two-seat Sopwith 1½ Strutter with a top speed of

Mass production. Sopwith Aviation Company factory in England. *(Peter Jackson)*

100mph. Its pilot had a Vickers machine-gun firing forward via an interrupter gear and the observer behind him with a Lewis gun on a swivel mounting. The machine had a bomb-load of up to 130lbs and a flying endurance of four and a half hours.

Arrival in service of the Sopwith 1½ Strutter, so called because of the W-shaped metal bracing wires between the struts, initially raised hopes of hitting steel works at Essen and Düsseldorf from Detling in Kent, a concept abandoned because violation of neutral Dutch airspace would be involved. Discussions had already taken place, however, about co-operating with French squadrons against German industrial centres from continental bases. Opposition within the Admiralty to diverting machines for 'inland work' away from 'coastal operations' delayed any positive movement until Spring 1916. Then Capt W.L. Elder RN travelled to Luxeuil-les-Bains, 25 miles (40km) north-west of Belfort, to form No 3 Wing RNAS, which became operational on 1 July, without ever reaching its planned strength. Arguments that attacks on 'blast furnaces and munitions factories in Alsace Lorraine' would impede steel production to the detriment of the enemy fleet, 'navigation over long distances was more in accordance with naval training' and the inability of the RFC to spare machines earmarked for support of ground forces were persuasive.

British airmen enjoy their first Christmas dinner of the peace. How many of these men had survived combat since 1916 or earlier? *(Peter Jackson)*

Evidently, No 3 Wing carried out an impressive array of raids. It claimed not only to have inflicted heavy damage on its targets, but to have forced the Germans to deploy searchlights, balloons and anti-aircraft batteries around sensitive sites, as well as to withdraw single-seat fighters from the Front to counteract the bombers.

The facts did not quite fit this story. For example, on 22 October 1916 forty-five RNAS and French aeroplanes took off in daylight against the Mauser production complex at Oberndorf. Fewer than half actually discharged their bomb load and some of those did so on an entirely different town. Nine of the attackers were lost, and the French decided that their slow pusher machines must henceforth be confined to night operations. Ewart Garland underlined the inaccuracy of all bombing operations, day or night, at this stage of the war: 'It was not unusual for bomb raid formations to lose sight of each other and either go over the lines and drop bombs on any target thought fit or return to the aerodrome and land with the bomb load.' Nevertheless, 'strategic bombing' would now form an integral and expanding part of British aerial warfare.

Back in England, the impact of German air-raids on industrial production continued to cause grave concern. During 1916, warnings of possible Zeppelin activity in thirteen separate weeks in the Cleveland area alone led to blast furnaces being extinguished, which contributed to the annual output of pig iron being lowered by one sixth. Now that the War Office had assumed full responsibility for aerial defence, No 39 Home Defence Sqn was created to defend London. In all, eleven defensive squadrons were located throughout England from Newcastle to Hove, each with its three flights at dispersed locations. A twelfth reserve and training squadron was stationed at Northolt. Action by squadrons south of Melton Mowbray was co-ordinated by the Home Defence Wing; those further north (with responsibility up to the Firth of Forth) acted on information from the Warning Controller in their area. The RFC's contribution to home defence was thus much more organised and comprehensive than before.

Nonetheless, in practice, airships still seemed able to roam at will. Urban centres were blacked out at the slightest hint of an attack. As one London journalist noted in his diary: 'We rode through the dismally dark streets – the Zeppelin menace has made London a medieval city again.' Recovering from an eye injury sustained in France, Algernon Insall took his wife to matinée theatre performances rather than risk exposure to airship raids in the evening. During April 1916, two airships had crossed north-east England. The official report read: 'Three aeroplanes went up but saw nothing and were all damaged on landing. One pilot was killed at Cramlington.' An appended comment was revealing: 'The usual result of flying at night against Zeppelins.' An onlooker, describing an attack on Portsmouth, wrote of searchlights from all sides of the harbour illuminating a 'big silver cigar', at which several anti-aircraft batteries opened up; 'You could see the puffs of the shells they were sending up as they were exploding, and the noise was terrific, but it was high so it got away.'

During the night of 2/3 September, fourteen airships were over England. Sixteen had set out for London, two turned back in the face of adverse winds, heavy rain and icy conditions at high altitude, which caused the remainder to become scattered. In all, four people were killed on the ground, twelve injured and £21,072 of damage wrought. Only one airship came within seven miles of Charing Cross, the others being spotted over East Anglia, the Midlands and as far north as the Humber. Searchlights attempted to illuminate them, aeroplanes to catch them. The RNAS flew six sorties and the RFC ten, but although several pilots caught sight of an airship, only one made conclusive contact.

The experiences of Harold Buss, a pilot since 1913 and veteran of both France and the Dardenelles campaign, undertaking defensive patrols from Westgate, Kent, illustrated the frustration of so many pilots. During the afternoon of 19 March, in a BE two-seater at 3,000ft, Buss 'sighted [a] German machine over Ramsgate at about 6,000ft', but he lost the enemy 'in mist'. Late that evening, he was ordered to Dover for a 'reported Zeppelin' without finding any trace of the intruder. During April, he flew ten patrols during which he saw no sign of 'hostile aircraft'. In fact, the fleeting sight of an airship in March proved the only visual contact he recorded in his seven months at Westgate.

Encouragement, though, was at hand. William Leefe Robinson (known usually by his second Christian name), born in India of British parents, was commissioned into The Worcestershire Regiment in December 1914. Three months later, he volunteered for the RFC and was posted as an observer to No 4 Sqn at St Omer. Wounded in action, he returned to England on 8 May 1915 and after recovering, qualified as a pilot in August. Sent to No 39 Sqn, which was involved in London's defence, several times he attempted to intercept Zeppelins before, on 25/26 April 1916, engaging one near Barkingside without bringing it down.

Capt Leefe Robinson took off from Sutton's Farm, Essex, at 11pm on 2 September 1916 with orders to patrol the Hornchurch-Joyce Green area. Shortly after 1am on 3 September, he caught sight of a Zeppelin illuminated by searchlights near Woolwich, gave chase, but lost his quarry in cloud. Back on patrol, just before 2am he saw a glow to the north-west which looked like a fire, and decided to investigate. As he drew nearer, Robinson found an airship lit up by searchlights and ringed by bursting anti-aircraft shells. Despite the clear danger of being struck by friendly fire, 'I flew about 800ft below it from bow to stern and distributed one drum along it,' he reported; to no avail, none of the internal gas bags were hit:

Off-duty RFC members relax outside a Nissen hut. *(Peter Jackson)*

I therefore moved to one side and gave it another drum distributed along its side – without apparent effect. I then got behind it (by this time I was very close – 500ft or less below) and concentrated one drum on one part (underneath rear) … I hardly finished the drum before I saw the part fired at glow. In a few seconds the whole rear part was blazing … I quickly got out of the way of the falling blazing Zeppelin and being very excited fired off a few red Very lights and dropped a parachute flare.

Lack of petrol forced Leefe Robinson to return to Sutton's Farm, where he landed at 2.45am.
Meanwhile, SL.11 had fallen in flames at Cuffley, Hertfordshire. A Schütte-Lanz wooden framed airship, it burned for two hours, attracting hundreds of excited spectators, reporters and photographers. Next day, Robinson's feat – the first destruction of an enemy airship over England – attracted widespread praise and acknowledgement that a major morale boost to military defenders and civilians alike had been provided. Two days later, Robinson was awarded the VC for his achievement. Enemy airships at night were not after all invincible, and by the end of November four more had been accounted for.

While the home defences had begun to make tangible progress against enemy intruders, at the front unpleasant developments were afoot. No sooner had the Fokker menace been countered than the Germans produced even more dangerous single-seat machines. They also expanded the system of specialist fighter squadrons manned by their best pilots.

With the approach of the third winter, there was much yet to be done.

7

Renewed Optimism: The Third Winter
'Hot milk and rum'

On 15 December 1916, eleven months of mammoth struggle at Verdun ended. The British operation on the Somme, designed to relieve pressure on the French there, had already come to a close on 18 November at a cost of 419,654 British ground casualties. In addition, the RFC lost 308 pilots and 191 observers killed, wounded or missing, with a further 268 'struck off strength from all causes other than battle casualties'. Yet the RFC's operational strength in France rose during the battle. The 410 machines serviceable on 1 July had become 550 on 17 November (306 fitted with wireless), available pilots up from 426 to 585, the number of operational squadrons from 27 to 35.

Individual replacement machines were ferried from England to St Omer, and this process did not slacken during the winter of 1916/17, as Stuart Keep, who had contrived transfer to the RFC while on sick leave from the trenches, testified. A qualified pilot awaiting posting, on 9 November 1916 he went from Farnborough as a passenger on one of the flights enjoying a 'splendid view' from the observer's cockpit of a pusher aeroplane. The route took the crew via Guildford, Redhill, the railway line to Ashford and Hawkinge aerodrome north of Folkestone. Two circles cut in chalk close to Hawkinge gave the compass bearing for the cliffs of Blanc Nez on the other side of the Channel, and from 14,000ft, Keep could 'easily' see the French coast. Once over France, the route took the FE2b east of Calais to St Omer, where the aerodrome was situated half a mile south within the confines of the old racecourse.

Keep reflected that the life of an observer in a ferry machine was 'not a happy one', and it could be boring in the extreme once the novelty wore off. Regulations laid down that an observer must be carried with a loaded machine-gun in case of trouble. But scarcely did a threat from the enemy materialise so far from the front line.

While the confrontation on the Somme was at its height, the Germans had undertaken drastic administrative restructuring, which would have grave implications for the British despite their increased capability. In August 1916, Maj Wilhelm Siegert was appointed Inspector of Military Aviation, tasked with overseeing the training and equipment of the Army's air division. On 8 October Lt Gen Ernst Wilhelm von Höppner became Commanding General of the Army Air Services, responsible for all aspects of Army aviation. The post of Head of Military Aviation was abolished, Lt Col Herman von der Lieth Thomsen made Höppner's Chief of Staff. Under Höppner's auspices, Thomsen rapidly addressed perceived shortcomings in aerial performance.

Acknowledgement that the Fokker E type monoplane had become 'far inferior to the new enemy fighting aircraft, such as the single-seater Nieuport, F.E [sic], and Sopwith biplanes' led to the 'thorough reorganisation' undertaken on Thomsen's authority. Boelcke has been credited with originating the concept, but Immelmann seems to have been think-ing along much the same lines shortly before his death. Thomsen ordered grouping of all German single-seat fighters into Jastas (fighter squadrons) each comprising fourteen machines. These formations were 'to overcome the superiority of the enemy in the air on the Somme' and in the longer term, 'make [it] possible at any time to counter-balance the constantly increasing numerical superiority of the enemy at least temporarily and on certain sectors of the front'.

More immediately, single combat encounters or fights when in a minority must be avoided, 'large formations up to a whole "Jagdstaffel" [Jasta]' be adopted. Squadrons should be trained to perform as 'a single tactical unit'. By the end of 1916, thirty-three fighter squad-rons would be deployed. Growing numbers of Halberstadt D.II (doppeldecker, biplane) and Albatros D.II (nicknamed *Haifisch* or Shark) machines with 120hp or 160hp in-line engines increased danger for the RFC. With a better rate of climb than the Fokker E, they had two fixed machine-guns firing through the propeller. The German fighter force on the Western Front had therefore fundamentally reinvented itself.

Further notice was served of impending disaster, when the RFC lost a proven veteran at the hands of a rising German star and protégé of Boelcke. After completing pilot training, Manfred von Richthofen had flown an Albatros C. III two-seat biplane for reconnaissance and bombing operations. But his primary aim, inspired by the exploits of Immelmann and Boelcke, was to fly fighters. He fitted a machine gun to the top wing of his biplane, which he fired via a cable in his cockpit, and like Albert Ball he seized every opportunity to go up in a single-seat machine.

On 1 September 1916, having joined Boelcke's Jasta 2, in a single-seat Albatros D.I biplane armed with twin machine-guns mounted above the fuselage forward of the cockpit (the type in which Boelcke claimed eleven victories in sixteen days) he accounted for an FE2b from No. 11 Sqn; his first confirmed victory. Richthofen continued to secure victories, and on 23 November in an Albatros D. II fought a prolonged aerial battle with a British DH2 in the Bapaume area before finally shooting it down. His eleventh victim was Maj Lanoe Hawker, who had won his VC near Ypres in July 1915; a loss not immediately admitted in the British press.

Richthofen applied his prowess as a wild animal hunter to aerial combat. He wrote about 'the same hunting fever that grips me when I sit in an aeroplane, see an Englishman and must fly along for five minutes to come at him. Only with the difference that the Englishman defends himself.' To commemorate his first kill, Richthofen ordered an inscribed silver cup from a Berlin jeweller; something he would repeat for future successes. The idea for this almost certainly arose from the practice of awarding an *Ehrenbecher* (Goblet of Honour) to an airman for his first confirmed victory.

British reluctance to reveal Hawker's loss may be explained by unwillingness to overshadow the news that, on 28 October, Oswald Boelcke had been killed in a mid-air collision with one of his own squadron's machines. Renowned for his qualities of leadership, organisation and innovation, quite apart from his impressive operational achievements, Boelcke was a prize scalp for the RFC. Erwin Böhme wrote that in trying to avoid a British machine in a melee over Flers, 'for an instant' he and Boelcke lost sight of one another. Suddenly Böhme saw his squadron commander and pulled up sharply, but the two 'grazed each other … only a gentle touch'. It was enough to send Boelcke plunging to his death; whereas Böhme's machine suf-fered only minor damage. Before and after bringing Jasta 2 to operational readiness, Boelcke had flown almost continuously for two months, often several times a day. Two days before his death, he had claimed his fortieth victory, the twenty-first since 2 September, and his final flight was the sixth that day. Like so many other airmen on both sides of the line, he may well have been suffering from mental and physical exhaustion. However, Erwin Böhme wondered whether Boelcke's habit of not strapping himself into an Albatros cost him his life.

Richthofen, who witnessed the incident, revealed in a letter to his mother that the Squadron (Jasta 2) had suffered six killed and one wounded in six weeks, in addition to two others being 'washed up because of nerves'. He added that Boelcke's loss had 'affected all of us very deeply – as if a favourite brother had been taken from us'. It had even wider implications, for Boelcke had been feted as a national hero.

Among the many official and unofficial messages of condolence received by Boelcke's parents came one from Countess Margareta von Spee, who lost her husband and two sons in the naval battle off the Falklands in December 1914: 'I sympathise with you from the depths of my heart. You too have trod the path that leads from victory to doom. I give you my hand in warmest sympathy.'

The end of the Somme battle and making plans for 1917 did not mean cessation of activity on the ground or in the air during the third winter of the war. After avoiding a transfer to a DH2 'spinning incinerator' squadron, Ranald Reid went instead as a flight commander to No 20 Sqn, where he received an MC for his work with No 25 Sqn and a Bar for that on his new squadron. Like so many other pilots, he reflected on the tragedy of aerial battle:

> On one patrol, I dived on a German biplane and opened fire. Either we hit him and removed his wings, or he was startled into a fatal dive which tore them off. As I watched the poor young chaps hurtling to death, I had all sorts of emotion, with pity overshadowing the triumph.

In October 1916, Tryggve Gran, then serving in his country's air force after his abortive attempt to join the British air arm two years earlier, successfully applied for attachment to the RFC to learn about night-flying techniques against Zeppelins. He therefore found himself at Northolt, Middlesex, with No 11 Reserve Sqn wearing an RFC uniform under the name of Teddy Grant.

Northolt, he discovered, only undertook daytime instruction; night-flying training was carried out at Rochford, near Southend, Essex. On 20 November 1916, he travelled to Farnborough to collect a new machine. Taking off in the late afternoon for the short trip to Northolt as darkness approached, it was cold and blustery but a tail wind encouraged him to press ahead. The first half-hour was fine, then suddenly, 'I flew into a howling snowstorm and all became inky and black and snow and hail whipped my face. Seldom in my life have I been gripped by such fear as assailed me now.' With night rapidly approaching, 'every minute that passed lessened my chances of a safe landing.' Gran turned off the engine and glided to escape the cloud. Finding himself only 200m (650ft) above the ground, he realised he was over a large built-up area: 'I saw flames from factory chimneys and a few lights gleaming in the thick darkness'; the wind having forced him north-eastwards over London. Quickly he turned round to look for a landing spot. Soon the house tops disappeared and 'in the gloom and fog I found myself flying over land which appeared to be flooded. The situation began to be desperate.' It was almost completely dark and he went down to 20–30m (maximum 100ft), where he picked up a railway line. Following it westwards, he saw a large locomotive 'spitting sparks and fire' and with 'a happy feeling of relief', a large field 'more or less free of water'. He put down and rolled to a halt. Suddenly came 'a frightful jolt and before I could tell what was happening both I and the aircraft stood on our heads.' So ended Gran's first experience of night flying in soggy terrain, but he was soon off for more conventional instruction at Rochford.

Gran's flight that day was without doubt uncomfortable, but flying conditions in France were infinitely more unpleasant, as Harold Taylor from Clapham, who fought with the Machine-Gun Corps on the Somme, recalled. In his observer's role that winter:

> I stood up in my nacelle, my feet and back were frozen, and in spite of my face being well greased with Vaseline my nose was frozen. On these flights if any German machine had left its aerodrome to attack us, I could not have fired my guns. When eventually we landed home, all feeling had left my face and hands and to bring the circulation back I drank very hot milk and rum.

Ewart Garland was also in action during these bitter months, on 29 January 1917 he spent his twentieth birthday flying a daylight photographic operation at 2,000ft over the enemy lines followed by a 'pretty cheering evening' in Béthune. One shortcoming of artillery observation was highlighted on 1 February, when he was using a motor car klaxon horn to communicate by Morse with the battery. When it broke, he had to return to base for a replacement klaxon, which disrupted and delayed the shoot. Five days later, after a photographic operation in the afternoon, he was detailed to bomb Provin aerodrome at night. Despite 'bright snow' he failed to locate that or any other airfield, so he released his load on convenient railway buildings; 'another instance of wildly indiscriminate bombing … fully accepted by Authority'. He was critical of using BE pushers in a bombing role. At best they could reach 12,000ft if light, but only 10,000ft with a bomb load. They 'laboured' for an hour to reach that modest altitude, which enemy fighters greatly exceeded. He felt more secure when, contrary to accepted doctrine, their own fighter escort remained with them rather than disappearing ahead in a sweep to deter and engage hostile machines.

Garland was happier with his photographic flights, recording on 3 November 1916: 'Went up on photo work for 2½hrs – took photos at 9,000ft. Was archied all the time I was over the lines. ALL [sic] the photos were successful.' It soon became evident that British advances in photographic reconnaissance and interpretation of photos were being matched by the enemy, and so more serious attention was paid to ground camouflage. Although hangars and aerodrome buildings could be concealed, tracks towards them or outlying latrines betrayed a military concentration. In February 1917, football matches were forbidden because players and spectators might become targets for aeroplanes and artillery shells.

Garland explained too how hazardous night flying could be. The only take-off and landing aids were paraffin flares, the aerodromes often rough fields and engines notoriously unreliable. Once aloft, the pilot's only instruments were those indicating ground speed, engine speed and height. Garland found compasses 'useless' at night, as they frequently 'spun madly'. He therefore relied on flying 'by sight', which could lead 'easily' to getting lost in cloud or fog.

Reflecting further on his operational environment, Garland wrote: 'Many of us looked upon our active service squadron as "home", much like sixth-form scholars or perhaps like a rugger team.' As repeated references to sport showed, the squadron was the centre of sporting and social as well as professional life, with formal dinners and mess parties being supplemented by concerts and shows by visiting actors, one of whom was the musical comedy star, Leslie Henson.

James McCudden's letters during the opening months of 1917 once more showed close concern for his family. Writing to 'Dear Dad' from 'Your affectionate Son Jim' on 23 January, he described how 'a few days ago' a 'Hun' airman had lost his way, landed on his Squadron's air-field, realised his error and blew up the machine before anybody could reach him. McCudden wrote that it was 'intensely cold' with a biting north-east wind and four inches of snow on the ground. He revealed that recently 'a few hits' had been achieved during 'two scraps'. One enemy aeroplane had broken away in a steep dive, as the other 'attracted all my attention'; though he gave no further details of the encounters. It was, he noted, his sister Cis's twenty-fourth birthday. He apologised for not having written, but he wanted her to know that '[his] thoughts are with her'. Thanking her for another 'welcome' letter, James McCudden wrote to his younger sister Kitty on 5 February 1917. Apart from a brief reference to 'bright' weather, which allowed much flying, he concentrated on family affairs. He wondered whether she had worn out the gramophone and whether there had been any good shows at the Empire since he was last home. He was pleased to receive a 'nice letter' from Eileen at Aldershot and another from Cis, which he would answer soon. It might have been a chatty communication from a holiday resort.

While Garland and McCudden were in action at the Front, back in England after his spell in France, on Wednesday 24 January 1917 at 2pm in the Parish Church, Saltwood, Kent, Capt Douglas Grahame Joy RFC married Beatrice Ernestine (Nesta) Gordon MacKenzie. Just over a fortnight later, his new mother-in-law, Kathleen Mackenzie, again went into battle on behalf of her sole surviving son. She noted in her diary on 15 February 1917 that having transferred to the RFC, John was currently on an observer's course at Reading. Presumably Kathleen MacKenzie thought this meant an imminent posting to the Front. For, two days later, she went to Adastral House to see 'Brigadier-General W.S. Brancker, Director of Air Organisation at the Air Branch' only to find him out. Undeterred, she returned by taxi a second time, and managed to see Brancker, reiterating the loss of her two elder sons in action. He advised her that John should train as a pilot, though Kathleen MacKenzie did not reveal the reason behind this suggestion – it was possibly because of the training involved, which would delay any involvement at the Front. If Brancker hoped that this would quieten Mrs Mackenzie, he was mistaken.

As Mrs MacKenzie continued her personal crusade, improvement in the monitoring of Zeppelin wireless traffic allowed up to three hours warning of an impending attack on Britain, though quite where the enemy airships would end up was at the mercy of their own navigators and the weather. The string of defensive successes commenced at Cuffley had not stemmed the aerial tide, and in November 1916, a worrying increase in aeroplane threats to south-east England also became noticeable.

Particularly at night, defensive patrols against airship or aeroplane intruders remained hazardous. During his attachment to the RFC, Tryggve Gran resigned from the Norwegian Air Force and was appointed captain in the RFC with seniority backdated to 1 January 1916. After completing his night flying training at Rochford, he was stationed at North Weald, where he found himself on anti-Zeppelin patrol one cloudy night. The flare path was lit to assist take-off, but surrounding searchlights were unable to penetrate the cloud base. Mechanics moving around the machine 'like wet crows' confirmed it would be impossible to go up. Whereupon, the OC appeared out of the gloom: 'My dear boy, you have to go.' Gran recalled, 'Seldom in my life have I felt my courage fail as I did that dark and stormy night … drawing on my will power I forced myself to sit in the pilot's seat behind the instruments apparently something like a normal person.' The 'pale-faced' OC told him to land again if the conditions proved too bad.

'I never had a more unpleasant experience in my life', Gran recalled of his take-off that night. As the last ground flare disappeared under the wing, he felt rain 'lash me in the face.

Then a chaos of fog and darkness closed round me.' The machine 'jumped about violently in the wicked cloud layer' before Gran realised he was flying upside down 'and dropping towards earth with dizzy speed'. Having managed to right the aeroplane, 'a cold sweat had broken out all over me and something inside me shouted "This is madness – go down".' But as his nerves settled, he turned into the wind and studied the phosphorous of the instruments in front of him. Glancing round, he realised that he was 'over an immense white sea ... a story-book world'. His orders were to 'patrol the line North Weald – London Colney at 12,000ft for 3hrs'.

The ground was invisible, but taking into account his own speed of 60mph, the speed and direction of the wind, he calculated that he must be 25 miles (40km) south-south-west of North Weald. He therefore set course northwards. It was so cold that 'from the wings and stays you could make out ice glittering through the stars'. After flying back and forth for two hours, the sky began to lighten. Suddenly, the engine stopped and despite his frantic efforts, could not be restarted. 'The machine began to plunge downwards and the wing shrieked in the guys and stay wires. Where in the world would this end? ... Like a drowning man, I cast an imploring glance at the stars and then the aeroplane sank into the fog and darkness.' Down to 2,000ft and still only 'the racing banks of cloud', Gran fired a parachute flare, which ignited – 'a ghastly flame shone through the murk and I was nearly dazzled by the glare.' However, 'as if by magic', a wood and river emerged and, miraculously, a flat field. 'What a wonderful sensation to feel the ground under the wheels again. It was almost impossible to believe it was true.'

Jumping clear, he threw off his flying kit and ran towards the two roads he had noticed. On the way, he met some farm workers: 'Where's the nearest telephone exchange?' 'Hull', came the reply, 'giving me such a shock of surprise that I nearly collapsed'. He was, to put it mildly, a trifle off course. Gran made his way back to North Weald that afternoon. 'I have seldom had such a heartfelt welcome,' he noted, which made him reflect that 'perhaps the tension and pressure had been worse for the ground staff than for the pilot.'

Without suffering Gran's tribulations, Maj A.R. Kingsford emphasised the frustration and discomfort of being on routine anti-airship duty. Serving with a detachment of No 33 Sqn at Brattleby (later renamed Scampton), Lincolnshire, 'our job was night patrols hunting for Zeppelins. My patrol was Spurn Head [a spit of land east of Grimsby] to south of Lincoln for 3hrs duration and we literally froze.' In his opinion, this exercise was absolutely pointless, as the ceiling of the FE2b was 12,000ft, whereas Zeppelins cruised at 18,000ft. Small wonder, he concluded, that he did not even glimpse an enemy airship throughout his time at Brattleby.

In France, as the new year dawned, Allied hopes turned towards the annual dreams of a decisive Spring breakthrough. In the east, Russia was to launch offensives against Germany and Austria-Hungary; the Italians would renew their campaign on the Isonzo river; the French (led by the confident, charismatic Gen Robert Nivelle) seize the dominant Chemin des Dames ridge; while the British advanced in the Arras region. In the British sector, the RFC would once more play a critical role, but it also had to support activity in other parts of the line, like the Ypres salient. Arras would be an important but not exclusive commitment. Hopes were raised of a more telling long-range bombing campaign with entry into service in November 1916 of the Handley Page (HP) O/100, product of a call from the RNAS the previous year for a 'bloody paralyser' of a bomber. With a crew of three, this formidable machine was powered by two 250hp Rolls-Royce Eagle engines, had a maximum bomb load of 2,000lbs, provision for Lewis guns in the front cockpit, rear cockpit and for downward and rearward firing through an opening in the fuselage.

On 7 January 1917, the RFC received a further morale boost with the award of another VC. Flying a FE2d at 9,000ft, Sgt Thomas Mottershead of No 20 Sqn remained at the controls

Manfred, Count von Richthofen (left). Transferred to German air service from cavalry in 1915. Nicknamed 'The Red Baron', due to his aristocratic origin and colour of his aeroplane, he was awarded *Pour le Mérite* in January 1917. The following year he led a large formation known as his 'flying circus'. Eighty confirmed kills. Here with his brother Lothar and father. *(Peter Jackson)*

of his burning machine, while his observer attempted to quell the flames. The citation for Mottershead's decoration explained:

> This very gallant soldier succeeded in bringing his aeroplane back to our lines, and though he made a successful landing, the machine collapsed on touching the ground, pinning him beneath wreckage from which he was subsequently rescued. Though suffering extreme torture from burns, Sgt Mottershead showed the most conspicuous presence of mind in the careful selection of a landing place, and his wonderful endurance and fortitude undoubtedly saved the life of his observer.

The citation ended sadly in noting that 'he has since succumbed to his injuries', leaving a widow, Lilian.

A week after Mottershead's act of bravery, on 14 January an ominous appointment occurred in the German ranks. Manfred von Richthofen, awarded the Prussian *Pour le Mérite* two days earlier for his sixteenth kill, assumed command of *Jagdstaffel* 11 and painted his Albatros D.III red – a colour destined to strike fear into many an Allied pilot. The British aerial successes of the Somme were about to be painfully reversed at Arras; the new Halberstadt and Albatros machines prove as devastating as the Fokker of yesteryear.

8

Months of Setback, March–July 1917
'Quelle guerre!'

Political upheaval in Russia arising from widespread dissatisfaction with the war, and which saw the Tsar replaced by a Provisional Government in March 1917, had worrying implications. The promised Russian offensive evaporated, and the collapse of the entire Eastern Front now seemed likely, making additional land and air forces available to the Germans in the west.

More immediately for the British air arms, the relative weakness of the pusher fighters compared with the new enemy single-seat machines and Jasta organisation caused mounting concern. During March 1917, 120 RFC machines were shot down, and Ewart Garland personally testified to the carnage. He returned from leave on 23 March to find that he had been posted to No 10 Sqn, which was still flying BE pushers. 'Casualties were so high we hardly had time to get to know one another. I was soon to know what it was like to be attacked by enemy fighters of far superior speed and ability.'

James McCudden missed the disasters that month, having returned to England as an instructor at Joyce Green, near Dartford in Kent. His pupils included Lt Edward 'Mick' Mannock, a future VC winner, and his own brother Anthony. All four McCudden brothers were now in the RFC, the youngest (Maurice) having become an apprentice. James was not unduly impressed with Anthony in the air: 'Very keen, but inclined to be over-confident', he reported. Less officially, McCudden smuggled a blonde West End dancer onto his machine for a joy ride, subsequently painting 'Teddie' on the aeroplane's fuselage in tribute to Miss Teddie O'Neill. The showgirl indirectly caused a moment of acute embarrassment for him, as he explained to his sister Kitty on 10 April: 'Miss E' had just phoned 'to see if I received her letter posted three weeks ago'. He told her it had not arrived and she therefore thought that Kitty had not forwarded it or it had been lost. 'Just play up to that', McCudden asked, 'so she will not have the satisfaction of thinking I got it'. Apparently, Miss E wanted 'to make up' and tell 'her version' of an incident, but McCudden had swiftly made his excuses and rung off. He admitted to Kitty that when he first heard a woman's voice on the phone, he thought it was Miss O'Neill and said: 'Is that you Teddie?' Miss E must have heard this, so 'don't let it out' that he knew a girl in the West End show *Lorne*, 'otherwise she will get a programme and see Teddie O'Neill's name'. Signing off 'in great haste', he pleaded with his sister: 'Don't tell anyone about Miss O'Neill will you.'

While McCudden – soon to be promoted to captain – was instructing at Joyce Green, test flying for Vickers at their nearby works and indulging in extra-curricular flirtations, promising technical developments were enhancing the RFC's operational capability. In May 1916, a Romanian inventor, George Constantinesco, began work on an idea for 'a gear designed to fire a machine-gun by means of impulses through a column of liquid contained under

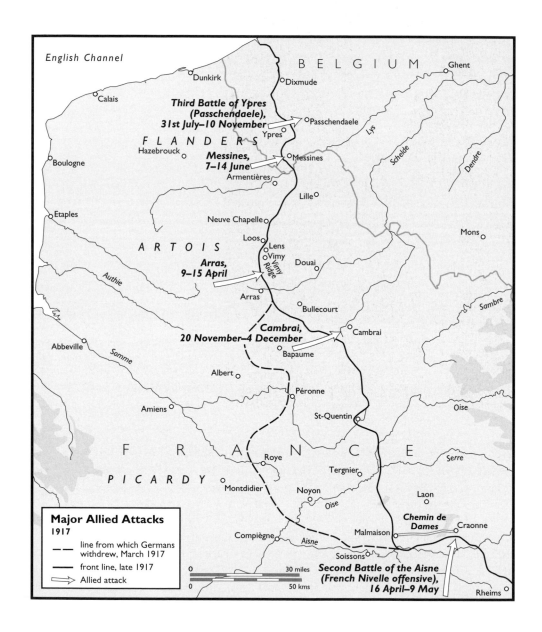

English Channel

BELGIUM

Dunkirk

Ghent

Calais

Dixmude

**Third Battle of Ypres
(Passchendaele),
31st July–10 November**

Passchendaele

FLANDERS

Ypres

Lys

Hazebrouck

Boulogne

Schelde

**Messines,
7–14 June**

Messines

Dendre

Armentières

Etaples

Lille

Neuve Chapelle

ARTOIS

Loos

Mons

Lens
Vimy
Ridge

**Arras,
9–15 April**

Douai

Authie

Arras

Sambre

Bullecourt

Abbeville

**Cambrai,
20 November–4 December**

Cambrai

Somme

Bapaume

Albert

Péronne

Amiens

St-Quentin

Oise

FRANCE

Roye

Serre

PICARDY

Tergnier

Montdidier

Noyon

Laon

Oise

**Chemin de
Dames**

Major Allied Attacks

1917

Compiègne

Malmaison

Craonne

— — — line from which Germans
withdrew, March 1917

Aisne

—— front line, late 1917

Soissons

Allied attack

0   30 miles

**Second Battle of the Aisne
(French Nivelle offensive),
16 April–9 May**

0   50 kms

Rheims

Lieutenant Kurt Wolff wearing the *Pour Le Mérite* at throat. Enlisted in the German army 1912, transferred to air service July 1915. Credited with thirty-three victories before being shot down, September 1917, aged 22. *(IWM Q 107390)*

pressure in a pipe'. In other words a variation of the mechanically-operated interrupter gear, which activated a machine-gun when the propeller blades were out of the line of fire. This synchronised system prevented the gun from firing when a propeller blade was in the way. The new arrangement was demonstrated on a BE2c in August 1916 and once teething problems had been smoothed out, reached France in DH4s of No 55 Sqn on 6 March 1917. Two days later Bristol Fighters of No 48 Sqn and a month after them, on 8 April, SE5s of No 56 Sqn arrived at the front similarly equipped. Before the close of 1917, 6,000 synchronised gears would be fitted to a range of machines, a further 20,000 before the Armistice.

This was a timely development in Spring 1917, when enemy formations like Jasta 11 under Manfred von Richthofen were harassing British squadrons. Richthofen nearly came to grief near Douai on 9 March, when his Albatros was damaged by an FE8 of No 40 Sqn, causing him to echo the dread of British airmen. He immediately lost height and switched off his engine, fearing that if the fuel tank were ruptured petrol would wash around his cockpit. In such a situation, he wrote, 'the danger of fire is indeed great ... One drop of fuel and the whole machine will burn.'

The next day, his brother Lothar joined Jasta 11, where the younger Richthofen commented on the superstitions of airmen. Manfred always wore the same old leather jacket in

A captured French Caudron G3 which was used for reconnaissance and training from 1914. This is an early-war shot judging by the style of German cross applied to the underwings and tail. *(Peter Jackson)*

the air, another pilot Kurt Wolff a nightcap and Lothar himself donned leather gloves given to him by his brother. Violations of such rituals could, apparently, prove fatal. Oswald Boelcke never had his photo taken before take-off until the day he was killed, and Kurt Wintgens of Jasta 11 perished on the only occasion he left behind his riding crop.

Boelke's death had not affected the ability of Jasta 2 (renamed Jasta Boelcke in his honour) to wreak havoc. On 27 November 1916, a newcomer Werner Voss claimed his first victim, bringing down a BE2c on the Allied side of the line. As the crew fled, Voss landed, scrambled aboard the wreck, unloaded the machine-gun and took it back to prove his triumph. Voss had begun the War in a cavalry regiment and in 1915, aged eighteen, volunteered for the Air Service. After a spell as an observer, during which he found artillery spotting unadventurous, Voss underwent pilot training which preceded his appointment to Jasta 2. After his first success in November 1916, he rapidly increased his score, between 1 February and 24 March 1917 registering nineteen victories, and shortly afterwards, his prowess would gain him command of his own squadron. The successes of Voss and Richthofen showed that loss of prominent airmen such as Immelmann and Boelcke had not operationally affected the Germans.

Away from the Front, Spring 1917 saw Kathleen MacKenzie once more on the offensive in England. Her diary entry for 25 March recorded that in response to a phone call from John, then training at Brooklands, 'that he needed me to go and see General Brancker', she had done so 'last Tuesday'. Tantalisingly, Mrs MacKenzie entered no more details. On 24 May, a proud mother noted that her son had gained his wings, but added a concerned foot-note: 'Fearing he might be sent to France, I planned to go to London tomorrow to see Col Warner to get him sent as an instructor to Canada or the States.' That morning, apparently in response to a communication from her, she received a letter from Lt Col W. W. Warner (in the Directorate of Military Aeronautics) stating that Brancker 'quite realises this is a special case and that as soon as he had graduated in flying [which had now happened], his name shall be put down for duty in Canada'. Perhaps unfairly, the impression conveyed by this decision is that the Deputy Director-General of Military Aeronautics would prefer not to face such a formidable lady for a third time. On 28 June 1917, John Mackenzie would sail for Canada, never having come within earshot of the guns.

April 1917 proved a traumatic month at the front. In late 1916, a German bulge westwards in the Péronne/Roye area looked vulnerable to a pincer movement. Plans were therefore drawn up for the British to advance south-east from Arras in the north, French troops north-west towards Guise in the south. Once the Germans were committed to these flank attacks, Gen Robert Nivelle would launch the decisive French thrust towards St Quentin in the centre. Unfortunately, poor security alerted the Germans to the scheme and they pre-empted it by withdrawing from the salient 20 miles (32km) east to a 60-mile (96km) long line of fortified positions, the Siegfried Stellung, known more generally as the Hindenburg Line.

On 4 April, a five-day artillery bombardment by 2,800 guns, orchestrated by RFC spotters, preceded a successful assault by Canadian forces on the dominant Vimy Ridge. During this period and throughout the ensuing battle the RFC carried out reconnaissance, escort and photographic duties, fighter operations, bombing of the enemy front line and rear areas: the entire range of activity now expected of it, and the cost was horrendous. Between 4 and 8 April, 75 aeroplanes were lost (105 men killed, wounded or missing), and a further 56 machines wrecked in crashes.

Ewart Garland was detached from No 10 Sqn to carry out photographic flights over Vimy. 'I got badly shot up by Hun fighters taking photos of the Ridge urgently needed by the Canadian Command just before their attack was launched,' he recalled. His letter to his parents about this 'narrow escape' was revealing. With no escort, he was taking photos at 6,000ft when two German scouts 'twice as fast as us ... came at me'. He and his observer had 'a sporting chance' until the observer's gun jammed. 'Well I flew for our lives – My God what an experience. This wonderful Hun machine just flying all over us and firing all the time while I tried to dodge in our clumsy bus.' Until, 'at last', five fighters came and drove it off. Just in time 'because I couldn't of [sic] dodged him any more.' Garland's aeroplane suffered '50–60 holes, but I had my photos'. Reflecting on this experience of 2 April, he wrote: 'Later in the war I met the General [Sir Julian Byng] in London at his house in Belgravia and he mentioned how vital the photos were.'

On 5 and 6 April, Garland was again over Vimy Ridge, on the second of these days watching two other BEs shot down before the comparatively slow FE escorts could come to their rescue. As soon as Garland saw three Albatros machines making towards him, he 'scuttled back over our side' and landed safely with 'the necessary photos'. He related his experience to his parents that same day: 'It was an awful sight to see the machines shot down in a mass of flames before your eyes.' Garland and his fellow flyers were 'continually harassed' by an enemy with 'far superior machines', and he went on to show how the strain was beginning to tell. So far away, his parents must have been desperately worried.

Garland confessed:

It is wearing me out. They expect too much from me. They give me photos and photos and photos every day to take, not once but twice a day. It's like being sentenced to death, because of the type of machine we have as compared to the Hun. I have got very thin but am quite fit although I have no muscular strength at all.

To overcome this, it was necessary to develop 'what we call "guts" ... By rights it is time I was sent home to England, but the Colonel will keep me until the push is over and working high pressure all the time.' An element of special bitterness then surfaced: 'You see the better work you do the more you get – until the end. So long as the colonels and people get a DSO then nothing matters.' Garland concluded, 'Yours fed up but with much love', adding a postscript: 'Excuse bad writing. I'm shaky to-day.' A sharp contrast to the ebullient newcomer to the Front of the previous year.

'*Quelle guerre!*' he wrote on learning the very next day, 7 April, that he was to return to No 10 Sqn so close to the 'big show'. He arrived that afternoon in time to lead his flight against Provin aerodrome on which he dropped two 112lb bombs (each with 40lbs of explosivess). Garland heard on 8 April that two RFC machines had been shot down by the Allied barrage near Vimy Ridge and after completing practice formation flying with his flight, went up to have a look at the scene. 'It was no exaggeration to say the sky was thick with shells ... little black spots.'

Harold Taylor was equally unimpressed with the 'obsolete' FE2bs, which No 25 Sqn were still operating. He had an added cause for concern, being in the 'unhappy position' of knowing that from 1 April he could be granted leave 'any day', which made life tense. 'Would I survive to have this leave or would I be wounded, taken prisoner, or be killed before the happy day arrived?' Early in April he met Lt E. Bell, who had been in the choir with him at St John's Church, Wimbledon, where Bell's father was vicar. The meeting was 'a wonderful surprise'. Bell was a pilot, though Taylor never flew as his observer. Shortly after their encounter, on 8 April, while on photo reconnaissance under 'very heavy fire', Taylor saw Bell go down on the other side of the line but make 'a fairly decent landing'.

Taylor did last until 20 April, when the 'wonderful day' came for him to travel via Boulogne to Victoria station and ten days leave. He took the opportunity to visit Canon Bell, but he had already heard that his son was a prisoner. Taylor received a 'marvellous reception' from his parents, brother and sister. Qualms, though, soon arose:

> I had been home two days and then I began to doubt whether this leave was really so wonderful. In a few days I would have to return to France ... I knew all the terrible dangers ahead of me. Still, whenever with my folks, I kept happy and I was rewarded by the look of joy in all their faces ... especially my mother.

The war was hardly mentioned in the house, 'and I think they realised that maybe I would be happier if the war was not discussed.'

When time to return to the Squadron came, Taylor bade farewell to his parents, but his sister went with him to Victoria Station. He found it difficult to restrain his tears. 'They were very emotional moments. Unless I was exceptionally lucky this would be the last time that I would see them as I was fully aware of what could be my fate.'

Although Vimy Ridge had fallen on Easter Monday, 9 April, high hopes for wider success were soon dashed. Further south, British troops did initially advance over three miles, but the Germans deployed strong reserves and soon more fierce fighting took place on the ground and in the air. On 9 April, the RFC had 365 serviceable machines (in twenty-two RFC and three RNAS squadrons) at its disposal in the Arras area. Exclusive of machines held in the army aircraft parks, the total strength at the front totalled 903 machines.

Casualties scarcely slackened, though, once the main battle commenced. Of particular concern was the patent inferiority of the DH2, Nieuport fighters and newly-arrived FE2d. One

DH2 report read: 'The hostile scouts with their superior speed and good handling were able throughout the fight to prevent the pilot from getting a single shot at one of them.' A formation of German two-seaters accounted for all five FE2d machines on an offensive patrol. Both the Nieuports and to some extent the new Bristol fighters, proved vulnerable, though greater experience of the pilots and a change of tactics (with pilots no longer primarily manoeuvring for their observers to open fire) would overcome this problem in time. In retrospect 'Bloody April' 1917 would be the worst single month of the war for the RFC. On the Western Front as a whole, 316 machines were lost.

Harold Taylor arrived back from leave on 1 May to discover that several of his friends had been killed or taken prisoner. He just had time to send a field postcard informing his parents of his safe return when, due to a shortage of personnel, he was ordered into the air at 5pm. His FE2b, flown by Lt B. King, was one of six detailed to bomb an ammunition dump at Inzel-Les-Eperchin. They had dropped their bombs and were on the way back, when Taylor's machine became detached from the others and was attacked by three Albatros scouts from behind.

> Within seconds I felt bullets in my thigh, which blew it to pieces, at the same time a bullet hit me in the right arm, going straight through the muscle. This paralysed my arm. Bullets were spraying everywhere. I felt them pass my head. My rear gun was hit many times and the petrol tank had been pierced and petrol was blowing all over the machine. I slumped onto the floor of the nacelle, bleeding profusely from my leg and arm and then there was oblivion.

Taylor came round as the machine hit the ground, ran 'a few yards, tipped on its nose and settled on its right-hand wing tip'. If it had gone completely over, he and the pilot would have been buried under the engine. King was unharmed and had crash-landed in the middle of Arras racecourse, where infantry dragged Taylor clear. As they did so, he passed out again and came to on a stretcher on the floor of Arras Cathedral, which was being used as a Casualty Clearing Station. The place was full of wounded men, and Taylor sensed that if he did not get attention soon he would bleed to death. 'But I was lucky,' he acknowledged. He had no idea how many days he lay unconscious, but when he woke up he was on a hospital train. Eventually, Taylor arrived at Charing Cross Station, where he would 'never forget' his homecoming: 'It had become the habit of many hundreds of men and women to meet the hospital trains so that they could welcome the wounded'; a truly heart-warming gesture Taylor thought. Cpl H.G. Taylor underwent six operations on his leg, during the last of which the surgeon stiffened the limb as the only way to save it.

On the day that Taylor was shot down, 1 May 1917, Capt Charles Brown wrote to his mother from No 40 Sqn. He was not flying at that time and had just learnt that he was to return to 'the Home Establishment' for at least three months. 'I am coming home for a rest as my nerves have practically gone so I am useless out here. We have been doing a terrific amount of work out here lately and it had been too much for me.' His logbook entry read: 'taken sick in the air … returned to England for rest'. Between 18 November 1916 and 1 May 1917 in France, Brown had flown seventy-seven operations.

Farther south than Brown, Capt Harold Balfour, the King's Royal Rifle Corps officer who had volunteered for the RFC from the trenches, flew on patrol near Vimy Ridge shortly after it fell to the Canadians. Misjudging the strength and direction of the wind in 'dull and overcast' weather, he found himself well over enemy territory facing a slow flight back in the face of a stiff breeze. Zig-zagging to avoid volleys from hostile rifles and machine-guns, he managed to escape serious damage until 'a harsh metallic clang' preceded the engine packing up and the propeller ceasing to turn, with Balfour still short of the Allied line. He could only glide and hope. Falling rapidly, his biplane scraped over the Ridge, and Balfour pitched head first into the mud on the edge of a shell crater. Momentarily stunned, he was found by rescuers wandering around thoroughly disorientated.

Balfour's survival owed much to a last-minute decision. Serious disagreement existed between aircrew as to whether belts should be undone before an inevitable crash. Until that day, Balfour had vehemently advocated remaining strapped in. Mid-air as his damaged machine plunged, he changed his mind, was thrown clear and lived.

The heavy loss of aircrew during April and the concluding phase of the Battle of Arras put added pressure on the training system to produce pilots more quickly. Yet John Jeyes, the former Oundle schoolboy who avoided an attempt by the RSM at Northampton to draft him into the army, suffered from its administrative quirks. On joining the RFC in August 1916, he had been sent on a three-month cadet training course, where 'I soon found it was no good showing any sign of fear or not trying by every method possible to stick to one's purpose.' He went to Jesus College, Oxford, for theoretical and practical instruction in the intricacies of engines and rigging, Morse, photography, navigation and map reading. Then it was off to Waddington, Lincolnshire, where he had flights with an instructor on Farman Longhorns and Shorthorns. 'I could not believe my eyes' to see flying types 'which had first caught my schoolboy dreams way back in 1915.'

He was shown 'how to cope with – or tackle – REs', which he found 'tremendously exciting'. The day came when six new RE8 machines, popularly known as 'Harry Tate' after a music hall comedian, arrived for the pupils to fly. The first, with the pupil in the rear cockpit, took off, stalled on its initial climbing turn, spun into the ground and put the pupil in hospital. To the horror of those waiting their turn, exactly the same happened with the second and third. For the fourth attempt, the instructor decided that the pupil would fly the machine with him in the rear seat. The aeroplane took off into the wind, but suffered the same fate as the others, except that this time both instructor and pupil were driven off to hospital. Not only had four potential pilots and one instructor been immobilised but four new machines had been wrecked in a single morning. Jeyes was fifth in line, 'filled with no confidence at all'. Asked whether he would like to go solo, he replied that he was willing to try if the instructor thought he could do so safely. Wiser counsels prevailed, and instead Jeyes was sent to Beverley, near Hull, to fly the BE2c, which he 'thoroughly enjoyed'.

Jeyes stayed in Yorkshire only a couple of weeks before going to the Brooklands Aviation School for artillery co-operation work and further instruction on the BE2c. After three weeks, he returned to Scampton, Lincolnshire, not yet having flown solo. After a few more take-offs and landings, he at last went up alone. To compensate for the absence of an instructor, two ½ hundredweights (127 kilos) bags of sand were loaded into the rear cockpit. Jeyes taxied out, checked the controls, turned into the wind, opened the throttle and took off. Climbing to 1,000ft, he executed a left turn and 'soon got the feel of the aircraft. Harry Tate, me and the sandbags were up and away on my first solo.' Scampton was a large aerodrome with plenty of room and a level surface, so he landed safely at 65–70mph. After 'five or six' more solos and 'two or three days more practice', Jeyes was told he had passed the necessary tests and gained his wings. However, eight months later, April 1917, he was still a long way from active service being instructed on the Avro 504K.

The experience of Lt Ferdinand Maurice Felix (Freddie) West, who joined No 3 Sqn as an observer in April 1917, proved somewhat different. Having travelled across France from Italy to

Felix Maurice Ferdinand 'Freddie' West. Son of British father and French mother, brought up in Italy. Enlisted in the RAMC, commissioned into the Royal Munster Fusiliers. Served in trenches before transferring to RFC. Lost his leg in action in August 1918 for which he was awarded the VC. Retired after Second World War as air commodore. *(IWM Q 68000)*

volunteer for service in England, he was arrested at Dieppe as a suspected French deserter due to his fluency in the language; the result of having a French mother. Released from custody, he was accosted by a sergeant at Victoria station and marched off to the nearest recruiting office, where Freddie 'heard the clink of silver' as the NCO claimed his reward. A further shock awaited the Anglo-French volunteer. Because he came from Italy, where he had been brought up by his mother and aunt following his British father's death in the Boer War, it was assumed that he had a knowledge of Latin and he found himself in the ranks of the Royal Army Medical Corps. Having advanced to sergeant, on 15 May 1915 West was commissioned into the Royal Munster Fusiliers; he claimed because his expertise as a fencer caught an influential officer's eye and as a Roman Catholic, he met a prime requirement of The Royal Munster Fusiliers, a regiment seriously short of subalterns due to heavy losses in battle.

From November 1915 until April 1917, West served in the trenches, in his own words 'crawling through slime, human refuse and human carnage in sweat-caked clothes'. This was, he decided, 'a war of rats and generals'. He began to envy the crews of aeroplanes, 'up in the clear, clean sky' and recalled his youthful enthusiasm for flying awakened by the exploits of Georges Chavez, who in 1910 killed himself after crossing the Alps. West bribed an acquaintance, Lt Edgar Golding, to take him up in return for a ride on the horse allocated to him as a company commander. West was 'hooked' and when a request for observers in the RFC appeared on the battalion notice board in March 1917, he promptly applied. However, his secondment was delayed for a month by a reluctant senior officer.

After attending a short Artillery Spotting Course at Brooklands, he found himself assigned to No 3 Sqn, where he teamed up with Golding. The Morane-Saulnier L Parasol two-seat tractor had an effective ceiling of 12,000ft and top speed of 90mph. To his pilot's consternation, West tended to concentrate on familiar landmarks from his infantry days as they patrolled the Béthune area, rather than scanning the sky for potential danger. After three months and having taken every opportunity to fly with any pilot short of an observer, West applied for pilot training.

At the Front, by mid-May 1917 the Nivelle offensive, launched so optimistically on 16 April to seize the Chemin des Dames highway overlooking the Aisne river, had failed, and the enormous losses incurred prompted serious mutinies in the French armies. About a half of the front line divisions (54/100) refused to obey orders and reputedly, one regiment which did, marched forward bleating like sheep. Fortunately these disruptions were undetected by the Germans and in due course, General Philippe Pétain would restore discipline. Inescapably, however, the grandiose Allied plans had come to nought. On the French left, at Arras, Haig's advance had managed a maximum 4 miles (6km) at a cost of 158,600 casualties by 27 May when it came to a halt, with the Germans still occupying high ground at Lens.

The Battle of Arras provided a particular shock for the RFC. Albert Ball had remained in England attending various courses and undertaking instructional work during the winter of 1916–17. He shrank from public recognition, wearing a trench coat to conceal his decorations when off duty. Ball did accept the freedom of his own birthplace, Nottingham, and became involved in the design and building of a single-seat fighter by the Austin Motor Company, which never saw service. On 25 February, Ball was posted to No 56 Sqn and went with it to France in April.

During the evening of 7 May, Ball was part of a force engaging German fighters in poor weather. He was seen chasing an opponent into cloud, but failed to return to base. His loss was confirmed the following day when Trenchard wrote to his father about 'the most daring, skilful and successful pilot the Royal Flying Corps has ever had … His good spirit was infectious, as

Albert Ball. Commissioned into The Sherwood Foresters he took private flying lessons and joined RFC in 1915. An accomplished fighter pilot, Ball was awarded the MC and DSO with two Bars. Killed in action after forty-four victories, May 1917, aged 20 and buried with full military honours by the Germans. Posthumously awarded VC. *(IWM Q 69593)*

whatever squadron his was with, the officers of it tried to work up to his level and reputation.' In his diary, staff officer Maurice Baring wrote: 'This has cast gloom through the whole Flying Corps.' Ball was only twenty and beyond the official forty-four victories, may have actually shot down forty-seven enemy machines and one kite balloon. Two days before his death, he had hinted at mental and physical exhaustion in a letter home: 'It is all trouble and it is getting on my mind. Am feeling very old just now.'

There is no dispute that Ball crashed fatally near the village of Annoeullin, though considerable doubt exists about the precise nature of his end. One eyewitness colourfully described how he tangled with three enemy machines, shot down two and the third made off, but Ball was then low enough for anti-aircraft guns to bring him down. One German account credited Lothar von Richthofen, Manfred's brother, with Ball's demise. Another reported that Ball emerged from cloud with his propeller stationary and simply glided to his death; his only injuries caused in the crash and no battle damage apparent to the aeroplane. This has prompted speculation that Ball may have become disorientated in cloud and even that, with his engine switched off, he was attempting a forced landing.

Albert Ball was buried by his enemy with full military honours. A cross placed above his grave read: 'He gave his life for his Fatherland.' On 3 June 1917, he was posthumously awarded the VC

> … for most conspicuous and consistent bravery, from 25th April to the 6th May, 1917, during which period Capt Ball took part in twenty-six combats in the air and destroyed eleven hostile aeroplanes, drove down two out of control and forced several others to land.

In June 1917, British attention switched from Arras to Flanders, where, occupying surrounding high ground, the Germans dominated the defenders of Ypres. To the east stood the prominent Passchendaele Ridge, but a shallower rise lay to the south from which the enemy could observe preparations for any assault on Passchendaele. The British planned to attack the Messines Ridge on 7 June after massive mines in tunnels under the German troops on the forward slope had been exploded.

To obtain control of this ridge, the British had to penetrate the German line to a depth of some 2½ miles (4km) over a 10-mile (16km) front. Three corps from the Second Army were allocated for this task, each closely supported by an RFC squadron with twenty-one machines.

For a week before the battle, 2,266 guns on a 12-mile (19km) front, three times the concentration on the Somme the previous year, pounded 3.5 million shells into enemy positions. They sought not only to neutralise troop formations and installations, but to cut defensive barbed wire. As well as spotting for the artillery, from 31 May squadrons other than those attached to a corps carried out reconnaissance as far east as Ghent and Bruges, offensive patrols and bombing operations up to 17 miles (27km) beyond the Messines Ridge. These operations were designed to minimise German aerial activity once the ground operations began and to prevent enemy machines from helping their own artillery to counter the British batteries before it.

After his spell at the front the Boer War veteran, Capt Harold Wyllie, received a first-hand account of a night attack on 30 May from Lt E.A. Worrall, who opened by revealing that 'Castle has been wounded and so has your humble.' He apologised for writing 'with my left hand as my right is hors de combat'. Worrall admitted to 'promiscuous bombing' after dropping a 112lb bomb 'on a Boche train' and derailing 'the blighter'. 'Naturally I was delighted and I tootled off to another spot where I knew there would be something worth strafing.' He never reached his second target. Searchlights were 'whipping the air and occasionally a few "flaming onions" [anti-aircraft shells] came up at me but they fell a few yards short.' In the half moon and at about 800ft, Worrall saw 'our recognition light fired from the ground'. On closer investigation, he saw what he took to be an FE machine in distress. 'Feeling rather elated and having room in the old FE for a passenger, I thought I'd land and give him a lift.'

As he prepared to do so, at 50ft from the ground 'a most colossal machine-gun fire broke out and made me realise I'd struck a Hun aerodrome. By gad, I opened the throttle and made off like stink.' As bullets hit his machine 'like rain … a spasm of pain in my right arm and leg told me plainly I was not wanted there'. Worrall rapidly 'got out of the way' until he remembered that he still had a 112lb bomb left: 'Well my rag was out and I wanted to square matters so I turned back.' The enemy were waiting 'with their blasted tracer bullets, but I got there and left an impression which will make them have a regard for us in the future.' With his right hand useless, he had to manipulate the controls with his left. The petrol tank must have been damaged 'for the old FE burst into flames and I thought the end had arrived. I jammed back the throttle and dived for earth and wonder of wonders the fire went out.' Worrall 'put her nose for home' and managed to get to 600ft, when 'she conked out' again. However, he switched to the service tank and the engine picked up. After evading a probing searchlight, 'I felt myself fainting and I decided to land.' Unsure of which side of the line he was, Worrall put down 'in a good field' only to have the machine burst into flames on landing. He 'made a jump for it', and knew nothing more until he came round 'in the hands of Australians half a mile behind the lines'. It was, he declared, 'a narrow escape and an experience which I don't want to have again. It will be a few months before I am ready again.'

Worrall's raid was only one of those in the build-up to the Messines Ridge attack. During the night of 2/3 June in bright moonlight trains and railway tracks were bombed at Menin and Warneton stations. On the evening of 6 June, airfields behind the battlefield were hit with 179 20lb or 25lb bombs; other formations used 112lb bombs against railway bridges over the Escaut river.

Due to the demands of the army at Ypres and the RNAS base at Dunkirk, in June 1917 Capt W.L. Elder RN's No 3 Wing established at Luxeuil the previous year with such high hopes of long-range bombing, was disbanded. Including the three squadrons supporting the corps and two attached RNAS fighter squadrons, there were 17 squadrons and a Special Duty Flight with 348 aeroplanes available when the Messines Ridge battle commenced. Two more squadrons with thirty and thirty-six machines were ready on the flanks, which represented an aerial superiority of almost three to one in the vicinity.

At 3.10am on 7 June, nineteen mines went up and the Germans were so disorientated that the ridge quickly fell. As the infantry advanced, the air forces played a critical role. Two flights from each of the corps squadrons directed artillery on enemy batteries, the third on uncut wire and trench positions. Escorts were provided for photographic aeroplanes, crucial for accurate assessment of progress. Two contact patrol machines were allocated to each corps area to communicate with the infantry; five fighters were given a roving role to attack troops, guns or transport at will. During the battle, the corps squadrons had responsibility up to 5,000yds (4,500m) from the enemy front line. Beyond that, other squadrons carried out deep penetration operations and day and night, continued to bomb aerodromes and railway facilities.

The work of the RFC kite (static) balloons, responsible both for providing tactical information and directing artillery fire, should not be overlooked. As Ewart Garland noted, these 'basket-carrying balloons with two men and used by both sides for observing were normally about 2 miles (3km) behind the lines'. At 2pm on 7 June, a British kite balloon identified enemy reserves advancing against II Anzac Corps on the British right and as a result, artillery batteries dispersed the threat. The Second Army intelligence report read:

> Most useful work was done by kite balloons on the 7th, reporting the intensity and extent of enemy barrages, progress of our own barrages, locations of hostile artillery activity centres and the progress and location of tanks.

Although the Germans did rally after the initial assault, British gains along the ridge were consolidated and after a week major fighting came to a halt. The right flank of the main thrust towards the Passchendaele Ridge had been cleared.

Before an Allied attack on Passchendaele Ridge could be launched, serious developments occurred in England which would have an immediate impact in France. In 1915, the German firm Gothaer Waggonfabrik had developed a twin-engine bomber, which the following year evolved into the Gotha II with two 220hp engines, 1,000lb bomb load, a top speed of 90mph and a three-man crew. Two forward firing guns were supplemented by a third capable of firing backwards and downwards through a channel in the underside of the fuselage. Stationed at St Denis Westrem and Gontrode airfields near Ghent, the Gothas had London within range. On 25 May 1917 twenty-three set out for the capital. One crashed on take-off, and the remainder were frustrated by poor visibility in the Thames estuary and spread out across Kent instead.

Twenty-one of the raiders attacked Shorncliffe and Folkestone, killing 95 and injuring 195 in the crowded Whitsun streets. The Chief Constable of Folkestone told an inquest:

> I saw an appalling sight which I shall never forget. Dead and injured persons were lying on the ground. Three or four horses were also lying dead between the shafts of vehicles, and fire had broken out in front of premises which had been demolished.

A public meeting condemned 'the wholesale murder of women and children of the town' and urged the Government to take action to prevent a repetition. On 5 June, twenty-two Gothas caused more devastation in Sheerness and Shoeburyness, killing eleven and injuring thirty-four. This time, sixty-six defending aeroplanes went aloft, five got near enough to attack but the only raider to fall was a victim of anti-aircraft fire.

London received a severe shock on Wednesday 13 June. In daylight, 17 Gothas dropped 118 bombs, hitting among other places Liverpool Street station and two schools: 160 men, women and children were killed, 408 injured. A further two men were killed and eighteen men, women and children injured by spent anti-aircraft shells. Fifty-two defending aircraft failed to bring down any of the intruders; just one was lost through mechanical failure. The following day, *The Times* printed full details of the debacle under headlines: 'The Trail of the Raiders' and 'Infants Killed in School' (one bomb on a school had killed ten and injured fifty children). Massive public meetings demanded immediate retaliation, 'to pay back the enemy in the same way as he has treated this country … a policy of ceaseless air attacks on German towns and cities'. One inquest ascribed the deaths to 'wilful murder'.

The Norwegian Tryggve Gran was one of the unsuccessful defending pilots. Flying a BE12 from North Weald towards Shoeburyness for 'shooting practice', crossing Sutton's Farm airfield he noticed ground signals indicating an enemy raid in progress and 'at the same time' saw smoke towards the south which he took to be exploding bombs. Approaching Maidstone

Gontrode airfield, near Ghent, Belgium. A former airship shed used to house Gotha aeroplanes, which raided London and south-east England, it was frequently attacked by RNAS bombers from Dunkirk. Lanoe Hawker awarded DSO for performing 'split arse spirals' to bomb it in April 1915. *(Peter Jackson)*

Richthofen's Fokker Dr.I triplane in original factory finish. He had the upper wing, cowling, tail and wheel covers painted red. Werner Voss, another ace, also flew this type of machine. *(Peter Jackson)*

at about 10,000ft, he saw German machines being pursued eastwards by two British pushers. 'I tried to manoeuvre myself across the enemy's course but got the sun in my eyes and in the strong glare accentuated by wisps of fog lost sight of him.' Turning north-east, he climbed to 12,000ft where there was virtually no fog and near Southend he saw a formation of 'six huge aircraft' about 1,000ft higher. In striving to reach the enemy's altitude, he fell behind and lost contact. Over Colchester, Gran turned right along the coastline and in the distance above the River Crouch saw a formation of aeroplanes, which he took to be British. 'Suddenly smoke dots began to appear round the formation and I realised I had made a mistake and made after them.' Flying at 12,000 ft, the same altitude as the enemy, he quickly caught up. 'With my back to the sun', from behind he approached 'the enemy phalanx' of twin-engine machines. At a range of 100ft, and still undetected, Gran

> ... let go with my two machine guns [Lewis and Vickers]. The observer in the seat aft fell over his gun and I concentrated fire on the mid-section. The German machine swung out to the side and disappeared below. At the same moment the three other machines opened fire on me and I thought it wise to remove myself. My motor seemed to have been hit and revs had dropped to 10,000 per minute. I steadily lost height and made for the airfield at Rochford where I landed at 1pm.

Gran concluded his report to the OC 39th Home Defence Squadron: 'My main struts were riddled with bullets and my motor slightly damaged.'

Two days after the raid, the Chief of the Imperial General Staff (CIGS), Gen Sir William Robertson, wrote to Sir Douglas Haig in France complaining that there was a lack of 'the right sort of machines' to defend London and 'the idea is that you should send over for a week or two one or two squadrons of good machines so as to give the enemy a warm reception.' Considerable debate took place in the War Cabinet about the feasibility of attacking German towns, but it was agreed that there were insufficient bombers to sustain a worthwhile campaign. However, in the charged atmosphere, expansion of the RFC from 108 to 200 squadrons was formally approved, and two squadrons were detached from the Front to defend the capital. One of these returned on 6 July, a day before disaster struck once more.

On Saturday 7 July, the Gothas came back to the capital, this time hitting commercial and residential properties on both banks of the Thames, including the City and Bermondsey. Twenty-one attackers dropped 73 bombs, killing 53 and injuring 190. Ninety-five defending machines shot down one of the attackers, and it emerged that the seventy-eight RFC pilots involved flew twenty-one different types of aeroplane. Greater loss was incurred by the defenders than by the Germans: two pilots were killed in action, one observer died of wounds, and another was wounded in the two aeroplanes shot down by the Gothas. Two more machines crashed on landing.

This time Tryggve Gran did not even get airborne. He was resting in his London club when 'a servant' told him that his base was on the phone. 'Is that you, old bean?' came the voice of the OC, Capt A. T. Hope. 'For goodness sake hurry up and come along ... The Huns are swarming across the Channel.' After fifteen minutes' effort with the starting handle, the engine of Gran's car failed to turn over. So he witnessed the second Gotha raid on London from the ground. 'The German formation was brilliantly led and every plane seemed glued in its place,' he remarked.

When he eventually got back to Sutton's Farm, the base 'did not give the impression of war and newly fought battles. The scorching sun of July covered everything.' Outside the door of

Bomb damage. Blazing
Central Telegraph
Office, following second
daylight Gotha raid on
London, 7 July 1917.
Note the horse-drawn
fire appliance bottom left.
(IWM Q 55535)

the mess, he found two pilots lounging in shirt sleeves. 'Any luck?' he asked. 'Colossal luck, old bean – we didn't see a Hun.' Apparently fog had blotted out visibility in the upper layer of air. Only in clearer conditions along the coast were the enemy machines spotted and attacked.

Once more a furore demanded the return of squadrons from the front (eventually one was agreed despite Haig's protests) and reprisal raids on German towns. The press again whipped up public opinion. Under the heading, 'Victims of Useless Raid', *The Illustrated London News* published photos of a terror-stricken mother fleeing with a child in her arms, and an injured man leaving hospital on crutches. Robertson, who attended War Cabinet meetings, wrote to Haig that 'one would have thought that the world was coming to an end … I could not get a word in edgeways.' The long-term impact was a commitment of more resources to home defence and the psychological legacy of a need for a bombing campaign against the German homeland far more comprehensive than the minor efforts of the Luxeuil wing in 1916. 'Reprisals on open towns are repugnant to British ideas, but we may be forced to adopt them' concluded a memorandum from Haig's headquarters. Amid the mayhem, Trenchard made a significant admission: 'Daylight bombing from a height is still very inaccurate and though large towns and big stations are easy to hit, it is very hard to hit a small individual shed.'

On his nineteenth birthday, 3 June 1917, John Jeyes was at length ordered to France, where he joined No 21 Sqn near Poperinghe. La Lovie airfield was very small, surrounded by hop poles and farm buildings. After half a dozen circuits and landings alone, he went up with Lt C.P. Wingfield, who showed him the front lines around Ypres. On 16 June, with Wingfield, he flew an artillery shoot in co-operation with a howitzer battery. Wingfield explained to him how an observer had to spot bursts from the guns and communicate necessary corrections to the battery. Jeyes thought the lack of dual controls for the observer a disadvantage:

> [He] could only contact his pilot by pointing out these positions at 3–4,000ft and indicate as best he could when to turn the machine towards our battery position and front line – and when to turn again and prevent the machine from flying over Hun territory.

All the time, the observer had to keep a sharp look-out for enemy machines coming out of cloud or bright sunlight while the pilot was fully occupied with flying the aeroplane. Preparing for the forthcoming Passchendaele battle, Jeyes was rapidly learning.

He was soon flying his own two-seat RE8, equipped with a machine-gun in each cockpit and racks for two 112lb bombs beneath the wings, and teaming up with Lt M.L. Hatch, who had been senior to him at Oundle.

> After our first detail together over the lines, we soon found that we could work together in the air … It gave me confidence to think that a boy like MLH, who had been my school prefect and also had been an officer in the Light Infantry, had confidence in my ability as a pilot.

Jeyes believed that boys from schools like Oundle, which taught engineering, 'had a better chance of coping in the RFC' than those from Eton or Harrow or 'any other classical school'.

At an operational airfield, Jeyes learnt the 'Drill of Vital Actions' necessary before take-off. Inspection of controls, camera and plates, machine-guns and ammunition; one and a half to two minutes run up of engine to test revs; maps and details of shoot all in place in cockpit; taxi into wind, another quick burst to test revs; proceed to far end of airfield, check engine not overheating, controls and trim; circle airfield for observer to test guns; confirm agreed call signs with the base radio operator and release aerial. If the aerial was let out too fast it might snap, which would entail a tricky landing again with a full load of petrol and ammunition to get it fixed. Repair could take twenty minutes, after which the whole checking procedure had to be laboriously followed once more. Jeyes recalled that an observer in another machine had let his aerial out too quickly so that it snapped and went through a tent on the outskirts of the airfield, hitting a man on the head and killing him. The observer, operating in a cramped space, had a difficult job to wind in the aerial before landing even in normal circumstances.

Overall, John Jeyes' participation in pre-Passchendaele work involved 'patrolling and doing shoots, photographs and bomb dropping' in his RE8. Often he combined three operations in one. Having set up an artillery shoot on the Allied side, he would slip across into enemy territory, take photos and 'drop my bombs on the German lines' before nipping back to complete the shoot. On these exercises, 'the ack ack fire was always intense, and the sky was black with gun bursts all around us, both on the way over and back again.' He and Hatch often considered themselves overworked during the long days of July. Dawn patrols, followed by two other operations the same day all of three hours' duration, in the face of enemy fighters and ack-ack were, to say the least, tiring.

During July, Jeyes recorded several close shaves. For example:

Reconnaissance Experimental (RE) 8. Two-seat tractor with machine-gun in rear cockpit, capacity for two 112lb bombs or equivalent under wings. Speed 98 mph at 6,500ft, ceiling 13,500ft. Nicknamed 'Harry Tate'. Operational 1916–18. *(IWM Q 63817)*

> One day I was up about 3–4,000ft quietly doing my shoot over Ypres with ML Hatch, when I got a sharp rap on the head from him. I jumped and he pointed at the Huns attacking us. There were three of them preparing to dive at us out of clouds. Hatch immediately took aim at them and I manoeuvred the machine so that he could get a good shot.

As Hatch exchanged fire with the enemy, Jeyes kept going in circles until he realised that his observer had stopped firing. Looking round he saw that his machine-gun had jammed and Hatch was frantically dismantling it; 'I immediately got my machine into a spinning nose dive with the engine full on'. The RE8 dropped 2,000ft but the Germans were still firing at it. They must have thought Jeyes was finished, regained formation and flew off. 'Mercifully' Jeyes pulled out of the dive at 1,000ft and as Hatch failed to get his gun working, made for La Lovie to land 'safely, none the worse but rather pale and wanting something strong to drink to calm us down'.

On 24 June, the German Fourth Army had gathered its four fighter squadrons into *Jagdgeschwader* (Fighter Wing) 1 under the command of Capt Manfred von Richthofen. What the British termed his 'circus' had been born. Unknown to the British, on 6 July 1917 Richthofen would be brought down and seriously wounded. In a tussle with a FE2d pusher, he was hit in the head, momentarily 'completely paralysed' and temporarily blinded. Richthofen regained his senses just in time to bring his diving Albatros safely down in a field near Wervicq, Belgium. He discovered, though, that he had incurred 'quite a respectable hole in my head' and a fractured skull which needed surgery. Incredibly, Richthofen would return to duty with JG 1 on 25 July to gain yet more victories in the coming months, although he would continue to be plagued by headaches.

On the Allied side of the line, during the run-up to Passchendaele, the volunteer from Australia Ewart Garland became a victim of what later became known as battle fatigue. On 2 July, when flying at 10,000ft under attack from enemy machines, he admitted to having a

Manfred von Richthofen with a bandaged
head following operation to repair a fractured
skull suffered in action on 6 July 1917.
Thereafter he suffered from severe headaches.
He was non-operational for six weeks.
(Peter Jackson)

'breakdown', though the very next morning he took up a Portuguese officer for instruction, did two hours artillery spotting in the afternoon and flew a night bombing operation.
Nevertheless, on 7 July he was posted to 'a staff job for a rest cure'. Before finally being sent
back to England in September, he wrote that 'my conscience pricks when I am recording
pilots' activity in action etc.'

Also operating in the Ypres sector, while serving at Boisdinghem, 8 miles (12.8km) west
of St Omer, Edwin Bousher – a former Rolls-Royce fitter who had enlisted in the RFC in
1915 and begun flying training the following year – recorded a catalogue of accidents suffered
by No 57 Sqn in the build-up to the offensive. Recalled from a bombing raid on 5 July due
to heavy cloud, one DH4 crashed on landing and caught fire. The observer jumped clear but
the pilot was burnt to death. The very next day, a machine crashed on take-off and both crew
members were burnt to death. On 12 July a DH4 developed engine trouble on a bombing
operation and force-landed behind enemy lines. Two No 57 Sqn observers were killed on
27 July though the pilots brought their machines back; the following day three machines
failed to return, one having been seen spinning down over enemy territory.

These and other losses had to be replaced. On 13 July 1917, Capt Orlando Beater, serving with the Royal Dublin Fusiliers at Ypres, responded to an appeal for observers and left
the battalion for the RFC. Returning to England, he had two weeks leave with his wife in
Dublin before reporting to the School of Military Aeronautics at Reading. Subsequently sent
to the Hythe School of Aerial Gunnery, on 1 August he learned that 'the big push' at Ypres
had begun the previous day.

9

Mounting Losses, August–October 1917
'The aircraft was smashed to pieces'

The plan to take Passchendaele Ridge entailed a parallel advance along the North Sea coast on the left, coupled with the British Fifth Army moving forward from the Ypres Salient roughly along the axis of the Ypres-Roulers railway. The Germans foiled the coastal phase by launching a successful attack there on 10 July, thus the assault on the ridge became an isolated operation. When the Battle of Passchendaele (or Third Ypres) opened, fifty squadrons (including five RNAS) and the Special Duty flight totalling 858 aeroplanes opposed an estimated 600 German machines, roughly one third of them fighters and including Richthofen's 'circus'.

Detailed orders were issued to squadrons directly supporting the corps and those acting further afield. During the preceding night, No 100 Sqn flying FE2b and BE2e machines would hit selected airfields and then on a second raid

> ... bomb any camps, billets, dumps, trains, railway stations or lighted aerodromes seen in the area Ypres-Menin Courtrai-Ingelmunster-Roulers-Bixschoote ... The type of bomb for both raids is left to OC, No 100 Squadron.

Other RFC squadrons were required to machine-gun enemy airfields at dawn to discourage German airmen from interfering with the ground advance. Underlining the separate nature of the British air arms, Maj Gen Sir Hugh Trenchard would 'be glad if the Senior Officer, RNAS Dunkirk, could consider the possibility' of bombing specified targets during the night.

In poor visibility moving north-east from Ypres on 31 July, twelve divisions of Gen Sir Hubert Gough's Fifth Army advanced a mile before heavy rain and enemy counter-attacks halted them. French troops on their left and the British Second Army on the right also made limited progress. Thereafter intermittent downpours so saturated the ground already churned up by artillery shells that Gough's troops failed to regain momentum. After three weeks of disjointed forward movement, the axis of the attack was switched southwards to Gen Sir Herbert Plumer's Second Army. In all, it would take thirteen weeks to overrun Passchendaele Ridge at a cost of 238, 313 men from the two armies, 65,319 of them killed or missing.

A cloud base of 500–800ft on the first morning and torrential rain in the afternoon, frustrated full execution of the aerial plans. Despite the conditions, fifty-eight patrols were flown over the battlefield. The reluctance of British infantry to reveal their positions forced the machines low in an effort to chart the extent of the advance. This exposed them to small-arms fire, and thirty aeroplanes were badly damaged. Beyond the battlefield, twenty-seven Martinsydes attacked enemy airfields with 20lb bombs and a 230lb weapon (110lbs of explosive) specially designed to be released from 400ft. Twenty-three aerial combats were recorded

Edwin Bousher in leather flying kit. RFC pilot and former Rolls-Royce fitter, Bousher flew a DH 4 two-seat day bomber during the Battle of Passchendaele. *(IWM Doc 760)*

on 31 July; eight enemy machines destroyed. Four British airmen were killed, three taken prisoner and eight wounded.

The contribution of the RFC for the remainder of the battle remained at the mercy of the weather. For example, strong winds and heavy rain vastly disrupted artillery co-operation for the five days after 1 August; low cloud, mist and smoke made flying difficult on 16 August when ground troops launched an attack in the Langemarck area. Similarly, rain and low mist reduced the air contribution to an assault along the Menin Road 19–20 September. However, during more favourable spells of weather, reconnaissance, patrol, artillery co-operation and bombing operations were carried out effectively.

On 3 August, Douglas Joy left England to join No 32 Sqn at Droglandts in the Ypres sector, where he would fly single-seat fighters. He had promised his wife, Nesta, that he would write each day and she fretted if he did not keep that promise. One delay was explained in a letter of 16 August: Joy had crashed into a shell hole in No Man's Land and lay there for a considerable time pinned under his wrecked machine, 'while shells rattled overhead', before help arrived. He was unhurt and soon flying again.

Sgt Edwin Bousher was not so fortunate. His operational career began and ended in the struggle to capture Passchendaele Ridge. A letter from Lt B.R.S. Jones of No 57 Sqn to Bousher's father on 22 August explained that his son had been wounded, but was 'progressing favourably'. Jones wrote that during a bombing raid with five other aeroplanes, his DH4 became separated from the others after Bousher realised that one of his bombs had not dropped. While trying to release it over the target, he was attacked by several German machines and 'put up a great fight'. Both petrol tanks were severely damaged and the engine stopped. Nevertheless, Bousher managed to put down on the Allied side of the line, despite having been badly hit below the left knee.

Jones had visited Bousher in a Casualty Clearing Station that morning, where he was 'full of grit', although the leg was 'rather painful'. He would soon be coming home, and Jones wrote that Bousher was 'one of the pluckiest young pilots in a squadron which holds a splendid record'. Jones was sorry to report that Bousher's observer had died of his wounds. He concluded: 'Allow me to congratulate you on being the father of such a grand young soldier, who will soon be with you to tell you the whole story in detail'. In his logbook, Bousher noted that the hang up occurred over an ammunition dump near Ledeghem aerodrome and that six enemy machines had attacked him.

Tryggve Gran very nearly did not survive even to reach the battle area. In August 1917, from their Essex base he and Capt J.I. Mackay took a machine to London to 'show off to friends … We looped, we rolled, we turned upside down and flew with heads down. The air of the capital made us quite tipsy and we were pretty shattered by the time we got back to Hainault.' Seeing fellow flyers on the ground, Gran could not resist going into a spin. 'Down I went like lightning and soon the ground was only 1,000ft below me', causing him to panic. Whatever Gran did, he failed to get out of the spin. Suddenly, he remembered words of wisdom once uttered to him: 'In emergency use your engine.' He pushed the throttle right forward 'and virtually let the plane look after itself. But the ground was already there and I heard a crash and saw stars and went over to a country of sweet dreams.' He came to with the sight of people crowding over him and the voice of Mackay: '"You lucky devil" – and he was right. The aircraft was smashed to pieces but as for me I escaped with mild concussion.'

Somewhat fortunately, therefore, on 1 September 1917 Tryggve Gran reported to No 70 Sqn flying Sopwith Camels at Estrée Blanche, Liettres. 'The flyers gave me a hearty reception, but from my reckoning not one which I could call encouraging'. The OC, Maj M.H.B. Nethersole, told him: 'Your arrival is heaven-sent. We lost five men today.' Allocated one of the dead men's tents, he recalled: 'A strange unpleasant mood got hold of me and I could have wished myself many hundreds of miles from Estrée Blanche'. He was a little cheered by the head of Frank Bickerton, a fellow Antarctic explorer who had been with Sir Douglas Mawson's Australasian expedition of 1911–14, being stuck through the tent flap. He suggested that next day they might 'shoot a few penguins together'.

Gran discovered that dawn and evening patrols were standard, the first at 6am before breakfast. One day two 'raw beginners' were lost. Never having been in action before, they separately 'lagged behind' the fighter formation. Gran mused: 'The first trip over enemy territory is, as a rule, the most fateful for a flyer'.

On another occasion, morning fog prevented operations until the afternoon when 'after tea four of us readied ourselves for a sortie behind the German lines'. Flying in formation they crossed the line at 10,000ft near Mount Kemmel. 'Fire from the ground was astonishingly weak and the whole expedition began to take on the appearance of a joy ride.' Crossing Courtrai they followed the Lys river southwards towards Menin, when the formation leader Lt C.F. Collett began wagging his wings and climbing so rapidly that Gran had difficulty following him. Almost immediately he heard 'a bang' behind him and saw Bickerton tussling with two enemy machines. 'On the horizon were still more planes and I realised at once that we were "going to have fun".'

Having failed to shoot down their intended victim and presumably confident in the impending arrival of support, the two enemy aeroplanes 'sailed alongside our formation' to the irritation of Bickerton. He made a sharp climbing turn to the right and got on the tail

German triplanes lined up on an operational airfield. *(Peter Jackson)*

of one of them from which 'a huge flame' appeared. 'Like a wizened leaf he sank down and then suddenly his nose dropped and he plunged down and disappeared like a burning torch'. Bickerton then attacked the second machine, which quickly made off 'in the direction of his friends, who were steadily getting nearer'.

Regrouping, the four Camels flew towards Ypres but were caught by the seven pursuing Germans short of it. With the sun 'in our favour', Gran was sure that if the enemy remained behind them all would be well. 'But fate would have it that a fight there would be'. Collett's Camel developed engine trouble, which slowed the formation and allowed the Germans to climb towards them. Something had to be done, and Collett signalled the other three to attack by wagging his wings once more. 'Like a wild animal leaping for his prey we cut into the front of the German line', which so surprised the enemy that they spilt up and turned away. Suddenly, Gran found one of the Germans in front at close range, 'gave him something to remember' and chased him as he dived away 'with me at his heels'. 'To my satisfaction', Gran recalled, he made an error which cost many airmen their lives: 'He steered straight down – and my task became simple. His machine lay before me like an anchored target and through my sights I followed my bullets' path into him. Poor chap, a tyro he must have been, but then so was I, his executioner.'

Gran had now descended to 2,000ft and lost the others. Setting course for base, he was relieved to catch up with his companions. Landing, they discovered that Collett was not back, and an anxious thirty minutes went by before he appeared with 'his engine stuttering and stammering'. Once he was down, it emerged that the Germans had pursued his crippled Camel and all the pilot could do was hug the terrain, hop over trees and houses 'while machine-gun fire from ground and air thundered in his ears'. Eventually the heavier German machines, unsuited to Collett's aerobatics, gave up the chase. Maj Nethersole was so delighted

William Avery 'Billy' Bishop (centre). Canadian who served in the trenches before transferring to RFC in July 1915. He became an observer, then had success as a pilot, gaining MC, DSO and Bar. VC gazetted on 11 August 1917, and before the Armistice he was also awarded DFC and three times mentioned in despatches. *(IWM Q 65422)*

at their exploits that he made his car available for the four of them. So as the sun went down, they 'drove at high speed through one of those typical North French towns, between high poplars, along canals and through innumerable dirty and dilapidated villages' until they found a suitable hostelry at which to celebrate.

Manfred von Richthofen indirectly acknowledged the effectiveness of the RFC on 10 August, when he complained that it was pointless taking off once Allied formations had crossed the line and the British were then flying at 14,000–15,000ft. 'Our machines do not have the climbing capacity to reach the enemy in time'. But he was cheered by arrival of the new single-seat Fokker Dr. I (*dreidecker*, triplane), with a maximum speed of 115mph (185kph), ceiling of 20,000ft and armed with two Spandau machine guns, one of which would become his distinctive aerial weapon. These machines could 'climb like apes and are as manoeuvrable as the devil', he wrote. Within two months, however, serious concerns were raised about their tendency to structural failure. On one occasion, Richthofen's triplane disintegrated as he landed.

On 11 August came another fillip for RFC morale and indirectly confirmation of Richthofen's unease about the current state of his own air force, when *The London Gazette* described an action near Cambrai on 2 June, which earned Canadian Capt William Avery 'Billy' Bishop a VC. Flying independently and finding no aeroplanes at the target airfield, he flew south-east to another, where seven machines with their engines running were about to take off. Bishop immediately attacked from 50ft. As one aeroplane became airborne, he opened fire and it crashed, then a second similarly fired on hit a tree. Two more successfully get aloft, but at 1,000ft Bishop emptied a drum of ammunition into one which crashed close to the aerodrome. He fired the rest of his ammunition into the fourth machine, then turned for home evading four more enemy aeroplanes on the way. The official account of the exploit ended laconically: 'His machine was very badly shot up by machine-gun fire from the ground'. Promoted major on 28 August, Bishop allegedly declared: 'Give me the aeroplane I want and I'll go over Berlin night – or day – and come back too, with my luck.'

Three days after the announcement of Bishop's VC, on 14 August James McCudden was cheered to learn of a posting to No 56 Sqn in France as a flight commander. There, he proved keen on discipline and high standards and led by example in his SE5a single-seat biplane. He was acutely conscious, though, that he lacked the experience and operational successes of Squadron pilots like Arthur Rhys-Davids, an old Etonian, and Richard Mayberry, a former cavalryman. McCudden knew Tryggve Gran from his Joyce Green days and complained to him of 'a rotten spell of gun trouble'. On one occasion he had been reduced to firing Very lights at an opponent, who 'put an explosive bullet' into his engine. McCudden thought the new Fokker Dr.I triplane 'an awfully comic old thing and I am awfully keen to see one out of control. I reckon it will be like a Venetian blind with a stone tied to it'. But he conceded that the German machine was 'very fast' with 'a good climb'.

On 10 September 1917, James McCudden once more thanked 'my dear Dad' for a 'very welcome letter'. His younger brother Jack (Anthony) was quite close, though not yet posted to a squadron. 'Splendid weather at present, and a lot of flying', he wrote. He repeated his complaint to Gran: 'I have had a lot of trouble with my guns jamming of late and have lost a lot of Huns over it'. He had manoeuvred into position behind an enemy machine that morning, pulled the trigger and nothing happened. He concluded informally, but affectionately: 'Well Dad old chap, I must close as I am up to strafe the Hun at 3pm.'

In the third week of September, McCudden claimed four victories. To Gran, whom he addressed as 'Dear old Bean', on 2 October he rather whimsically announced the award of a Bar to his MC. He modestly presumed it was 'because I saluted the colonel smartly last time I passed him'. After achieving his eighteenth victory on 21 October, he took the silk cap of the pilot home, when he went on leave, to be displayed as a trophy of war in the family house.

Following his transfer from The Royal Dublin Fusiliers to the RFC in July and subsequent posting as an observer to No 55 Sqn, Capt Orlando Beater's first operation was delayed by poor weather. He spent 19 September marking German aerodromes on his map, but the following day did take off on a bombing raid in a DH4. Even then a last-minute postponement occurred. The 5.30am take-off was put off due to 'dull cloudy' conditions until 2.30pm, when difficulty in starting the engine left Beater's machine 'several minutes' behind the other five. Nevertheless during a two hour and ten minute flight it caught up and bombed the briefed target, coming back via Armentières and Ypres. Beater found it 'very cold indeed' at 16,000ft. 'The wind pressure was simply terrific, my fingers ached, and I lost two valuable silk handkerchiefs, which were literally sucked out of my overcoat pocket and disappeared in a second'. He was astounded to see that movements on roads and even people ploughing were 'quite distinct'. He decided that 'flying would be extra specially nice if one could eliminate the cold, noise and draught'. The bomber force that day had been 'fifteen or so' with 'numerous scouts' as escort. 'So we could fairly laugh at the thought of any Huns daring to attack us: none did as a matter of fact.'

Three days later Beater was on another type of operation, 'a wide-eyed stunt' of photographic reconnaissance. This time the engine would not start, so he and the pilot had arduously to transfer the camera and machine-gun to another machine. Once aloft, the machine laboured in 'thick cloud' and intense cold, which coated Beater's gun with ice, the struts and bracing wires with hoar frost. For an hour the pilot strove to get above the cloud, but failed and they landed again not having crossed the front line.

On 27 September, Beater received distressing news from Elsie that her brother, Jack Manley, had been killed in action with No 19 Sqn. When heavy rain prevented flying on 4 October, his Squadron commander 'very kindly' gave Beater transport to visit his brother-in-law's grave and former unit at Bailleul. The loss of his wife's younger brother deeply affected the family.

On the other side of the line, on 7 September Gen Erich Ludendorff had the sad task of identifying the body of his stepson, Franz Pernet, and informing his distraught wife of her loss. Having recovered from serious injuries in a crash on the Eastern Front, Pernet displayed signs of stress when he resumed operations in the west. Writing to his mother shortly before his death in action, Pernet disclosed his feelings at the end of each day as he prepared for bed: 'Thank God! You have another twelve hours to live.'

In the same month that Beater and Ludendorff suffered family bereavements through losses in action, Maj Harold Wyllie took command of No 102 Sqn, which formed at Marham, Norfolk, on 11 September 1917. Personnel of the Squadron travelled to Southampton shortly afterwards and on 18 September embarked for France. The steamer, bound for Le Havre and protected by escorting destroyers, was 'very crowded with various drafts', but as a field officer Wyllie spent 'a comfortable night' sharing a cabin with one other occupant. The Squadron disembarked at 9am the following day and marched to a rest camp on a hill just outside Le Havre. Officers were allocated tents and use of a mess run by the YMCA, where to Wyllie's disgust, the 'cook hadn't any imagination'. Suffering from his culinary ineptitude did not last long, though.

The Squadron was ordered to Rouen on 21 September and duly boarded a paddle steamer on the Seine for a pleasant journey. 'Perfect day with a hot sun and little wind and the trip up the river was one of the most interesting times I have ever spent,' Wyllie recorded. He was 'very sorry when sunset came and shut out the glorious vista of wooded hills and winding river with ever and again glimpses of quaint chateaux or churches peeping out from the mantle of green.' Landing at Rouen that evening, Squadron personnel were met by transport which had preceded them from Portsmouth. There was no time to study 'the wonderful medieval architecture' of the city. The following afternoon, 'looking like a travelling circus on the move', No 102 Sqn and its transport set off via Foucamont and Abbeville for St André-aux-Bois, close to RFC HQ.

Wyllie once more enjoyed the scenery. He admired 'a succession of most lush woods growing on steep slopes. I have seldom seen anything finer'. In clumps, which grew up to the side of the road, could be seen 'endless tree trunks gradually dying away to ghostly grey shadows in the gloom of the inner wood. I am sure fairies play round those tree trunks.' Arrival at St André on 24 September to take possession of the Squadron's aeroplanes brought an abrupt

German groundcrew pose with bomb load. *(Peter Jackson)*

end to his fantasies. Four days later, No 102 Sqn flew its FE2b pushers to the operational air-field of Le Hameau, 10 miles (16km) north-west of Arras.

Only hours before Wyllie reached St André-aux-Bois, during the evening of 23 September 1917 James McCudden came upon a dog fight between an SE and a Fokker triplane. An official account of the subsequent exchanges noted that his and five other machines came to the SE's aid and for some time the German skilfully coped with the seven British aeroplanes. Other British and German aeroplanes appeared and a mass of machines were soon wheeling and diving with the Fokker triplane prominent. After a while 2/Lt Arthur Rhys-Davids got into position slightly above the German and opened fire at close range with his Vickers and Lewis guns. He reported that the German 'passed my right-hand wing by inches and went down. I zoomed. I saw him next with his engine apparently off, gliding west. I dived again and got one shot out of my Vickers.' Rhys-Davids continued to fire as the German sped past him, but then became involved in another combat. McCudden watched the triplane 'disap-pear into a thousand fragments' as it hit the ground on the British side of the lines. When the wreckage was examined, it contained the body of Lt Werner Voss – credited with forty-eight victims, the last gained that morning. The fatal flight was his second of the day in a replace-ment Fokker, his own being under repair. Rhys-Davids wrote that Voss 'fought magnificently' against heavy odds and McCudden that 'his flying was wonderful, his courage magnificent'.

While McCudden was enjoying success in his SE5a fighter, Tryggve Gran's brief spell with No 70 Sqn ended with transfer to No 101 Sqn, a night bomber unit flying the BE2b, which he found 'splendid and stable'. Prior to his first operation, he spent 'a long day … in tense waiting', before taking off at 9pm. Heading for Ypres, 'the landscape turned red from huge fires and gun flashes'. The night was so dark that even at 2,000ft the ground could not be clearly picked out. 'Suddenly I saw below me a wonderpiece of fireworks like a blue-gold river of fire coming up towards me'. As it got closer, Gran altered course, noting that the sky was lit by searchlights and twinkling stars. A searchlight caught him briefly as he approached the target, where he 'made out the shapes of the railway lines and a station'. He recorded, 'I let go a 112lb bomb. A pair of seconds and a flash – then the heavy thud. Again I pressed the lever and my last bomb went away. I heard a tremendous explosion and my work was done.'

Gran now 'set course for full speed homewards', pursued for some time by searchlights. Once clear, he 'sat and stared into the night' before he picked out the flashes of the British guns, and guided by the landing lights of his base, he put down safely.

Not long afterwards, a flight was not so routine. Operating again from Clairmarais Forest, near St Omer, Gran was badly hit in the leg, he managed to land safely, but soon found himself in hospital. There he caught sight of a report, which revealed that his injury was worse than the staff were telling him and he could well lose his foot. Gran was not uplifted by the fact that when the hut door opened, he could see the hospital cemetery where Chinese gravediggers were hard at work.

> One morning a group came and stood right outside the door. Among them was a little broad-shouldered chap, who out of curiosity stuck his head inside the door. When he caught sight of me, a broad grin spread over his ugly face and in broken English he stammered out: 'Me think you die next – me dig deep.'

He was promptly driven off by an angry orderly, but each morning he peeped in with the cheerful comment: 'English officer not dead'. Gran managed to elude his professional attention although he would spend a further four months in hospital.

England, meanwhile, was being subjected to a disturbing bombing campaign, the Gotha force in Belgium having been supplemented by a unit of four-engine *Reisenfluzeug*, R-type or Giant, machines with a crew of five, 5,000lb bomb load and speed of 85mph. During the night of 2/3 September, two Giant bombers launched a night raid on London, causing eleven casualties and £3,486 of damage, but the shock outweighed the material impact. Between 24 September and 2 October London experienced eight night air-raids. Other parts of the south-east suffered too. One bomb on the naval barracks at Chatham, Kent, killed 131 and injured 90. In Folkestone, on the Channel coast, Kathleen MacKenzie complained of 'such a lot of thud, thud and bang, bang, bang'.

The industrial penalty of these incursions was underlined when Winston Churchill, as Minister of Munitions, analysed the effect of the 24/25 September raid on production at Woolwich Arsenal. That night and the following day, interruption to work and absenteeism dramatically reduced the output of small arms ammunition by four-fifths. A post-war estimate, looking at the whole country, held that once the warning of a raid had been issued, 75 per cent of workers in the threatened area downed tools.

In the wake of the daylight raids on London in June and July, Lt Gen J.C. Smuts, the South African statesman and 'de facto' member of the War Cabinet (for legal reasons officially 'in attendance'), had been tasked with examining 'the air organisation generally and direction of aerial operations'. In detail he was to look at the response to air raids on Britain and the future roles of the RNAS and RFC.

On 19 July, Smuts' first report concentrated on home defence. He deplored the lack of 'a very heavy barrage of gunfire' before raiders reached London, where only 'a sporadic gun fire' met them. Similarly, 'very spasmodic or guerrilla attacks [by aeroplanes] failed to make an impression on the solid formation of the enemy'. Pilots, he believed, were ill-trained and too many separate authorities exercised responsibility for the capital's protection. He recommended a single senior officer to co-ordinate London's defences under the C-in-C Home Command, immediate attention to the disposition of anti-aircraft guns, the training of squadrons to fight in formation and sufficient air defence units to cope with any attack on the capital.

Smuts' second report, dated 17 August 1917, looked at the future of aggressive air power. Two special influences could be detected behind it: the tumultuous demands for reprisal raids on Germany, and the calculation that soon a 'considerable excess' of aeroplanes would exist over the requirements of naval and land forces thus creating a 'Surplus Air Fleet'. In June 1917 the Controller of Aeronautical Supplies, Sir William Weir, forecast that six months later British and overseas' manufacturers would be producing 2,600 aero engines, against a combined RFC and RNAS requirement of 1,859. Smuts concluded, therefore, that in Spring 1918, 'a great surplus' would be available for 'independent operations'; in other words, long-distance bombing. 'The air battle front will be far behind on the Rhine and … its continuous and intense pressure against the chief industrial centres of the enemy, as well as his lines of communication, may form an important factor in bringing about peace'. A tantalising vision for the war weary.

It did not take long for an embryo long-range bombing force to materialise. In October, Lt Col Cyril Newall took command of the Forty-First Wing stationed at Ochey, 15 miles (24km) south-west of Nancy. It comprised No 55 Sqn with DH4s, No 100 Sqn flying FE2b pushers for day and No 16 RNAS Sqn with HP O/100s for night operations. Orders were to attack the coal and iron industries of Lorraine and Luxembourg, responsible for 80 per cent of German iron ore supplies. In reality, this small force suffered not only from lack of numerical strength but also the limited range of the FE2b and the winter weather. Its formation seemed a gesture rather than a serious undertaking. But, however unsatisfactory in practice, the principle of a separate long-range bombing force had been established and the Ochey wing formed the basis for later expansion.

Orlando Beater found himself part of this new organisation. On 10 October, No 55 Sqn was ordered south to 'Nancy or some such place', which entailed a 2–3 day train journey for the observers. En route, they passed through Colombey, 'crowded with Yank troops'. Eventually they reached the aerodrome near Ochey, which No 55 Sqn would share with No 100 Sqn. Both squadrons had been withdrawn from the RFC Order of Battle, adding weight to the argument that a separate bombing force would weaken support for ground troops.

Former French billets were taken over, where Beater counted himself lucky to find a bed: 'Sleeping on the floor is no catch at all'. Two RFC squadrons and one RNAS squadron were to occupy the airfield. On Tuesday 16 October, six HP O/100s flew in, 'the last one in took the top off a tree on the edge of the aerodrome and levelled a telegraph pole, but landed with only slight damage to the lower wing'. The naval contingent had arrived.

Beater was soon in action, the next day taking part in the Wing's initial raid on Saarbrücken, 80 miles to the north-east, leaving Ochey at 1.10pm. The bombers encountered a 'fair dose of Archie' shortly after crossing the line and more near Toulquemont. The batteries around Saarbrücken

… put up a good barrage, and I could hear them go wouf-wouf-wouf, and on one or two were near enough to make the bus rock. Looking over the side, I could see the guns winking away below and fully sympathised with the feelings of a hunted pheasant. We dropped several bombs on Burbach [works] and the remainder on Saarbrücken, and I saw one delightful explosion in a big factory, which must have half wrecked the place and certainly started a large fire, which I could see burning long after we left the town.

Beater spotted 'Hun scouts several thousand feet below', but none worried them. He was not impressed by the flying conditions: 'I was cold in the air, for we touched 17,000ft coming back and as usual my cheeks and chin were frosted'.

The operation on 21 October, Beater's tenth, to a target just west of Saarbrücken was less peaceful. Taking off at 2pm, the bombers circled for an hour and a half to gain height, crossing the line at 3.30 and enduring 'the first whiff of Archie'. They duly dropped their bombs at 4.10, but as they turned away 'a circus of Huns' appeared 'fairly asking for trouble and they certainly got it'. Beater fired a double contraption, which comprised two Lewis machine-guns clamped together. He raked a German to his right 'fore and aft … When I last saw him he was spurting smoke in curious trailing wisps from engine and petrol tanks'. Another enemy dived below 'and standing up on the seat I managed to rattle a few shots round him'. Beater found the double-gun 'a bit awkward and too clumsy for rapid movement. After firing half a magazine one gun stopped with a broken extractor'. He did have one minor personal success, having fitted his helmet with a face mask, 'which kept my chin beautifully warm'. As they had not exceeded 13,000ft, he fired his guns with bare hands 'and did not freeze my fingers'.

During an operation on 30/31 October against the Volkingen steel works, Beater's compass froze at 15,000ft 'and my fingers weren't far off either'. But he did have a fur-lined mask over his lower face and a fur collar of which he was glad 'for the wind was icy'. The month ended on a depressing note with the 'very bad news from Italy' that the Germans had won a major victory at Caporetto on the Isonzo River. Between 24 October and 12 November German and Austrian troops drove the Italians back 70 miles (112km) to the Piave river, where the line was stabilised. By then, the Italians had suffered 45,000 killed or wounded and 275,000 captured.

After detaching squadrons to Ypres and the new bombing wing at Ochey, the RNAS continued to attack enemy targets from Coudekerque, its base near Dunkirk. Harold (known also as Horace) Buss, who began the War patrolling the Channel from Kent, had been flying operationally in HP O/100s from Coudekerque since April 1917. In July, August and September he took part in night raids dropping twelve or fourteen 112lb bombs on the Gotha airfields at Ghistelles and St Denis Westrem. These were punctuated with attacks on the Ostend railway sidings, Middlekerke ammunition dump, Thouront railway station, Bruges docks and the Zeebrugge harbour mole. Often alternative targets were attacked in adverse conditions. On 13 July, 'unable to find aerodrome owing to bad visibility', Buss deposited six bombs on 'a row of lights showing at Bruges on the canal bank' and eight more on Thouront railway junction. During the night of 2/3 September, he had more success at Bruges, where 'numerous direct hits on the docks, submarine shelters and railway sidings and the quay were obtained', which brought Buss a Distinguished Service Cross (DSC). Ghistelles suffered an unscheduled attack on 4 September: 'Started to raid Bruges Docks, but found smoke screen completely covering this objective so dropped bombs on Ghistelles aerodrome. Good results were obtained, bombs exploding among sheds and on the aerodrome.' On 10 September, an attack on St Denis Westrem in 'poor visibility' was completed after circling for an hour to identify the target.

Bernard Arthur Smart RNAS pilot awarded the DSO for destroying Zeppelin L.23 in a Sopwith Pup flown off HMS *Yarmouth* in August 1917. Warned his parents that their 'poor old heads' would 'ache with excitement' at the news. *(IWM Doc 763)*

Buss would remain at Coudekerque until January 1918, when he took command of No 16 Naval Squadron (later No 216 Sqn RAF) at Ochey.

The threat to Britain and warships at sea from Zeppelins had by no means disappeared, and success against one of these airships still caused a stir. FSL Bernard Smart RNAS, flying a Sopwith Pup off HMS *Yarmouth* on 21 August 1917, accounted for L.23 with machine-gun fire close to Lodjberg in Denmark; a feat which brought him the DSO. Writing to his parents, he began: 'I'm afraid that when you get the latest bit of news your poor old heads will begin to ache with excitement, still you must take it as calmly as possible.' He revealed that he was 'that portion of our light forces which brought down the Zep [sic] off Jutland'. Smart admitted not to having 'slept a wink since' as he was 'so bucked with myself'. He apologised for his tardy letter, 'but have spent all my time since my return visiting Admirals and Commodores and the big men of the fleet, and have not had a chance to get ashore or even the time to

David Lloyd George. Minister of Munitions (1915), Secretary of State for War (July 1916), Prime Minister (December 1916). Inspecting guard of honour at Birkenhead, 7 September 1917. Seven weeks later he declared that airmen were 'the cavalry of the clouds'. *(IWM Q 54026)*

write. Saw [Admiral] Beatty this morning, and he is awfully bucked and spoke very decently.' Smart concluded: 'This is only a note to give you the wheeze,' for they must 'keep it dark … as the longer the Huns think it is brought down by gunfire, they will merely give orders to keep well clear of our warships, and so there will be many other chances'.

By the close of October 1917, with the battle for Passchendaele Ridge entering its final stage, as a result of Lt Gen J.C. Smuts' two reports and influenced by the German night attacks on England, a fierce debate was taking place in London about the future of the air services. Senior naval and military officers, politicians and influential advocates of air power argued vehemently on paper and in person about the wisdom of amalgamating the RFC and RNAS into a separate air arm – a third service beside the Royal Navy and Army – and the establishment of an independent Air Ministry.

Irrespective of this manoeuvring, at the Front an enemy still had to be fought by the airmen, who in Lloyd George's flowery tribute of 29 October represented 'the cavalry of the clouds … the knighthood of this war'.

10

Yet More Plans: The Fourth Winter
'Low clouds and misty weather'

The struggle for Passchendaele Ridge, which had started with such high hopes on 31 July, culminated on 6 November when Canadian troops took the village of Passchendaele. Its buildings were in ruins, the surrounding countryside devastated, but the low rise which overlooked Ypres lay in Allied hands. Four days later, the battle officially ended.

Major fighting now switched 50 miles (80km) south to Cambrai, an important enemy communications centre 6 miles (10km) behind the front line and 20 miles (32km) south-east of Arras. Supposedly weak enemy positions offered the attractive prospect of a swift breakthrough: tanks would be used to spearhead the assault, and great emphasis was placed on a short, sharp preliminary artillery barrage. Comprehensive photography by the RFC meant that targets were identified silently, without need for shells to register their positions, the range and elevation from British batteries being worked out in advance.

At 6.20am on 20 November 1917, the Battle of Cambrai commenced, with 374 tanks leading six infantry divisions into action. Five hours later soldiers of the British Third Army were in the enemy's support trenches. That day a significant inroad was achieved, but 179 tanks were disabled and no decisive breakthrough made. Lack of tank reserves proved critical. The advance in the south was subsequently halted for troops to concentrate on penetrating German defences in the north of the battle area. However, difficulty in transferring heavy artillery to the new axis of attack and arrival of enemy reinforcements combined to frustrate the change of plan, and by 29 November significant forward movement had finished.

The RFC deployed 289 aeroplanes to support the attack: six squadrons for close cover of the troops, seven of fighters, one fighter-reconnaissance squadron and two flights of DH4 bombers able to carry two 230lb or four 112lb bombs. Covering the Cambrai area, the Germans had only seventy-eight aeroplanes of which just twelve were fighters. Exclusive of forty-nine bombers with the Forty-First Wing at Ochey, the RFC now had 912 aeroplanes available on the Western Front.

The aerial plan for 20 November envisaged fighter patrols to observe 'any movements by road or rail'. If the weather was too bad for formation flying, aeroplanes were to fly singly or in pairs. Sopworth Camels would bomb and machine-gun selected German airfields at low level, offensive patrols against enemy troops and installations be carried out by Armstrong Whitworth FK8 and RAF RE8 machines. DH4s were to bomb the railway station at Le Cateau. More Camels and DH5s would attack enemy artillery batteries, and SE5s stand by to shoot down enemy observation balloons. During the first night of fighting, Douai and Somain stations were to be bombed.

Remains of a German rigid airship, clearly showing its metal structure. Note its size in relation to the maintenance crew. *(Peter Jackson)*

On the day, conditions were far from ideal. A Camel pilot of 46 Sqn recalled that

… low clouds and misty weather made flying difficult … In the battle area the smoke rose to the mist and formed a barrier not very pleasant to penetrate at so low an altitude. A few casualties occurred through pilots flying into the ground, but the majority were from ground fire.

The first 'show' that morning involved passing over tanks through a 'thick haze of smoke'. Capt Arthur Lee retained

… vivid pictures of little groups of infantry behind each tank, trudging forward with cigarettes alight, of flames leaping from disabled tanks with small helpless groups of infantry standing around, of the ludicrous expressions of amazement on the upturned faces of German troops as we passed a few feet above their trenches.

'Owing to the low clouds' Lee explained, 'it was not easy to retain one's bearings especially after a few startled turns to avoid collision with one's companions.' During this first operation of the day, Lee became separated from his formation and after flying by compass and unexpectedly crossing the battlefield on the way back, he landed in a field 'to discover my bearings'. He realised that he was actually east of Cambrai behind enemy lines, after spotting a nearby road packed with German troops and vehicles, 'I had to make a hurried take-off …'

German airship. Rigid-framed Zeppelin being manouevred on ground. Note two gondolas beneath. *(Peter Jackson)*

German observation 'sausage' balloon. Used to spot Allied troop movements, defensive positions, artillery locations and aerial activity. Prime target for fighters. Note basket for observers beneath the envelope. *(Peter Jackson)*

Ready to fight. German air crew planning a flight in warm clothing. *(Peter Jackson)*

With a synchronised Vickers machine-gun mounted above the front fuselage, the DH5 single-seat fighters of No 64 and No 68 squadrons, the latter one of three Australian squadrons on the Western Front, were involved with No 46 Sqn's Camels in the opening action on 20 November. None of the pilots had experience in low-level attacks. From the three squadrons, nine machines failed to return, four were wrecked on landing, thirteen badly damaged by small-arms fire – approximately 30 per cent of those which set out and an average figure for all such low-level operations throughout the battle. On 23 November, the Germans committed Richthofen's wing to the fray, with their aerial strength by now significantly enhanced after the initial shock.

When the advance petered out on 29 November, the British had gained approximately 3 miles (5km) of ground in the centre of a new undulating line. The next day the Germans launched an assault south of this battlefield across the St Quentin Canal towards Gouzeaucourt with strong air cover. According to one infantry brigade: 'The massing of low-flying aeroplanes going immediately in front of the enemy's infantry caused many casualties and proved very demoralising'. Richthofen's 'circus' was prominent in support of the two-seaters which so effectively bombed and strafed British infantry; a tactic adopted by the RFC ten days earlier. Before their incursion had been stemmed on 7 December, the Germans ejected the Allies from previously hard-won territory below the Cambrai pocket.

November 1917 thus brought mixed fortunes for the British. Although two thirds of those committed were disabled through mechanical malfunction or enemy action, the potential for formations of massed tanks had been demonstrated. The growing importance of aerial operations had once more been heavily underlined. On the other hand, the Battle of Cambrai incurred 47,596 casualties (including 15,886 killed or missing).

Above: Benz-powered DFW CV photo-reconnaissance and artillery observation aircraft in snow. This aircraft entered German service in 1916 and remained in production through to the war's end. *(Peter Jackson)*

Left: British 0.303-in machine gun mounted atop a search light. Probably used for airfield defence. *(Peter Jackson)*

Capt Harold Balfour had reached the front once more during the battle without being closely involved in it. Following his crash on Vimy Ridge in April 1917, he spent several weeks in hospital. While convalescing he received the MC, which gave him 'an inordinate sense of pride'. After a spell of instructing, he briefly served with No 40 Sqn before rejoining his old squadron, No 43, in the Vimy-Armentières sector.

In France for the fourth time, the third as an airman and still aged only twenty, Balfour confessed to bouts of introspection and doubt. Walking around the airfield one still night, he experienced 'pangs of intense and inexplicable sadness and loneliness'. He pondered that he had known only boyhood prior to enlisting and on another occasion, as he looked at the Milky Way one 'brilliant starlit night', asked a fellow pilot 'if he could imagine what life would be without a war'. Not the first, nor the last, combatant to pose that question.

Relocated at La Gorgue, seven miles behind the front line and flying a Sopwith Camel with four 20lb bombs slung underneath, Harold Balfour took part in low-level bombing and strafing of enemy infantry, artillery and motor transport. But his days at the Front were numbered. He began to feel 'seedy', was unable to sleep and half fainted in the Mess. The doctor diagnosed a heart murmur, a legacy he believed of diphtheria. Balfour conceded that 'with nerves near to breaking strain [sic] I will admit that in the Doctor's verdict I found nothing unpleasant,' and he was invalided home in March 1918.

Further north, the RNAS was still attacking targets in enemy-held Belgium, especially airfields. Flying with No 7 (Naval) Sqn from Coudekerque, on 16 February 1918 Observer Sub Lt Aubrey Horn took part in his first night bombing raid on Mariakerke aerodrome north-west of Ghent in a HP O/400 (improved version of the O/100), carrying a crew of four and fourteen 112lb bombs (totalling 560lbs explosive). The twin-engine bomber had an internal bomb-bay capable of carrying one 1,650lb bomb (800lbs explosive) or the equivalent in smaller bombs. One or two machine-guns were fitted both to the front cockpit and that behind the wings, and another fired backwards and downwards through a trap door in the fuselage.

In the direction of take-off for Horn's machine lay 'an immense T of electrical cable illuminated at intervals by glow lamps'. The bomber, accompanied by one other, flew 'up and down the coast a few miles north and south of Dunkirk' to gain height. Sitting in the rear cockpit although

> ... very limited in detail ... the view was rather striking. The exhaust pipes were red hot and red flames capped by blue stabbed viciously into the darkness. Sometimes a long string of sparks was flung far behind the tail planes, and one begins to think that perhaps the Huns could see the sparks and flames being shot out into the night and then pick it up when over enemy country.

Below, the moon shone on flooded ground and star shells fired after they crossed the enemy lines colourfully reflected off the water as they fell. Crossing Ghistelles airfield two powerful lights 'flashed like rapiers' but were probing well above the British bombers. 'They swept over us and stood for a fraction of a second with a dazzling glare upon us, but evidently we were not seen' and the searchlights vainly stabbed the sky well behind them as they flew on south-eastwards. Glancing to his left, Horn saw

> a wonderful protective display over Ostend. Here was a spectacle that even the greatest lover of fireworks could feast his eyes upon and find no fault with. The scene is indescribable and

put shortly is made up of a cluster of powerful searchlights, green balls fired up in groups of three, rockets, and a most extraordinary chain of green fireballs.

Evidence of an air-raid in progress. The scene at Bruges was 'equal to Ostend' with a vast number of

> ... 'flaming onions' as the strings of fireballs are called. They appear to break into flame at some height above the ground and soar up into the air in ever-increasing spirals to 9,000ft ... [It was] not definitely known whether they are connected by wire or are separate ... They are certainly no source of amusement when one looks over the side and sees one or more of these sinuous forms worming and screwing its way up towards one at an astonishing speed.

Doubling back over the docks at Ghent, the bomber attacked its target. Two bombs hung up and were subsequently deposited 'somewhere in Belgium' on the way back. Over Mariakerke aerodrome the shrapnel did not bother Horn, but the machine was held in a powerful search-light. He opened fire with his Lewis gun without effect. Then the pilot 'by a weird series of banks, turns and side-slips at last evaded him [the searchlight], and the Lewis gun was no longer needed, as tracer bullets give the position away ... This was perhaps the most exciting time of what was a very quiet evening.' That is, until landing.

Horn knew that this was the pilot's first night solo. Arriving over base, the illuminated T was in place, a searchlight shining across the ground. A Very light was fired asking permis-sion to land, which attracted a red rocket indicating 'stand off'. The searchlight picked out an aeroplane nose down after landing in a ploughed field, which could hardly have inspired the inexperienced pilot as he circled. When the HP O/400 did so, Horn saw the aerodrome brightly illuminated

> ... and looking over the side we observed a machine gliding in with dazzling landing flares under each wing. These lit up all the ground and enabled the pilot to judge his distance. The machine, which was landing, presented an almost uncanny sight as she glided in noiselessly like a huge ghost.

Then a white rocket went up clearing them to land. The pilot circled down to 15ft above the ground and with 'a touch of an electrical button, over wing flames spluttered and burnt into dazzling brilliance'. Horn wondered how the pilot would cope. He slightly overshot to within 15yds (14m) of the canal, but otherwise 'a splendid landing'. Horn climbed out 'well satisfied' with his first night raid and made for to the mess 'to satisfy a good appetite'.

Two days later, he was off to another bomber aerodrome, St Denis Westrem, with a crew of three, a bomb load of four 250lb and six 112lb bombs with Horn acting as 'rear gunlayer' (naval term for gunner).

> The green ball station at Ostend was sending her signals soaring into the air. Looking over the port side, I saw far below a round dark blot on the ground. While wondering what town it was, a red rocket soared up and burnt into a million scintillating stars. This was the signal for undisguised hate on the part of the Hun occupants of the town.

Shrapnel and luminous balls of fire 'made their way upwards as well as the inevitable flaming onions'. He admitted that he had got the description of a flaming onion wrong: fired from three or four guns, the net result was a spiral. This night they were too close for comfort: 'I cannot but say that I had "the wind up", the strength of the latter not known on Beaufort's scale, for they almost seemed to envelop the tail.' The machine passed over the Brugeoise works, where it was treated to 'a vertically hostile anti-aircraft' display.

The bomber released its load from 9,000–10,000ft, one 250lb bomb causing a 'terrific explosion' which Horn could just hear. 'The appearance of this explosion was a thick oily dark reddish ring of flame, which surrounded a bright red flash. Judging from the size of this flame, the explosion must have been tremendous.' Immediately after the bombs landed, searchlights began to probe 'feverishly' and a further array of flaming onions shot skywards.

On the way back, the bomber encountered an Albatros, which

… provided the 'star turn', the grand finale to the evening's dark deeds. My first intimation of an unusual event was when the machine suddenly nose-dived, thus bringing my meditation to a rude and abrupt end, at the same time laying the foundation for a 'vertical hurricane up'. The next surprise was the rattling of our forward machine-gun, and this completed the strength of the cyclone which raged around me. I flicked my flying gloves off, which I had secured by a long cord round my neck, and seized my gun butt but too late. I then scrambled down to the lower deck and got behind the gun there, fully convinced that the Hun was on our tail.

From here he could 'rake with impunity' the Handley Page's blind spot. But the bullets never came.

Apparently, Observer Sub Lt Hudson in another bomber saw the enemy 200ft below deliberately turn ahead of his aeroplane and fly straight up towards Horn's machine. Crawling from his seat into the forward turret, Hudson 'fitted a pan and put a burst of 100rnds into the fuselage of the Hun, who was about 50ft below us. The Hun's nose turned vertically upwards, stalled and did a vertical nose dive.' Hudson poured a second burst into the Albatros, 'which was crashing earthwards along with the pilot's vision of Iron Crosses and other decorations'. Horn thought this might have been the first time that a Handley Page bomber had attacked an enemy scout, in an action which took about ten seconds 'but it seemed to be hours'.

Life at Coudekerque, one mile south of Dunkirk, was often interrupted by enemy action against the aerodrome itself and the port, raids on Calais and Gravelines and long-range artillery. Horn recorded that the anti-aircraft defences put up a 'deafening defence', which the airmen watched from a distance until 'Hun machines' got too close, when they 'hastily' ducked into a sandbag-shelter or dugout.

The approach of an enemy aeroplane, was signalled by 'Mournful Mary … an appellation fitting' for the siren. Its 'piteous wail … closely resembles the bellowing of a cow, which has been lost from its herd, and is in fact dubbed by the French *La Vache*'. With its first note, 'searchlights feel round the sky, each searching a little while a suspicious area, then finding nothing there to satisfy it takes a long sweep backwards and forwards intently until it is lucky enough to pick up a Hun, which it tries to hold', for anti-aircraft gunners to engage.

About 25 miles (40km) east-north-east of Dunkirk, close to Ghistelles air base, was the *Pièce de Leugenboom*, a 17 inch cannon. 'The first indication that this machine is taking part is a deafening crack immediately followed by a rolling noise exactly similar to a heavy roll of thunder, and it rolls for some seconds afterwards.' When in action, one shell arrived every seven minutes from this cannon, and Horn noted that a bombardment in 1917 went on throughout one night. Over Dunkirk, an enemy aeroplane spotted for the gun and occasionally the 'local

Left: Navigational error. Unusual landing for German biplane. *(Peter Jackson)*

Below: An RE 8, nicknamed 'Harry Tate', forced down in German lines in late 1917/early 1918. *(Peter Jackson)*

wireless station' would jam its transmissions. In the war, Dunkirk would endure 177 air raids, during which 5,092 bombs were dropped, four off-shore naval bombardments and thirty-two attacks by the long-range gun.

FSL Watkins (christened Siegfried by his father – a devotee of Wagner's operas – but known as Toby) took part in the aerial operations against the enemy positions in Flanders, details of which he recorded in a journal. He sailed from Dover in the afternoon of 13 January 1918: 'Jess [his wife] behaved like a brick. Felt like jumping overboard,' he confessed. Reporting to No 12 (Naval) Squadron at Dunkirk, enigmatically he recorded receiving a 'chilly reception'. The aerodrome was awash and on the evening of 15 January an enemy aeroplane came over machine-gunning from 1,000ft. 'No time to get to the dug out, so played touch round a tree trunk'. The airfield remained water-logged until 23 January, before which several more hostile raids took place.

On 24 January, Watkins did his first 'flip' in a Sopwith Camel, only catching sight of hostile formations in the distance. The following morning, he went up again but could not catch a German photographing the station. He had just gone to bed on 26 January, when the 17-inch cannon described by Aubrey Horn opened up: 'Hell of a din and a general rush for the dug out'. 1 February proved, 'a red letter day – had a bath in Dunkirk, the first in three weeks'. Five days later proved eventful for a different reason, when an enemy machine dropped a letter from FSL Carr, who had been posted missing a few days earlier. Carr had been shot down by somebody he knew at Oxford, was unhurt and writing from 'an Air Service Mess', where he was being well-treated.

Watkins, like Horn, was soon engaged in raids on enemy airfields of which that on 15 February, when flying a DH4 as flight leader, proved rather uncomfortable. 'Archie active and accurate as soon as crossed lines near Dixmude', he noted. The main rear spar of his machine was shattered by an anti-aircraft shell and the formation was attacked by ten German machines as it turned away from the target. Seeing an Albatros under the tail of the bomber ahead, Watkins dived and fired tracers at it. The enemy 'half-looped away', and Watkins suddenly found him under his own tail, and 'bracing wires on the left side' being shot away. Fortunately, the German did not persist, but Watkins' 'wonky' machine fell behind the others and was repeatedly attacked by more fighters. In the DH4's damaged state, Watkins 'dare not go full out', so he 'had to side slip and stall continuously to enable my gunlayer to get his own gun on them'. Having reached the Allied line, he saw another DH4 surrounded by eight enemy fighters and turned back to help. On getting closer, he realised that the whole formation was German, 'so retired as hurriedly and as quickly as I could'.

On the last day of February, No 5 (Naval) Sqn and Watkins were ordered south to Villers Bretonneux, 35 miles (56km) west of St Quention, to reinforce the air component preparing to counter the anticipated German ground attack.

Back in England, the training of aircrew continued to give concern. Maj Robert Smith-Barry followed up his criticism of the low standard of pilots being sent into action, voiced while commanding a squadron in France, with a comprehensive critique of the training syllabus. He insisted that it was unrealistic, as well as too short. Pupils were given no real impression of what awaited them at the Front. They should be instructed in 'every possible manoeuvre from taking off across wind to spinning', instead of encouraging them not to get into difficulties, they ought to be taught how to extricate themselves from dangerous situations.

Smith-Barry's outspoken views brought him command of No 1 Reserve Sqn at Gosport, where he put his ideas into practice. Possibly his most important legacy, however, was the 'Gosport tube', a length of tubing inserted in dual control machines for instructor and pupil to communicate verbally. So successful was this experiment that it became standard in all two-seat machines not only for training but operations.

Steps were also taken to improve training elsewhere. When Douglas Joy had learned to fly, facilities in Canada were sparse. With the need to provide many more pilots for the RFC, that country now experienced a vast expansion of training venues. The Curtis Center near Toronto had long been inadequate, and many Canadians underwent their entire training in Britain. In October 1916, the Canadian Government recommended the establishment of 'an aeroplane factory and aviation school', the former supplying the machines for the latter. With pressure to greatly expand the number of squadrons in France, it now seemed prudent to form twenty reserve squadrons in Canada, each in effect a training school. By February 1917, 1,000 applicants were in the administrative pipeline and that month the training flights were ready for action. On 16 March 1917, the first pupils went solo.

Although the USA had entered the war on 6 April, for the seven months from June 1917 American citizens could enlist in the RFC directly from a recruitment office in New York. The United States agreed to make aerodromes in Texas available for RFC training squadrons in the winter months. It undertook to purchase 180 machines from Canada for this pro-gramme and provide petrol, oil, lighting and power so long as everything was left in good order when the squadrons left. As part of the deal, American squadrons would be trained at the Texas airfields and in Canada during the summer months. The RFC advanced training HQ was opened at Fort Worth in September 1917, and on 19 December the first American squadron of twenty-five pilots, having passed qualification tests, with its own back-up staff, left for England. Nine more American squadrons would follow by March 1918. In the year up to 26 January 1918, the Canadians sent 744 trained pilots to the RFC in England, had 2,923 more in the training system, and recorded only thirty-four fatal accidents. The initiative, therefore, proved highly beneficial.

At the Front, flying a single-seat machine, during December 1917 James McCudden added fourteen victories to his existing twenty-three, one day shooting down four, and on another three. On 28 December, Trenchard signalled: 'Well done again. I wish I could have seen you to have said what I think.' McCudden's success attracted less welcome attention after the visit of an agency reporter to No 56 Sqn on 30 December. Articles subsequently appeared in the *Daily Chronicle* and *Daily Mail* at the beginning of January 1918 trumpeting the deeds of a 'Wizard of the Air … [a] fair-haired, slight, shy and delicate-looking youngster' and broaden-ing the story to laud 'beardless boys of Britain', who flew 'high in the icy sky' over France 'proving that they belong to the breed of the unafraid'. Indignant scribes complained that official policy prevented them from identifying the 'hero' who had achieved thirty-seven vic-tories. Not for long. On 7 January, McCudden was named and his photo published. Readers learnt that this 5ft 6ins tall 'slim figure is athletic and his boyish pinky-white complexion gives a touch of delicacy to a countenance that is full of character'. McCudden's father William was of Irish origin and from a military family, his mother (née Amelie Byford) from 'Scottish stock', her father and grandfather former Royal Marines. His elder brother, F/Sgt W.T.J. McCudden had been killed at Gosport, 2/Lt Anthony McCudden MC had brought down 'several German machines' and Maurice Vincent McCudden (aged sixteen) was already in the RFC 'pining to be a pilot'.

In an interview, James' proud mother revealed that 'he tells us hardly anything in his letters about what he has done. Sometimes, he just puts in a line – "brought down two more Huns to-day" – but nothing more'. He had written: 'Hear I've been recommended for the DSO' without telling them what for. Few of McCudden's letters to anybody exceeded a single page.

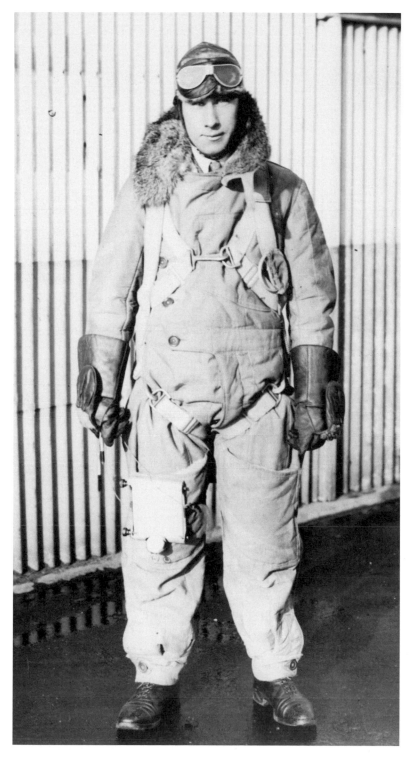

Maurice Vincent McCudden. Youngest and only survivor of the four brothers, who served in the RFC or RAF during the First World War. Seen here as a test pilot at the RAE Farnborough post-war. *(IWM Q 68560)*

On 24 December 1917, he had thanked his elder sister Cis for her Christmas present, but gently chided her for getting something 'so expensive'. He hoped she had 'a nice Christmas', before briefly noting that he had done 'very well lately', receiving congratulations from 'several generals' on receiving the DSO and raising his total number of victories to thirty-two. He wrote a postscript: 'I believe mother thinks that a DSO is the same value as a Band of Hope Medal' (an award from the temperance movement which discouraged alcoholic consumption).

Writing to Kitty on 5 January 1918, McCudden expressed concern that his mother was 'not up to the mark' and hoped 'this letter finds her better'. He dismissed 'all the bosh in the papers about me', wondered how London was 'looking at present', wished Kitty 'good luck and plenty of fun' before apologising for such a short letter. A stern postscript followed: 'On no account whatever are any particulars or photos of me to be sent to the papers, as that sort of thing makes one very unpopular with one's comrades.'

The letter arrived too late to prevent what McCudden feared. He wrote to the Air Ministry protesting his innocence, and on 11 January Sir Hugh Trenchard replied: 'I do not for one moment think you had advertised yourself in the paper knowing you and your work.' He asked McCudden to call on him when next in London. 'I have watched your career for a long time now, and I look upon you as one of the people who are making their weight felt with a vengeance on the Hun.' Now Chief of the Air Staff (CAS), and preparing for establishment of the independent RAF, Trenchard wrote: 'Sorry I am severing my immediate connection with you all in France, but I hope that you and all your brother pilots will still look upon me as a personal friend to help you if I can.' At the Front, by 30 January 1918 McCudden's total of victories had risen to forty-seven, making him the highest-scoring British airman.

As the New Year dawned, far-reaching changes were in motion for the British air arms. The intense military debate and political manoeuvring, which had followed the publication of Lt Gen J.C. Smuts' two reports, resulted in passing of the Air Force Act on 29 November 1917, which paved the way for a separate Air Ministry (created on 3 January 1918) and in due course the Royal Air Force – an amalgamation of the RFC and RNAS. As a result, in 1918 there would be dramatic events both in, and away from, the field.

In January 1918 extension of the British line on the Western Front by almost 30 miles (48km) to the south further strained RFC resources. Following the devastating Italian defeat at Caporetto in October 1917, which put Venice at risk, five squadrons had been sent south of the Alps at a time when campaigns in the Near East, Middle East, East Africa and Salonika also required support. Pressure to mount more long-range bombing operations was also rising, to Trenchard's dismay. He warned about relying too heavily on a weak bomber force: 'I want to bomb Germany, but please remember that if we lose half our machines doing so, the good moral effect which is three-quarters of the work will be on the German side and not ours.'

Writing to Lloyd George on 13 January 1918, he returned to this theme. There was 'in some quarters very serious misapprehension' as to what could be done. At present, three squadrons were operating from an aerodrome at Ochey 'temporarily lent to us by the French'. During the winter 'this limited force' had dropped 20 tons of bombs on Germany, but the proposed reinforcements due to be sent out quickly were 'meagre and disappointing'. Only the RNAS's HP O/100 machines had the ability to reach Mannheim 'unless the weather is very favourable'. The DH9, a longer-range version of the two-seat DH4, due to be the mainstay of the bombing force had not yet proved itself, particularly at heights over 13,000ft. Charles Callender, air mechanic with No 27 Sqn, agreed. While acknowledging that there had been 'bags of snow and ice', he referred to 'a rough winter' with the Squadron's DH9s. 'A bigger machine for bigger bombing … and a hell of a lot of trouble they brought too'.

Arrangements were in hand for twenty-five squadrons to be based around Nancy from May, with provision for a further fifteen two months later. But, realistically, given the need for sorting out teething troubles, special training of crews and always assuming that delivery dates were met, Trenchard estimated that at the end of May only four additional squadrons would be operational. By 31 October 1918, he hoped that eleven Handley Page and nineteen DH9 squadrons 'will be actually at work', a figure to which Gen Sir Henry Hughes Wilson, British military representative to the Supreme War Council at Versailles, added a DH4 squadron to make a total of thirty-one.

Capt Orlando Beater, a No 55 Sqn observer, illustrated the nature of the limited bombing operations from Ochey, near Nancy, as winter closed in. On 1 November 1917, during a bombing raid his formation clashed with enemy fighters. As one of the Germans attacked another DH4:

> I fired two magazines into him, on which he made an almost vertical turn, nose-dived for the ground and a few seconds later his wings fell off and the whole machine broke in pieces to our great gratification and relief. It was a wonderful sight to see him dropping like a stone, leaving a trail of smoke and fire behind him, then his wings fluttering and finally disintegration and death 14,000ft below.

A triumphant reaction not always expressed by aircrew responsible for an enemy loss. On 5 November, Beater practised dual control, taking over the 'bus for a short time … I made some turns, pretty bad ones they were too'. On landing, he learnt that a friend was missing after seven weeks on a Bristol fighter squadron, 'and so my old pals go, one after another, and I wonder which of us will be the next to go.'

The Squadron moved two days later to a new aerodrome close to Tantonville 'of brewery fame', and Beater's experience there suggested that Trenchard's optimism might be a trifle overstated. His arrival was not auspicious: 'We walked over to the mess hut through a sea of mud, which reminded me of Bally Hooley [in Ireland] at its worst, and scarcely tended to raise our rapidly sinking spirits.' The quarters were in a wood for camouflage purposes, and Beater constructed his own bed out of stray pieces of timber. He also 'knocked up a few shelves for my things' above the soaking wet floor in a large hut 'like a big horse barn minus the stalls'.

When landing, many of the aeroplanes sank up to their axles, and it took up to twenty-five men to drag one machine free. 'How they expect us to take off with bombs on board beats me.' Beater thought it would be 'hopeless' until the frost came. It rained steadily on 9 November, so that everything in the hut was 'saturated with moisture'. Four days later, Beater was still trying to get his cubicle finished 'before we all freeze to death'.

Others, he recognised, had their own problems, reflecting on the 'poor beggars', who had reached Victoria station in a leave train only to be returned to Folkestone at once because of 'the Italian situation' – the perilous plight of Italian troops in the face of the German and Austrian onslaught in the north-east of Italy. Depressingly, too, he had heard that the Russians were suing for a separate peace 'and incidentally that Kerensky had got the chuck', a reference to the Bolshevik Revolution under Lenin.

Shortly afterwards, Trenchard visited the Squadron and addressed its members in one of the hangars. 'He told us not to get bored or fed up with our surroundings, but to keep our spirits up and prepare for great things next Spring.' Trenchard had assured the Prime Minister that from Nancy, in co-operation with the French, 'the big industrial centres on the Rhine and in its vicinity' were to be hit. When the weather was unfit 'for long-distance bombing', closer targets in the Saar would be targeted. Short-range bombing 'in immediate connexion [sic] with the army' would take place too, as well as FE2b bombers carrying out night attacks on enemy aerodromes in Belgium.

On 16 January 1918, Trenchard reminded the whole RFC of its day-to-day role on the Western Front: 'The first and most important of the duties of the Royal Flying Corps ... is to watch for symptoms of attack,' which involved reconnaissance and photography and crucially, accurate interpretation of the results. To establish the scope of any such impending enemy assault, the construction of the following should be particularly noted: railways and sidings, roads, dumps, aerodromes, camps and gun positions. Once activity of this nature had been detected, increased co-operation with the artillery would be needed, so would 'extensive bombing attacks to hinder the enemy's preparations, inflict casualties upon his troops and disturb their rest' and 'an energetic offensive' be mounted 'against the enemy's aviation'.

If a major German assault did develop, the RFC should attack enemy reinforcements 'a mile or two behind the assaulting line', harass troop concentrations on roads and at assembly areas, and fly low level operations in co-operation with infantry combating advancing troops. The next stage, assuming the enemy advance had been checked, would be support for a counter-attack by low-flying machine gun flights against enemy trenches and artillery positions.

Trenchard emphasised that superiority in the air must be secured and maintained, adding that a reserve of four squadrons would be based at RFC HQ to reinforce a particular area under threat. Only by consistently attacking the enemy's air force could ascendancy be assured. Even if the ground forces were temporarily on the defensive, the RFC would 'always remain essentially offensive'. This was the declared aerial doctrine in France for 1918.

With reports of increasing enemy activity in the vicinity of the Fifth Army in the south, on 2 February Maj Gen J.M. Salmond, who had succeeded Trenchard as RFC commander at the front, ordered additional reconnaissance flights, which identified extension of light railways, unusual concentration of air units and signs of greater action in the rear areas at night. Clearly something was afoot. From 16 February, day and night bombers attacked aerodromes, railway stations, barracks and troop concentrations based upon photographic and reconnaissance information.

On 12 February, 20-year-old former bank clerk Victor Yeates joined No 46 Sqn flying Sopwith Camels from Filescamp Farm, 10 miles (16km) west of Arras. His journey to France had been neither swift nor smooth. He had volunteered in November 1915, stating a preference for the RFC, but not until 24 February 1917 did he commence his service with the Inns of Court OTC. Exactly three months later, he progressed to RFC instruction at Oxford, then Reading, enduring drill sessions interspersed with study of aero engines, navigation and Morse. Graduating to flying as a probationary 2/Lt at Ruislip, Middlesex, he encountered the Farman Shorthorn, mastery of which involved 'a mixture of playing a harmonium, working the village pump and sculling a boat'. Reputedly its nickname 'Rumpty' evolved from the rumpus caused by its air-cooled pusher engine as the machine rattled over the ground while taxiing.

While at Ruislip, Yeates married Norah Richards, five years his senior, whom he had met before joining the RFC. After Ruislip came spells at Northolt and Croydon, where he delighted in flying the Avro 504J and Sopwith Camel. On 2 February 1918, Yeates completed his pilot training following 11 hours 50 minutes dual and 52 hours 30 minutes solo (including 13 hours 10 minutes on Camels). Five days later he sailed for France and Filescamp Farm, one of three airfields collectively known as Izel-le-Hameau, and was there assigned to a Nissen hut, with an officer's bed in each corner and temperamental stove in the centre. It was the depths of a freezing winter, which lessened operational activity after the Battle of Cambrai. Yeates, therefore, had ample opportunity to practise formation flying and carry out low-level bombing exercises with the four 20lb Cooper bombs, which each Camel carried.

Before Yeates saw action, he had a domestic concern to address: Norah was pregnant with neither her parents nor parents-in-law close enough to give support. Her aunt, Florence Bard, filled the breach which Yeates appreciated. In thanking her, he wrote:'I am afraid she is having a lonely period just now, and she needs companionship … She seems to feel the need at the week-end chiefly.'Yet another family affected by wartime separation.

As a means of strengthening the RFC on the Western Front, in February 1918 the establishment of squadrons was raised to twenty-four aeroplanes and the number of pilots from twenty to twenty-seven with the aim of putting up eighteen machines at any given time. That month Salmond re-emphasied the thrust of Trenchard's doctrine:'offensive tactics are essential in aerial fighting. The moral effect produced by an aeroplane is … out of all proportion to the material damage it can inflict … the moral effect on our own troops of aerial ascendancy is most marked.' In addition to attacks on 'centres of military importance' close to and further away from the front line, offensive patrols were 'to drive down and destroy hostile aeroplanes'.

Even as the RFC was preparing for the war's fifth calendar year in France, enemy air attacks on England were causing renewed unease. By the close of November 1917, the Germans had 144 twin-engine machines available for long distance bombing. On 28 January 1918, a night raid by one Giant and three Gothas on London killed 51 and injured 136; 11 more were injured by spent anti-aircraft shells. At the Odhams Printing Works in Long Acre, which was being used as a shelter, thirty-eight were killed and eighty-five injured. Panic in other shelters, where warning maroons (rockets) were thought to be falling bombs, added a further fourteen killed and fourteen injured to the list. Overall, £137,000 of damage occurred to buildings, 311 of which were hit by falling shrapnel. On 16 February, bombs fell in the grounds of Chelsea hospital. These were timely reminders that the homeland remained vulnerable and that the bombers' bases in Belgium must not be neglected in the pressure to support ground forces elsewhere. One observer recalled 'the tension, the overworked nerves, the horror' caused by 'the noisy, droning winged monsters'. Years later, the Air Ministry would claim that the German air raids on London in early 1918 'had a strong effect upon our air policy, and deserve to be remembered for that reason alone'.

Whatever the other pressures, the primary concern of Salmond and the RFC in the field was to identify the strength and location of the German offensive in the offing, and help to frustrate it once launched. As feared, disintegration of the Russian theatre had allowed the Germans to transfer ground and air forces to the Western Front. All the signs were that a massive attack could be expected before American units reached France in strength.

As February 1918 drew to a close, the precise area of the anticipated assault remained uncertain. RFC HQ therefore laid down contingency plans for deployment of squadrons in one of three sectors covered by the four British armies: north, centre and south. Within days, the sector most likely to bear the brunt of the onslaught would become clear, and movement of designated squadrons to it would begin.

11

German Offensive, March–May 1918
'Backs to the Wall'

On 3 March 1918, Russia signed a peace treaty with Germany and Austria-Hungary at Brest-Litovsk in Russian-held Poland. Within four days, Romania and Finland had also made peace, opening the way for further enemy reinforcement of the Western Front.

By the beginning of March, it was believed that the expected attack in France would most probably fall in the south, where the British Third and Fifth armies were spread thinly for 70 miles (112km) astride the Somme from Gavrelle near Arras in the north to Barisis just south of the Oise river. The Fifth Army front covered 42 miles (67km) of this distance, with French troops on its right (south).

Including reserves, Gen Sir Hubert Gough's Fifth Army had fourteen divisions, Gen the Hon Sir Julian Byng's Third Army sixteen (three of them cavalry divisions), amounting to approximately 440,000 men. Opposite them, including reserves, in their Seventeenth, Second and Eighteenth Armies the Germans deployed seventy divisions (about 840,000 men) and enjoyed roughly three to one superiority in artillery. General Erich Ludendorff, deputy to the 68-year-old German Chief of the General Staff, Field Marshal Paul von Hindenburg, and in practice commander of the armies in the field, calculated that American troops would not be fully effective until the summer, and that the British had not recovered from their heavy losses at Passchendaele and Cambrai nor the French from their failed offensives in 1917. With an additional twenty-three divisions available to him from the east, Ludendorff reasoned that a decisive breakthrough could be achieved on the Western Front in Spring 1918 by driving a wedge between the British and French before sweeping north towards the Channel ports.

Within five days of Russia's formal withdrawal from the war, three single-seater Sopwith fighter squadrons (two of Camels, the third with Dolphins), a reconnaissance squadron of Bristol Fighters and two DH4 day bomber squadrons flew as reinforcements to aerodromes behind the southernmost of the two British armies, the Fifth. One night bombing squadron of FE2b machines was already there and another moved to the Third Army area on 5 March. This left two FE2b night bombing squadrons to support the RNAS against enemy airfields in Belgium.

Mist over the likely area of attack between 17 and 20 March restricted air activity. However, limited air reconnaissance together with captured documents and debriefing of prisoners pinpointed 21 March as the fateful date. Gough wrote home on 19 March: 'I expect a bombardment will begin tomorrow night, last six to eight hours, and then will come the German infantry on Thursday 21st'. British squadrons were required to carry out 'extensive bombing attacks to hinder the enemy's preparations, inflict casualties upon his troops and disturb their rest'. So, during 20 March, DH4 bombers attacked Cambrai and other railway centres in a bid to disrupt German troop movements.

On that eve of the Kaiserschlacht or Ludendorff Offensive as the German attack has become known, the RFC had sixty-two squadrons and one special duty flight in France, excluding forty-one kite balloon sections but including three Australians, one Canadian and three RNAS squadrons. Arrival of another squadron on 22 March raised the nominal strength to 1,232 aeroplanes. Of these, 579 including 261 single-seat fighters were positioned in the area of the Third and Fifth armies; opposing them were an estimated 730 German machines including 326 single-seat fighters.

Orders to the squadrons in the Third and Fifth armies' sectors reminded those supporting the individual corps that once the battle commenced they should concentrate on counter-battery work, contact patrols, artillery co-operation, photography, harassing enemy movement with bombs and machine-guns and after day operations, night bombing behind the German lines. Squadrons more generally supporting an army were to prevent interference with the corps' machines, attack concentrations like 'detraining points and debussing centres', carry out low-level attacks on enemy troops and fly patrols high over the area of operations as additional protection.

Capt S.R. 'Toby' Watkins, who was involved in the run-up to the battle, had arrived at Villers Bretonneux in No 5 (Naval) Sqn from Dunkirk on 6 March, and was not over-impressed with his new abode. 'Awful aerodrome mostly soft ploughed, bomb holes and ditches the whole garnished with hundreds of red warning flags'. Three DH4s crashed on landing, two being write-offs. On a familiarisation flight that afternoon, Watkins found it a difficult 'to find one's way' with a map because the terrain had been so altered by the Somme battles. He had no time to settle in, the very next day for the first time leading 'a stunt' to Mont d'Orginy aerodrome, east of St Quentin. Heavy cloud obscured the results of the bombing and Watkins discovered on his return that all other squadrons detailed to attack this target had abandoned the operation due to the conditions.

Watkins was kept busy, sometimes flying twice a day and often combining photography with bombing. Going to Mont d'Origny again on 9 March, he endured 'a very warm time' due to engine trouble and Albatros attacks before the target, on the way back and well over the British lines. A bullet had passed between his observer's feet, missing the seat of Watkins' pants by inches to hit the engine. Four days later, he noted that No 42 Sqn had encountered Richthofen's 'circus' near Cambrai and lost six machines. 'Hope to goodness we don't meet them,' he wrote.

British airmen carried out several raids against Etreux aerodrome from which twin-engine Gothas attacked Paris. Bombing operations on this and other airfields had prompted the Germans to concentrate Richthofen's 'circus' of single-seat fighters in the area, 'out for our blood'. This led the RFC to despatch bombers to a target, ordering them to circle after release of their load to entice enemy fighters into the air. Whereupon, a formation of SE5s lurking above would dive on the enemy. This particular 'stunt' did not always work. On 16 March at Busigny, the fighters failed to appear, so the bombers had to fight their way back at times outnumbered four to one. The following day, the scheme did function, leading to 'the biggest scrap I'd ever seen' according to Watkins:

> The sky seemed to be full of machines looping, cartwheeling, spinning, diving in flames and going down without wings. Saw one Hun go down in vertical dive from 15,000ft and crash in the middle of a village. The net result was eight Huns bagged without a single British loss.

Siegfried 'Toby' Watkins with sister Gladys (right) and Phyllis (left). The RNAS pilot flew DH4s during the Ludendorff Offensive (March 1918) and narrowly escaped injury when his own airfield was shelled. He completed forty-four bombing operations in under two months; leading to exhaustion and medical repatriation to England. *(June Watkins)*

However, on 18 March, he acheived 'not such a good result as yesterday'. The Germans put up sixty machines against thirty SE5s and Camels with eight DH4s. The British lost five Camels, two SE5s and a DH4, with unconfirmed claims of eleven Germans shot down. At this stage, No 5 (Naval) Sqn had lost nine DH4s in nine days and Watkins diary entry betrayed the strain: 'Whose turn next?' For the next two days came 'rain all day. Thank God!'

Second Lieutenant Hervey Rhodes joined No 12 Sqn in March 1918, shortly before the German offensive. Son of a factory worker from Saddleworth, Yorkshire, he left school aged twelve to work in a mill and subsequently spent two years labouring in Canada. Returning to England, he enlisted in the Army in August 1914 ten days short of his nineteenth birthday. As an NCO in the King's Own Royal Lancashire Regiment, Rhodes saw action at Loos and on the Somme before being recommended for a commission. At an Officer Training Unit in a Cambridge college, he recalled mixing with men of vastly different social and educational back-grounds which 'gave me enormous confidence, when I realised I could hold my own'. Rhodes finished in the top ten of his course and was commissioned into The Yorkshire Regiment.

Returning to the trenches, with their combination of knee-deep mud, vermin and the thud of bullets hitting bodies as men went over the top did not seem attractive. Instead, 'sick and tired of the infantry', he volunteered for the RFC, which ultimately led to his posting as an RE8 observer to No 12 Sqn. There he teamed up with South African pilot, Lt Croye Pithey. Pithey and Rhodes would form an effective partnership in the air and become firm friends. Inexperienced when the enemy's March offensive commenced, pilot and observer contrived quickly to master climbing to 12,000ft, taking photos of the battlefield, communicating with

Left: Hervey Rhodes. Served in trenches, then as a gunner/observer in No 12 Sqn. Pictured here as a private in the Signals Platoon, 7th Battalion, The King's Own Royal Lancashire Regt. before joining RFC. *(Adam Sutcliffe)*

Below: Hervey Rhodes (back row, second right) seen here as a member of No 12 Sqn's concert party, when not flying with South African pilot, Croye Pithey, in an RE 8. *(Adam Sutcliffe)*

artillery batteries, bombing and strafing German positions during 'very hazardous' low-level contact patrols. As a former regimental signaller, Rhodes was proficient in the sending and receiving of Morse, which proved invaluable when spotting for the artillery. The crew's success soon caused them to be dubbed 'the Pithey and Rhodes Line'.

After a dry spell, on 19 March rain fell and a heavy mist settled over the area, which contrived not only to conceal but to muffle enemy movements. At 4.45am on 21 March, a ferocious barrage including gas shells drenched troops astride the Somme for a depth of 20 miles (32km). Gough's Fifth Army bore the brunt of the assault and a new tactic. The Germans increased the machine-gun complement of their divisions and used quick-moving storm troopers to bypass strong points and attack command centres in the rear leaving infantry to consolidate gains in their wake.

The enemy bombardment severed important telephonic communications, and in the murk visual warning signals went unseen. The first that most forward troops knew of danger was the sudden emergence of Germans from the fog between 8am and 10am. By noon the storm troopers had gone through the Fifth Army's forward zone. By evening, the enemy had advanced an astonishing 17 miles (27km) and taken some 20,000 prisoners. To avoid being cut off, the Third Army was obliged to fall back and straighten the line. The relentless advance continued. By 4 April enemy formations were within 10 miles (16km) of Amiens having penetrated 40 miles (64km) along a 50-mile (80km) front in just two weeks. The assault, in the face of Allied reinforcements and effective inner defences, now stalled.

On the opening day of the attack, 21 March, visibility was sufficient in the Third Army area for RE8 crews to report enemy activity from as early as 6.15am, and later that day artillery co-operation machines were also active. On the Fifth Army front the mist lifted in the afternoon, which allowed patrols to engage enemy aeroplanes and other machines to spot for the artillery and machine-gun German troops. Below them, though, British infantry were falling back rapidly.

As they did so, squadrons had swiftly to change airfields and a co-ordinated response proved increasingly difficult. Cpl Charles Callender, the mechanic from Stockton-on-Tees who experienced such traumatic training at Farnborough and Brooklands, recorded that at one point No 27 Sqn moved to another station, which in turn had to be abandoned. Left there were eighteen 'large HP bombers' with folding wings, then on the secret list and 'never been used', which were burnt because there was nobody to fly them.

Low cloud on the opening morning frustrated German airmen, too. Richthofen's wing was scheduled to take off 45 minutes before the infantry attack, tasked with protecting reconnaissance machines, dealing with Allied fighters and attacking observation balloons. It did not get airborne until 12.30, and managed only fifty-two sorties to account for just two balloons.

On 21 March during the artillery overture to the German attack, 6-inch shells demolished three hangars and an office on Toby Watkins' airfield, only protective earth banks saved the accommodation huts:

> One big shell burst about 10yds (9m) from my hut as I was packing. I heard it coming like an express train, and just had time to fall flat down behind my tin trunk before the world fell about my ears. Most astonished to find that I was alive and unhurt.

Watkins confirmed that the mist cleared at about 2.00pm, when dodging shell holes his and other machines took off to bomb troops crossing pontoon bridges over the St Quentin Canal. The DH4s landed at an emergency airfield on their return and from there attacked enemy troops and the pontoon bridges again the following day. On 23 March, No 5 Naval Sqn flew four operations against advancing enemy columns before falling back to Bertangles, west of their old aerodrome. By 24 March the St Quentin canal bridges were 25 miles (40km) behind the front line and that day Watkins saw enemy scouts leaving the squadron's former station at Mons-en-Chaussée, but could not reach their height to intercept. In the evening, when the formation leader got lost in thick mist en route to a railway target, Watkins took the lead and guided the formation back on course; 'Engine fell to bits on landing, so did not fly on the 25th.' He took up a new machine on 26 March: 'She will be top hole, when the engine is tuned up, but no time for even cleaning machines these days,' There was opportunity only 'to rebomb and refuel tanks, when we land from a raid, then all machines off again on the next … Result: machines and pilots going to pieces'.

After leading a raid on bridges across the river on 26 March, Watkins recorded that 'the Huns were well over the Somme – somewhere between Brie and Villers Bretonneux'. That afternoon he went by car to Villers to collect one of the Squadron's machines, which had landed there with engine trouble. He found the road 'packed with retreating troops, transport, villagers with their goods and cattle, and ambulances'. The aerodrome was deserted. 'There had been a stampede from there the night before and thousands of pounds worth of stores, furniture and officers' personal belongings were left behind undestroyed'. Returning to base, Watkins led two more raids that evening against enemy transport on the Albert-Bapaume road, but clearly the Germans were still making rapid progress.

> More dead than alive by evening, could scarcely get out of machine. Food is nearly as scarce as sleep – we're mostly too tired to sleep at night – but no one thinks of giving up. I find that leading one raid tires me more than doing three when following another leader.

On 27 March, the squadron was ordered to adopt a new tactic, 'which frightens me stiff'. A low-level contact patrol was, in his view, 'highly dangerous work' for scouts, but 'on DH4s it's suicidal'.

During three raids that day, he flew below 1,000ft 'bombing and shooting up transport, troops and batteries two or three miles behind the lines. We passed our scouts shooting up the trenches from <u>our</u> [sic] side of the lines, with no Hun scouts or Archie to worry them'. On the first, he dropped his bombs from 900ft, then flew up a road to let his gunlayer fire his two guns at columns of troops marching up in support. Watkins watched the enemy scatter along the roadside and get their machine-guns 'busy on me … Little holes began to appear in my planes (could hear the "zip" every time the machine was struck), so zoomed up to 2,000ft having first dived on a machine-gun crew and dispersed them with a burst from my front gun.' Watkins then attacked a kite balloon, one of several 'strung up' close to the lines. As his gunlayer had run out of ammunition, Watkins left the balloon to another pilot, who got fifty rounds away as it was being hauled down. Suddenly Watkins realised that nine enemy scouts were closing on his tail, and swiftly made for the safety of friendly territory.

His second operation of the day was 'a repetition of the first stunt, but with more Hun hate, in the form of pom pom tracer shells, which leave a thick green trail of smoke'. After dropping his bombs and firing at troops from 1,000ft along the Amiens-St Quentin road, he spotted a group of triplanes 'coming down nearly vertically onto me'. Having loosed off fifty rounds at the leader, 'I was beginning to say my prayers, when I saw an enormous plume of black smoke from a burning dump drifting towards the lines. So immediately camouflaged myself in this and got safely back over lines at about 800ft.'

'Archie'. Mobile German anti-aircraft unit in protective trench. *(Peter Jackson)*

Watkins' third raid engendered 'a very warm reception'. He dropped bombs on transport from 1,500ft 'then fooled about shooting up troops and batteries from 1,000ft'. However, the Germans had brought up 'a lot of anti-aircraft guns, which made some wonderful shooting'. When enemy scouts appeared and 'things got hot', Watkins took refuge in clouds at 2,000ft. In a 'large clear patch' over Foucancourt, 20 miles east of Amiens, he was 'ringed with bursts in no time'. He side-slipped, half looped, dived and zoomed, 'but still the "woof, woof, woof" continued all around me'. He managed to get back into clouds on a left hand turn and while hidden, turned sharp right. When he emerged into sunlight, he saw 'dozens of Archie bursts well to my left. The blighters had followed me up on my original course'. Watkins repeated 'this performance' several times, aware that triplanes were waiting to pounce on any machine coming out of cloud. One of his fellow DH4s had three on his tail, and Watkins was delighted to see two of them collide 'and go down locked together in flames'. Another DH4 shot down a triplane, 'which fell with one wing folded back'. However, Watkins witnessed a bomber hit by 'Archie, burst into flames and go down', and a second was missing believed shot down.

In a 'low stunt' on 28 March, Watkins' bombs hit motor buses bringing up troops near Foucancourt and in a second sortie, pontoon bridges over the Somme. He saw anti-aircraft fire score 'a direct hit' on a bomber, which disintegrated in the air. After a 'critical state of affairs' developed at Morcourt, just north of the Amiens–St Quentin road, the 'situation was saved by a brilliant cavalry charge. I was over the charge at 1,000–800ft and led the charge firing my front gun in to the Hun troops.' But, due to the enemy's continuing advance, the squadron had to move back again to a field east of Abbeville, which had primitive facilities.

As it rained all day on 29 March, Watkins motored into Abbeville 'for bath, hair cut etc'. Despite the weather, he also managed some sight-seeing: 'Fine old town. Cathedral disappointing. Had topping dinner at the Officers Club – first good feed <u>for weeks</u> [sic]. Club

This Mercedes-powered LVG B I reconnaissance aircraft machine has suffered a heavy landing judging by the collapsed right undercarriage leg. Pilot to left is a lieutenant with an Iron Cross (black ribbon visible under second button of tunic). Observer with hand on propeller.

full of officers straight from the retreat. Heard some blood curdling yarns.' Back at the new airfield, there was no news of five missing crews, but four other men were known to be recovering in hospital.

In the air again on 30 March, Watkins bombed transport on the Amiens–St Quentin road from 2,000ft and shot up troops from 1,000ft. The following day, his target was a German advanced landing ground between Caix and Rosières, roughly 20 miles south-east of Amiens. Low cloud obscured the site, 'so dropped my pills on hutments and troops near Froyant, spotted through hole in clouds'. After releasing his bombs, 'found myself sharing the sky' with seven hostile triplanes, so Watkins dived below the clouds and escaped to the lines, where he flew back and forth while his gunlayer 'pumped lead into Hun trenches'. Nobody fired at him 'or if they did were very bad shots'; a tame end to 'a most interesting little tour', he mused.

Toby Watkins' experiences were part of a confused picture in the wake of the German advance. On 23 March, the day that long-range artillery shelled Paris and as the Fifth Army tried desperately to stabilise its front, SE5s carried out offensive patrols on enemy troops and their transport. No 84 Squadron reported 'large swarms of enemy troops … advancing across fields near Viefville' shortly after midday. For 20 minutes, its SE5a machines relentlessly attacked until their ammunition ran out. Elsewhere, Spad aeroplanes of No 23 Sqn stampeded mules and scattered cavalry. As they did so, RFC DH4s were attacking an ammunition dump near Cambrai and a transportation centre at Quéant. RNAS DH4s dropped 25lb and 112lb bombs on troop reinforcements massing in the rear areas, while other day bombers focused on railway stations.

Improved visibility dictated that more aerial combats took place on 23 March than during all of the days preceding. Thirty-six enemy machines were reported shot down in the battle area. That day, the RFC lost five aeroplanes, plus thirty-three wrecked 'from all causes'. Next day, 24 March, forty-two German machines were reputedly shot down for the loss of eleven RFC aeroplanes with another forty written off in crashes. Capt J.L. Trollope in a Camel of No 43 Sqn, supporting Third Army, alone accounted for six of the enemy. Four days later, Trollope would be one of five pilots reported missing from ten who set out on an offensive patrol. His mother would later receive a letter from a PoW camp, in which he was keen to tell her that he had accounted for two more enemy machines before being shot down.

Desperate attempts were made by the RFC and RNAS squadrons to slow the Germans as crisis after crisis developed. With hail and snow blanketing the area, on Monday 25 March RFC HQ signalled: 'A concentration of enemy troops has been located just west of Bapaume. Every available machine will leave the ground so as to attack this concentration at dawn with bombs and small-arms ammunition and break it up before any attack develops.' The following day, Maj Gen J.M. Salmond ordered: 'Bomb and shoot up everything you can see … very low flying essential. All risks to be taken. Urgent.'

The harassing work of low-flying machines was illustrated by the activity of Camels from No 4 (Australian Flying Corps) Sqn on 27 March, whose sixteen pilots achieved a total of seventy hours flying that day. Troops and transport on the move, ammunition dumps and static concentrations were bombed and machine-gunned to effect. In the period of 25–28 March an average of fifteen pilots in total flew operationally over 200 hours.

German airmen were by no means toothless. On 25 March, Richthofen secured his 69th and 70th victims, two days later his wing flew 118 sorties in the vicinity of Albert and shot down thirteen aeroplanes. That day, the Germans claimed thirty-three machines, seven of them to anti-aircraft fire, one to 'a railway sentry post'. The RFC recorded sixteen confirmed 'kills' with four more driven down out of control. During the night of 26/27 March, German bombers heavily struck Doullens aerodrome.

James McCudden was not involved in any of this activity. On 2 March, he noted that he had flown 777 hours 20 minutes as a pilot. Since he joined No 56 Sqn 16 August 1917, this unit had claimed 175 enemy machines either destroyed or driven down out of control, but these successes came at a cost. In that period, fourteen of the Squadron's pilots had been killed or were missing, seven made PoW. Shortly afterwards, McCudden went on leave to England prior to a non-combat appointment, a rest which would soon be cruelly interrupted.

On 19 March 1918, his mother received a letter from No 84 Sqn commander, Maj Sholto Douglas. 'I am sorry to say your son [John Anthony, known as Anthony in the RFC and Jack to his family, aged 21] went missing yesterday.' Douglas could not be certain about what happened, 'everybody was busy scrapping. All we know is that he did not return.' The Squadron commander tried to be encouraging: 'We can only hope for the best'; but it was 'quite likely … a lucky shot hit his engine or radiator'. In which case, he could have come down and been taken prisoner, 'One cannot say. I sincerely hope that you will get definite news of his safety very soon.' Douglas rated him 'quite one of my best pilots, and I am sure that given a little luck he would have emulated the success of his elder brother.' He went on unconsciously to echo the concerns of James, when he assessed Jack's ability at Joyce Green. The younger McCudden was 'extraordinarily brave – too brave if anything. He often took risks that 99 per cent of humanity would refuse to take.'

Anthony McCudden had taken off at 10am on 18 March in one of the operations against Busigny. He became involved in a melee with fifty enemy machines and was one of eight RFC machines that failed to return. James wrote to Maj Douglas from the RFC Club in London on 22 March. He hoped that his brother 'may be alright [sic]. Rather bad luck. I wish you would let me know as soon as possible any news received concerning him.' Unknown to Douglas or the McCudden family, the body of John Anthony had already been buried by the Germans with full military honours.

On 26 March, five days after the initial German assault, a major move was made to improve Allied activity on the Western Front, when the French general, Ferdinand Foch, was appointed 'to co-ordinate the action of the British and French Armies', an arrangement to which the Americans and Italians subsequently adhered. Foch, therefore, became Generalissimo or over-all Allied commander. Another highly significant development from the British standpoint was amalgamation of the RFC and RNAS into the Royal Air Force on 1 April 1918; RNAS squadrons being renumbered by adding 200.

That same day, Foch drew up directives 'with the object of assuring co-operation between the British and French Air Services'. He wanted reconnaissance extended to the line St Quenton-Cambrai-Douai to ensure 'air observation covers *every part of the area of approach to the battle zone*'. As to bombing, 'the *essential* condition of success is the concentration of *every resource* of the British and French bombing formations on such few of the *most important* of the enemy's railway junctions as it may be possible to put out of action with certainty, and to keep out of action.' So far as the British were concerned, this meant attacking the stations at Péronne, Cambrai, Aubigny-au-Bac and Douai.

Foch emphasised that 'the first duty of *fighting machines* is to assist the troops on the ground by incessant attacks, with bombs and machine-guns, on columns, concentrations or bivouacs.' He believed that the Allies had failed to make their numerical superiority count, by too wide a dispersal of resources. On the British front south of Arras, 822 German machines currently faced 645 RAF. Exclusive of aeroplanes on both sides committed to naval operations, to the north 393 RAF opposed 185 German machines. At the same time, some 2,000 French aeroplanes were deployed against 367 German. So it was, in Foch's view, utterly illogical that on the Somme battlefront the enemy should currently enjoy superiority of numbers. However, within days, German advances in the north would undermine the logic of Foch's analysis.

More immediately, on 1 April Toby Watkins' RNAS squadron became No 205 Sqn RAF and celebrated its new status with a return to 'high level bombing in formation … well behind the Hun lines'. Unfortunately, the bombing was 'very inaccurate. Everyone too worn out to take a good line'. Enemy anti-aircraft fire was heavy and accurate and 'nearly every bus hit by splinters of HE or shrapnel'. Watkins 'experienced my closest Archie burst on this raid. Was tooling along half asleep, lulled by the coughing of many Archie bursts.' There came a big flash 'followed by a gigantic cough and a tremendous shock right through the machine which made me think that I'd "bought it" in a direct hit.' He was through the smoke of the burst almost before he had seen it 'spreading out from nothing (like a huge umbrella point towards one being quickly opened) in the uncanny way of the HE Archie'.

On 2 April Watkins bombed Rosières aerodrome. When attacked by a large force of Pfalz scouts, he 'managed to cloud dodge them'. It would be his last operation. The following day, suffering from exhaustion, he was ordered to hospital at Etaples. His first operation had been flown on 16 February, so the intensity of completing forty-four operations, given breaks for bad weather and travel between airfields during the retreat, had clearly been overwhelming. On 7 April, he wrote: 'Spent most of the last 96hrs sleeping … was examined by a Medical Board – a fearsome test lasting several hours, and … ordered home for a month's complete rest and a spell of Home Service to follow.' Watkins would not return to operations before the Armistice.

Even as British airmen strove to counter the German onslaught, operations were continuing against enemy port installations and German bomber bases in Belgium. Flying in an HP O/100 from Dunkirk Observer Sub Lt Aubrey Horn noted 'about twenty' Gotha 'jumping off places' in the Bruges-Thourout area; Thourout being 'a favourite port of call'.

The dangerous progress of the German forces farther south meant that during the night of 26/27 March, Horn's crew was ordered to attack Valenciennes railway junction through which enemy reinforcements were moving. Armed with twelve 112lb bombs, the Handley Page would be in the air from 9.45pm on 26 March until 07.30am on the 27th. Horn carried out the bomb dropping duties on this operation.

> The bomb sight and dropping lever had been moved from the forrard [sic] gun pit to a place amidships … Lying down on the floor I slid back a panel thus revealing the landscape below. We ran down wind, turned and got nose into the wind again. So strong was the breeze that the machine just held its own making very little headway.

Eventually the aeroplane reached the target and 'I slowly loosed the medicine'. So far so good.

On the way back, enveloped in mist and buffeted by strong winds, suddenly and unexpectedly at 4,000ft the crew found itself over Ghistelles aerodrome. The pilot swiftly climbed into the cloud again for 'being as low as we were, we should have been an excellent source of amusement for the gunners for we were silhouetted against the mist'. Above the thick mist at 7,000ft, the sky was clear. But the bomber had to descend through it when nearing Dunkirk. At 2,000ft Horn identified a large glow as the Belgian furnace near Furnes, east of Dunkirk inside the British lines. On closer inspection, it was a well-lit town, which confused him. He had seen Ostend with its colourful anti-aircraft defences some distance behind and therefore discounted the possibility of a compass error taking the machine over neutral Holland. The crew decided this must be Calais, 25 miles (40km) west of Dunkirk, but there was no response to their Very lights. When the starboard engine began to misfire, the pilot put down on a convenient stretch of sand. After the crew clambered out, a council of war became 'slightly obsessed with the possibility of not being on Calais sands at all'. Eventually, they found a telephone and to their intense relief, got through to a nearby British aerodrome.

The day after its formation, the RAF received a welcome morale boost, when news was published that twenty-three-year-old James McCudden, already holder of the Croix de Guerre, MM, MC and Bar, DSO and Bar had gained the VC. The citation explained that 2/Lt (Temp. Capt) McCudden had to date accounted for fifty-four enemy machines, of which forty-two were 'definitely' destroyed, twelve driven down out of control. On two occasions, he shot down four two-seaters in a single day. Single-handedly he attacked five German scouts on 30 January 1918, destroying two and only breaking away when the ammunition for his Lewis gun had run out and the belt of the Vickers had broken.

> As a patrol leader, he has at all times shown the utmost gallantry and skill, not only in the manner in which he has attacked and destroyed the enemy, but in the way he has during

several aerial fights protected the newer members of his flight, thus keeping down their casualties to a minimum.

Maj Gen Sir Hugh Trenchard sent a hand-written note from the Air Ministry, Hotel Cecil, Strand, London to McCudden still on leave in England: 'I am glad not only because you have got what you have so well deserved but because of all the others in your old squadron and in the whole Flying Corps who get the reflected credit and are encouraged.'

McCudden's correspondence once more revealed dismay that 'the papers are making a fuss again about the ordinary things one does ... I'm so tired of this limelight business'. McCudden soon escaped to an instructor's post at No 1 School of Aerial Fighting in Scotland, where he was reputedly prone to filling a waste paper basket with the contents of his in-tray. Another exploit was less conclusive, when he contrived to take another young lady for an aerial joy ride, this time the sister of a fellow instructor. The engine of the Avro 504 cut out, forcing McCudden to land in a suitable field. Except that the machine rolled into a gully and turned over, leaving an abashed RAF captain and Mary Latta to crawl from under the wreckage.

Across the Channel, the end of the enemy thrust towards Amiens did not signal the abandonment of German aggression. On 9 April Ludendorff opened another 30-mile (45km) front astride the Lys river in Flanders, threatening to encircle Ypres in the north and aiming at the railway junction of Hazebrouck in the south. The day before, Lt Henry Blundell with No 21 Squadron had written in his diary: 'Great excitement caused by an S.O.S. call being received on wireless'. His mood changed dramatically on 9 April:

In the afternoon we had a great alarm. News came through that the Boche had broken through and taken Armentières and all machines were got out, four bombs on each. Every pilot had to stand by his machine ready for instant flight. It was arranged that B Flight should leave the ground first and fly down to Armentières sector and drop bombs on the Huns and fire from above 500ft all our ammunition on advancing troops. Everyone had fearful wind up. After ½hr suspense I went up on a weather test. I found the clouds at 500ft and could only see the ground immediately underneath. As a result nobody went up.

So serious had the situation become that on 11 April Sir Douglas Haig declared: 'With our backs to the wall and believing in the justice of our cause ... every position must be held to the last man. There must be no retirement.' The Germans advanced to within 5 miles (8km) of Hazebrouck, retook Passchendaele Ridge on 13 April and twelve days later captured Mount Kemmel south-west of Ypres. On 13 April Blundell's airfield was abandoned: 'the Boche started shelling us badly, so we cleared off quickly in our machines'. In the haste, two aeroplanes crashed on take-off, their crews burnt to death. At length, on 30 April, faced by resolute action from reorganised British, French and American forces, the German attack came to a halt, but not before it had driven significant inroads into the Allied line.

Shortly before the Germans' Flanders incursion halted, the RAF enjoyed a memorable triumph. For months, Manfred von Richthofen had been the scourge of British airmen exploiting the power of his 'circus' and personally notching up eighty kills on 20 April 1918 (a total unsurpassed by any other airman on the Western Front). The very next day leading a flight of six machines against eight Camels of No 209 Sqn near Arras, Richthofen's aeroplane was brought down, as he chased an 81st victim. Canadian Capt Roy Brown was credited with his demise, but an Australian artillery battery also claimed to have shot him down and yet another source has credited an Australian machine-gunner with Richthofen's loss. The Germans were convinced that ground fire brought him down.

During his last leave, Richthofen had shown distinct signs of strain, such as being uncharacteristically temperamental. His mother remarked, 'I believe he has seen death too often.' Noting that his hair had thinned and the after-effects of his head wound were still troubling him, she added: 'He does not look good … Previously it seemed to me he was like young Siegfried and invulnerable.' As Richthofen's sister Ilse bade him farewell at the station, she urged him to take care, 'as we do want to see you again'. The suspicion must linger that, battle-weary, mentally exhausted and never having fully recovered from the wound suffered in July 1917 which left him with recurring headaches, Richthofen's judgement failed on the fatal day. For, contrary to his own standing orders, totally without support he pursued 2/Lt Wilfred May's lone Sopwith Camel over the Allied lines. At the very least, he miscalculated the strength and direction of the wind blowing unusually from the east. Richthofen was two weeks short of his 26th birthday and allegedly after his eightieth victory the day before his adjutant had urged him to take a non-flying post. 'A paper-shuffler? No. I am staying at the Front,' was the reply.

At 4pm on 22 April, the Allies buried Manfred Count von Richthofen at Bertangles with full military honours. Capt Freddie West witnessed part of the action which concluded with Richthofen's death. In March 1918, although he did occasionally fly with other observers, he paired up with Lt James Alexander Gordon (Alec) Haslam, nine months younger than him, who like West had enjoyed a chequered war. After attending Rugby School and destined to read medicine at Cambridge, instead he opted for the shortened wartime course at The Royal Military Academy Woolwich, was commissioned into The Royal Artillery in 1916 and subsequently served in France. Recognising the value of aerial co-operation for gunners, Haslam volunteered for the RFC but was turned down for being too tall and heavy. He was eventually accepted in 1917, though the War Office ruled that as gunner officer he would be more use as an observer than a pilot. Ironically, by then pilots were conducting the artillery spotting duties, observers were primarily manning machine-guns. In these roles, West and Haslam flew in an Armstrong Whitworth FK 8 during the Ludendorff Offensive. They were, as both admitted, 'like chalk and cheese'; West energetic and restless, Haslam scholarly and meticulous but each immensely respected the other and would do so throughout their lives. As Haslam remarked: 'Here was somebody who would get me into many scrapes, but he would get me out of them too.'

During the morning of 21 April 1918, West and Haslam flew to a designated location close to their airfield to carry out aerial machine-gun practice. On the way back, West saw a 'scrap' involving a red triplane but skirted the danger. Over lunch, the rumour spread that Richthofen had been brought down. Possibly because he realised that his observer would disapprove, West took a fellow pilot Lt Richard Grice to validate the story. They duly found the wreckage and were shown the German pilot's body by Australians, who gave West a small piece of the triplane's fabric cut into the shape of their home country.

The very next day, enemy anti-aircraft guns 'shot away' the aileron controls of West and Haslam's machine, so that they force-landed near Bertaucourt and were fortunate to walk away unscathed from the wreckage. On 1 May West and Haslam were called into the office by Maj Trafford Leigh-Mallory, the squadron commander, and to their embarrassment ('many others had done far more than us') were told that they had both been awarded a MC. The citation for each noted that, while on patrol, they had spotted fifteen enemy motor vehicles. Unable to call up artillery support, West and Haslam flew 4.5 miles (7km) into enemy territory at 3,800ft 'in the face of strong opposition from the ground, and dropped four bombs, obtaining direct hits on the lorries and doing considerable damage to their personnel'. A fortnight later, reconnoitring the area of an expected enemy attack they flew below the 200ft cloud base to obtain 'most valuable information' and successfully directed artillery onto a concentration of German infantry. 'Throughout the operations their work in co-operation with our artillery was always of the greatest value, and their enterprise in attacking enemy troops and transport with bombs and machine-gun fire was splendid.'

Also on 1 May 1918, 2/Lt Alan McLeod gained Canada's second aerial VC. Attacked by eight enemy machines on 27 March, he manoeuvred so that his observer could drive down three out of control. By now McLeod had sustained several wounds and soon afterwards, as he continued the fight, the petrol tank was set alight. According to the citation:

> He then climbed out onto the left bottom plane, controlling his machine from the side of the fuselage, and by side-slipping steeply, kept the flames to one side, thus enabling the observer to continue firing until the ground was reached.

The machine came down in No Man's Land, where it was fired on from the enemy trenches. Although seriously injured, McLeod dragged his wounded observer from the wreckage 'before falling himself from exhaustion and loss of blood' and being rescued by friendly troops. Shortly after receiving his award from the King in London, McLeod went home to Stonewall, Manitoba. Still recovering from his wounds, he contracted pneumonia and would die five days before the Armistice.

Gen Erich Ludendorff's ambitions had not been curbed by failure at Amiens and in Flanders. On 27 May he attacked the French in the Chemin de Dames sector in his third spring offensive. Following the mauling they had taken in March, supported by an RE8 squadron five British divisions had been redeployed in this region. Between 22 and 24 May, distant clouds of dust in front of the French were reported by the RE8s, which, due to an agreed demarcation of responsibility with the French, they did not investigate further. Thus, enemy heavy artillery units were able to conceal themselves together with infantry regiments in thick woods. The 1am barrage along a 27-mile (43km) front from Brimont to Leuilly, which shattered the night silence on the Aisne, and the enemy's infantry attack at dawn, came as a surprise.

At the end of the first day, two British divisions had been wiped out as the Germans advanced 12 miles (9.6km). No 52 Sqn discovered that enemy machines were sweeping ahead of the infantry at low level and lost its first aeroplane just after dawn but rallied to identify the positions of German units coming up. The British artillery was too disrupted to respond effectively. With air superiority, the Germans attacked Allied airfields, which were also hit by long-range artillery. During the afternoon of 27 May, No 52 Sqn were driven out of Fismes to Cramaille and endured two more rapid moves before settling at Tecon south of Reims on 29 May. For two days it was non-operational and did not re-join the battle until 30 May. By then, German forces had penetrated 40 miles (64km) and were on the banks of the Marne river with Paris in their sights.

Throughout the Spring in which the three German offensives took place, the bomber force at Ochey (renamed VIII Brigade) had continued to attack Germany. The first raid of Lt Stuart Keep, a DH4 pilot with No 55 Sqn, was scheduled on 16 March against Mannheim until 'unsuitable weather' switched the target to the closer Zweibrücken. Keep wrote:

> The start of a raid is an impressive sight. The twelve machines, six in each formation, set out in battle flying order on the aerodrome, the props revolving easily with engine throttles right

back; the streamers of the leader and deputy leader fluttering from the struts, heavy ominous looking bombs slung under the wings, machine-guns pointing upwards; pilots and observers tense and waiting for the signal to start and last but not least Rodger the Squadron's dog running excitedly around. Then the scene changes, the low note of the engines becomes a full throttle roar and the leading machine followed by the rest of the formation move forward rapidly, gaining speed, leave the earth behind and soon become specks in the blue.

Keep had 'plenty to do' keeping formation and avoiding a collision. The DH4s climbed for an hour to cross the line at 13,000ft. 'Below we could see the shell-pocked earth and the wriggling lines of trenches and here and there the smoke of a bursting shell.' He was soon reminded that enemy batteries 'were by no means unmindful of your existence. What had previously been clear air now became filled with puffs of black and white smoke preceded by a little flash of flame.' The sensation of an 'Archie' barrage he found weird. 'The little round black puffs of smoke apparently appear from nowhere with nothing to herald their approach,' as no shell burst could be heard above the engine noise. But they were soon through and heading for the Vosges mountains before crossing the Rhine and on to the target. Everything was now going smoothly, 'when with a cold thrill I saw a red light soar into the air from the leader's machine'; this meant 'enemy aeroplanes approaching, close in and prepare to fight.'

Black specks to port 'speedily resolved themselves into hostile aeroplanes … and a few seconds later spurts of flame appeared from the leading machine'. Stuart Keep heard the 'never to be forgotten crackle' of machine-guns and saw 'blue smoke from the tracer bullets'. He was soon embroiled in an aerial fight as a German machine came up behind him with Keep's observer 'blazing away' with his Lewis gun. 'To put it mildly, I was frightened and quickly decided that I must be something worse than an ordinary fool to have voluntarily given up my safe testing job at St Omer to come into this.' (After ferrying replacement machines to France from England, Keep had been posted to St Omer as a test pilot. His fellow pilots there included 'a wild good-hearted Irishman', a Canadian 'with a dry sense of humour' and a former Oxford don.)

One bomber with a damaged petrol tank turned back, but the Germans failed to stop the others. Over the target, the leader fired white lights, the signal to attack. Shortly afterwards bombs began to fall 'and with great joy [I] released my own with a vigorous tug of the release gear. The worthy citizens of Zweibrücken vigorously plastered us with Archie shells but without much effect', as they 'wheeled for home. I experienced great satisfaction in seeing flames in various parts of the town where our bombs dropped,' Keep observed. He landed after 2 hours 40 minutes, in time for lunch, 'feeling very satisfied with the morning's work'.

Stuart Keep flew on several bombing raids during March and named his DH4 'Buff Orpington' after the fowl, which was a good egg layer, and the machine 'certainly laid some very healthy eggs'. On 29 March, he undertook his first photo operation to an industrial complex inside Germany. 'The trick,' Keep explained, 'was to fly at 22,000ft' to avoid danger. There it was undoubtedly cold despite 'our electrically heated clothing and towards the end of the trip owing to failure of my oxygen apparatus my heart gave trouble'. Nevertheless, the DH4 landed safely and Keep suffered no permanent ill effects.

Shortly after this episode, Keep described a moment of light relief. The presentation of the Croix de Guerre to some squadron members was 'duly carried out with appropriate ceremony' by a French general. He kissed the recipients on both cheeks 'to their disgust and the huge delight of everybody else. As the worthy general was about 5ft nothing and Capt Collett one of the victims stood 6ft or more, the kissing was worth seeing.'

In May 1918, Keep went on leave.

Only those who have been on the line can appreciate what this means. One marked one's life by the times of leave … Never had I been more glad of leave than this time. The strain of the big raids was telling and I wanted a rest for body and mind and had ten perfect days in England.

When he returned, the Squadron had moved to Azelot. While on leave, Keep (a former pupil of King Edward's School, Birmingham, and graduate of Birmingham University) was awarded the MC for displaying 'great skill and determination' while raiding enemy towns. By Keep's own admission, though, the repeated, long-distance operations were taking their toll of airmen.

As more squadrons reinforced VIII Brigade and hopes of a decisive bombing campaign against Germany rose, a change of emphasis became apparent. No longer were purely industrial reasons advanced. On 7 March the War Cabinet declared that 'in the interest of the world's peace in the future, it was not desirable that the civil population among the belligerent nations be immune from the worst suffering of war.' Eighteen days later, Sir Henry Norman, 'additional member' of the Air Council, responded to the Secretary of State's request for his 'impression upon the general question of long-range bombing of German towns, the air situation and prospects'. Referring to 'the destruction of the national <u>moral</u> [sic] and means of production by the bombing of his [the enemy's] towns', Norman recommended that six major towns be repeatedly attacked. They should be 'reduced to virtual collective ruins', so that the rest of Germany would 'approach a state of panic', their military strategy 'largely paralysed'. The reliability of this assessment may be gauged from Norman's judgement of the fragility of 'the German civilian <u>moral</u> [sic] … I speak from personal knowledge, dating from my school days.'

Notwithstanding the conduct of the bombing campaign, support to ground forces remained crucial. The Germans had been rebuffed at Amiens and around Ypres, but they retained significant gains in these sectors. Furthermore, following their third offensive on the Aisne, enemy troops were on the Marne for the second time in the war poised to assault Paris.

HP O/400, wings folded; 400 would be delivered before the Armistice. Such was the psychological impact of the bomber that post-war all large British aircraft were often referred to as Handley Pages.

12

Forward March, June–August 1918
'Flaming onions and archie'

Enemy air activity at the beginning of June suggested an impending foray along the Oise river, north-east of the main confrontation on the Marne. The British had fourteen squadrons with the Fourth Army in a position to intervene and, responding to a French request, between 5 and 8 June heavily-escorted formations of day bombers attacked the communication centre of Roye and nearby ammunition dumps. German ground forces launched their expected assault at 3.20am Sunday 9 June and in two days advanced 6 miles (9.6km) until halted by a French counter-attack. During this brief battle, the RAF carried out mainly low-level attacks against troop targets, dropping sixteen tons of bombs and firing 120,000 rounds of ammunition.

As they did so, Maj Gen J.M. Salmond commanding the RAF in the field, drew conclusions from the German assault on 21 March. He was particularly concerned at the shortcomings of air intelligence. Salmond reminded commanders of the 'vital necessity that his [the enemy's] approach march must be discovered'. Reconnaissance should be carried out on all likely routes twice a night and the slightest movement noted. The same areas had to be covered immediately before dawn, which meant pilots risking low flying in poor light. Nevertheless, 'responsibility that the British Army is not surprised is on the Royal Air Force.'

In the third week of June, several of the squadrons that had supported the French near Noyon on the Oise were moved north to the La Bassée-Ypres area preparatory to an air assault on the German lines of communication by five day and three night squadrons. Railway junctions and large depots, wayside stations and sections of track between stations were specifically identified for attack. Between 24 June and 2 July, the day squadrons dropped nineteen tons on allotted targets and ten tons on alternatives when primary targets could not be reached; night squadrons forty-two tons and five tons respectively. However, a study of aerial photos on 1 July confirmed the pilots' views that attacking railway lines was not productive, railway junctions a better option. Wet weather over the following week restricted bombing designed to hamper the enemy's troop concentrations prior to a renewed British advance. Furthermore, an outbreak of influenza provided a sharp reminder that availability of aircrew did not solely depend upon losses in battle or accidents. No 46 Sqn had thirteen pilots (half its strength) in hospital with the bacterium between 18 and 21 June.

Back home, Douglas Joy, now the proud father of baby Jean Kathleen, indirectly revealed the strains that war service could put on a marriage, even though the husband was not at the Front. Having survived two spells in France and been promoted major on his return to England, command of No 93 Reserve Sqn had prevented Joy from spending Christmas 1917 with his family. In June 1918, to Nesta's evident dismay, he was posted to command No. 105

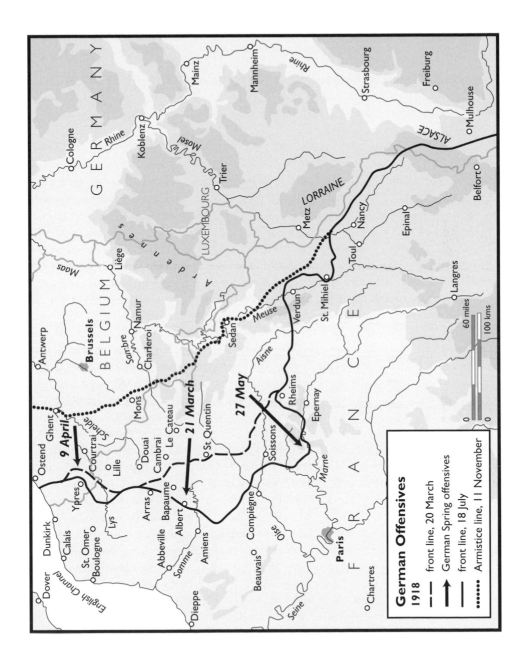

German Offensives
1918

- front line, 20 March
- German Spring offensives
- front line, 18 July
- Armistice line, 11 November

Sqn in Omagh, Ireland. Her reaction led Joy to address a testy letter to 'My bad-tempered wife ... You should have censored your own letter and yet my sincere wish is that you and I should be living together again.'

Across the Channel, it soon became clear that the Germans were preparing a major effort on the Marne. Therefore, on 14 July, despite the rain nine British squadrons flew there to reinforce the French. At midnight that day, a massive enemy bombardment commenced and as dawn broke on 15 July Ludendorff launched his attack, which had been thrown back by the evening of 17 July with the help of American troops, and Paris had been saved once more. During the Second Battle of the Marne, British aeroplanes attacked battlefield targets at low level, especially footbridges over the river. German single-seat fighters shot down eleven British machines; four others were wrecked on landing.

Lt Anthony Kilburn, eight months after commencing his RNAS flying training at Eastchurch and now serving with a Handley Page squadron at Ochey, was not involved in this action. On 26 June, his first planned operation as pilot of his own machine against Metz was aborted due to bad weather. Despite poor visibility, two raids on that target were subsequently completed before Kilburn was briefed for an operation on Mannheim, which did not have a successful outcome. During take-off, his machine struck Ochey church spire and crashed with a full bomb load, fortunately without exploding or anybody being injured. Kilburn explained that 'an extra person came on board at the very last moment, as I was preparing to take off. No compensation was made for this extra weight by the removal of two 112lb bombs with the result that the machine would not rise.'

'A very misty night' was a complicating factor during a six-and-a-half-hour round trip to Stuttgart on 30 July. At the target, 'two fires' were started despite 'a great deal of Archie and a good many searchlights'. On the way back though, the crew lost its way, ran out of fuel and came down in hilly country 4 miles (6km) from the Swiss border. Kilburn noted that the 'machine crashed and ran into river. Caught fire, but put out by back gunlayer'. Kilburn and the observer were 'pinned in water under the machine for one and a half hours. Not badly hurt.' Perhaps not, but one HP O/100 had been written off without enemy intervention.

That was certainly not the case on 24 July, when flying a contact patrol Pithey and Rhodes of No 12 Sqn also had a narrow escape from injury. Rhodes accounted for one of the four attacking Fokker D.VIIs, but a bullet pierced the RE8's petrol tank. As fuel streamed out, the likelihood of reaching safety seemed remote until Rhodes climbed out of his cockpit onto the lower wing of the biplane. He stuffed one of his gloves into the hole and clung precariously to the wing until Pithey managed to put the machine down at their base. An incandescent squadron commander greeted Rhodes, his ill-temper fanned by a report from an anti-aircraft battery that one of his airmen had been seen doing aerobatic stunts. Maj T.Q. Back calmed down when Rhodes showed him the gaping hole in the tank. 'Ho! Ho!', he said, 'forget it.' Rhodes admitted, though, that aircrew were not above 'skylarking' on other occasions. A petrol can was often placed on top of a garage and the proceeds of a sweepstake given to the first aircraft to knock the target off that perch with its wheels. In off-duty hours Rhodes, who during his infantry days had sung duets with the future celebrity Stanley Holloway, joined the No 12 Sqn concert party, whose shows provided much-needed relaxation from the stress of battle.

With Soissons retaken on 6 August and the Allied line straightened, Gen Pétain called a halt to the French counter-attack. Two days later, Haig mounted a strong assault on the Germans around Amiens. Again profiting from effective preliminary aerial photography, the initial bombardment at 4.20am caught the enemy by surprise. Soon afterwards, covered by mist along a 14-mile (22km) front, the British Fourth Army left its trenches, supported by the artillery,

Fokker D VII. Formidable single seat fighter, entered service April 1918. Two Spandau machine-guns, 124 mph at sea level, ceiling 22,900ft. *(IWM Q 66380)*

which fired a creeping barrage in front of the advance, 530 tanks and a strong RAF presence. On that first day, the British went forward an unprecedented 8 miles (12km), causing an estimated 27,000 enemy casualties and capturing some 400 guns. It was, Ludendorff declared, 'the black day of the German Army'.

On 8 August Salmond had 88 squadrons and two flights totalling 1,696 machines on the Western Front. Of these, 810 were committed to the Amiens attack. Not until 9am did the mist clear sufficiently for squadrons to take off, then the low-flying machines found ample targets. At 10.30am two Camel pilots dropped 25lb bombs on three trains near Harbonnières village. Two escaped but the third was surrounded by British cavalry, its passengers returning from leave captured. Other low-flying aeroplanes bombed an 11-inch railway gun busily firing on Amiens. When the 5th Australian Division reached the cannon, they found the entire gun crew either killed or wounded.

One pilot flying a SE5 machine of No 24 Sqn was reputed to have scattered 300 infantry with bombs and machine-gun fire. Another spotted eight armoured cars held up by an enemy anti-tank gun, attacked and silenced the weapon allowing the armoured cars to proceed. Later in the morning, the same pilot had his petrol tank damaged by small arms fire causing him to land for running repairs. Grey uniforms speedily approaching alerted him to a geographical error. Discharging his revolver at the hostile pack, he rapidly switched to the gravity tank and had just enough petrol to get to an advanced party of British cavalry, which promptly charged the would-be captors. In the afternoon, attacks were made on three major bridges over the Somme and wider afield, escorted bomber operations hit other crossing points. To cope with the aerial onslaught, the Germans summoned reinforcements from the adjacent Seventeenth Army, including the Richthofen wing (JG 1) now commanded by Capt Hermann Göring.

The RAF did not escape lightly on 8 August. From ninety-seven aeroplanes shot down or written off, seventy belonged to squadrons engaged in low-level attacks, a 23 per cent loss rate. That day, fifty-seven men were missing, besides four known to have been killed and nineteen wounded. This prompted the headquarters of the RAF's IX Brigade at St André-aux-Bois to issue a variation of orders for the morrow. Noting that enemy scouts had 'molested our bombers by diving on them from the clouds and preventing them from carrying out their missions effectively' wing commanders were required to 'detail scouts for close protection of bombers to ensure the latter are not interfered with by enemy aircraft, while trying to destroy bridges'. This would be 'the sole duty of these scouts', who would not themselves carry bombs.

Something went wrong with this arrangement at first light on 9 August. Between 5am and 5.15am, DH9s of Nos 27 and 49 squadrons took off to attack three bridges from 500ft, but failed to rendezvous with their escorts. Harassed by the enemy, the bombers dropped half their loads on other targets and scant, if any, damage was done to the primary objectives. Incredibly, none of the DH9s were lost. One No 49 Sqn report referred to between ten and fifteen enemy machines attacking from the south-east as the formation approached its target, another ten to fifteen joining them from the east as the British turned for home, so that 'a running fight ensued'. This DH9 crew, pilot Lt J.A. Keating and observer 2/Lt E.A. Simpson, had a torrid time:

> We were persistently attacked by a large number of enemy aircraft; observer fired a good burst into the first enemy aircraft which was only 50ft from our tail, and it turned over on its back and burst into flames: this was over Marchelepot.

This success was confirmed independently by another pilot. Just after this encounter,

> … another enemy aircraft dived on us and when he got to about 60 or 70ft distance, observer fired about 100 rounds into him, when large quantity of flames burst out and machine went down ablaze near Soyecourt. When over Soyecourt, observer fired a further long burst into another enemy aircraft at a very short distance which stalled, went into a spin and went down hopelessly out of control, and was seen to crash near Soyecourt.

Keating and Simpson's adventures were not yet over:

> Immediately after this machine disappeared, observer saw another aircraft diving on our tail, and before he could change drums the enemy aircraft had approached to within 40ft of our machine. Observer then fired about 60rnds straight into this enemy aircraft which fell over on its side and spun right into the ground west of Soyecourt.

Keating concluded his report in which he had effectively claimed four enemy shot down: 'During the combat our machine was so badly shot about that we were forced to land near Lamotte-en-Santerre with damaged engine, tail, propeller and undercarriage.'

From the outset of the Battle of Amiens, a special effort was made to establish close co-operation between aeroplanes and tanks. Maj Trafford Leigh-Mallory's No 8 Sqn, equipped with eighteen Armstrong Whitworth FK8 two-seat reconnaissance machines, had been attached to the Tank Corps since 1 July. Each of the Squadron's three flights was allotted to a tank brigade. Leigh-Mallory, a contemporary of Arthur Tedder at Magdalene College, Cambridge, reported that

> a thoroughly good liaison was established between the flights and the unit with whom they were working. Tank Officers came to stay with the flights, and were taken up in aeroplanes, and pilot and observers stayed with the tank battalions and went for rides in tanks.

However, attempts to communicate by wireless proved unsatisfactory.

Leigh-Mallory explained that 'the great difficulty' for the tanks 'was to produce an aerial which would be practicable both for battle use, and at the same time be of sufficient length to develop the full efficiency of the wireless telephone'. Results were 'indifferent', so resort was made to visual signals. Despite all the preliminary work, in practice the most reliable means of communicating between air and ground proved the dropping of messages. Leigh-Mallory concluded: 'It was a pity that there was not longer than one month in which to prepare for the battle … [however] this liaison work stood the Squadron in very good stead as soon as the fighting commenced'.

Once the mist had cleared on 8 August, flares were successfully employed by the infantry to indicate progress to contact patrol aeroplanes. When the supply ran out, alternative coloured metal disks and strips of cloth quickly became tarnished or dirty. The fluid nature of the battle posed even more problems for airborne observers inexperienced in the nature of the battlefield, especially in identification of enemy movements. A post-operational RAF report acknowledged that

> nothing at present in the training of corps contact observers can compensate for the lack of
> army experience … As an example, the enemy puts down a barrage – the observer does not
> connect this with a raid or counter attack and misses the approach of the enemy infantry.

One lesson emerging from the Battle of Amiens, which lasted 8–12 August, was the need to deal quickly with enemy anti-tank guns. Single guns had been responsible for 'knocking out' up to eight tanks and seriously destroying the momentum of an attack. Thus, eliminating these weapons became 'of paramount importance'. All machines 'engaged in low-flying attack … conducting Artillery, Contact, and Counter-attack patrols' were required to watch the ground in front of advancing British tanks 'for their appearance and for their flashes. It is not possible to emphasise too strongly the duty and responsibility of pilots and observers in regard of the foregoing'. Leigh-Mallory confirmed that for the remainder of the war

> … our policy changed. Instead of sending all machines up on contact and counter-attack
> patrol, as many machines were reserved for anti-tank gun work as possible, and just the
> number of machines were reserved as would ensure the battalions and brigades being sup-
> plied with all the information they required.

Hair-raising adventures were not confined to the Front, as the former Oundle schoolboy John Jeyes discovered, after having completed a prolonged spell in France and been posted as an instructor to Worthy Down, Hampshire, in January 1918. Returning to the aerodrome one day, he decided to call on his parents, as he was flying alone. He identified a convenient field, 'but found it was not an easy approach and not a big field'. On the third attempt he did manage to put down in the middle of the pasture, 'but there was a sharp dip in the field, so just as I was coming to rest on landing, my machine tipped up on its nose and bent my prop'. There was 'great excitement when they found out who had arrived', but unfortunately he missed his sister, who had returned to Northampton that morning. Jeyes had to off load equipment from the machine, which was in no condition to fly, and wait for a party from the nearest RAF station to collect it. Fortunately before the party arrived somebody siphoned off the petrol, which made it look as if he had run out of fuel.

When there was no flying at Worthy Down, Jeyes and a fellow instructor would go up to London and take two nurses out on the river in the afternoon or to a show in the evening. In July one of them, Grace, secured a hospital post in Winchester, not far from Worthy Down, and asked Jeyes to take her for a flight. She was not allowed on the airfield so Jeyes arranged to make the trip from a field close to Micheldever station. In due course, he landed; Grace having taken a train from Winchester and walked the half mile from the station. Jeyes saw her approaching as he put down and left the engine ticking over while he removed the sandbags used as ballast from the passenger's seat.

As Grace settled in her seat, Jeyes swung the prop and rapidly jumped in because the idling engine was in danger of overheating. Due to this he dare not taxi, so began to take off at once. 'We went down the field which rolled down to a sort of valley,' Jeyes recalled. 'Faster and faster we went, then up the slope to the other side of the field towards a big 12–20ft hedge. The wheels of the machine were still on the ground and we were touching 60–70mph. I think the wind was quite strong and we were still not lifting, and bang – we went through the hedge and the struts between the wings were full of branches and twigs.' The aeroplane started to leave the ground with these various unscheduled attachments, prompting Jeyes to abandon plans to climb. He throttled back and put down quickly in the adjoining field, not quite smoothly: 'The crash through the hedge had completely bent my undercarriage, so of course the machine just slid along the ground and the wings wrapped round the fuselage. We came to rest in a bit of a mess.' Surprisingly, pilot and passenger emerged from the wreckage unscathed.

Grace immediately tramped back to the station, thoughts unrecorded: 'I did not want her hanging around when the police arrived.' Once she was out of sight, Jeyes went to telephone for help and then kept guard over the remains of his machine, which was another write-off. 'I knew quite well that I could get into a spot of bother if it was found out what I had been doing … Fortunately nobody had witnessed the landing or the attempted take-off and crash.' Jeyes and Grace did meet again in Winchester 'for tea and a chat, [but] I felt I had not made a very good impression'.

In France, Capt Freddie West had three crashes in somewhat different circumstances. Taking off at 5am on 8 August, according to squadron records 'the valleys were already coated with thick mist, and within an hour the whole country for miles was obscured.' Nonetheless, West and his observer Haslam stayed up and flying low saw through gaps in the mist that tanks had captured Demuin where the bridge remained intact. After dropping a message detailing the progress of French troops on the right, West made for base, which he located by rockets sent up to aid him. Getting the AW FK8 down was more difficult. On the third attempt, he virtually stalled the machine as he came in and suddenly a hangar appeared ahead through the gloom. West side-slipped, scraped the side of the building and hit the ground. He suffered a badly cut lip, Haslam a damaged knee.

Despite their injuries, the two returned to duty next day and 'again did excellent work'. At 10.45am they dropped another message reporting the progress of French troops. Fifteen minutes later, West spied a German train being set on fire by an advancing tank. Shortly afterwards, he came across four tanks under attack from 'a great number of hostile infantry with machine-guns'. West dived five times on the enemy, 'who retired in disorder'. However, his engine had been put out of action by small arms. With difficulty, he made his way to safety and crash-landed for the second day running.

Undaunted, on 10 August West and Haslam were up on tank contact patrol again. Just after identifying enemy armour near Rosières, West spotted considerable activity around

Roye almost 5 miles (8km) behind the enemy front line. He made for the spot and 'wrought great havoc among [artillery] limbers and transport with his bombs and machine-guns'. On the way back, the Armstrong Whitworth was attacked by seven fighters. West's left leg was smashed by an explosive bullet and the wounded limb 'flopped around' until the pilot wedged it beside the control column. Haslam, who was hit in the right ankle, continued to fire on the enemy, as West gradually edged across the lines. In spite of his grievous injury, he managed to get the damaged machine down and make his report on the location of the German reserves before passing out. As he remarked, 'I was very keen to get the information back.' When he came round, he was lying on a stretcher in a ruined church. Without anaesthetic (he was given a bottle of whisky to induce unconsciousness), his leg was removed. Some time later, waking from a nap in hospital, he heard a 'tick-a-tick-tick' sound and realised that the other patients were rattling toothbrushes in their mugs. An orderly then brought him a newspaper announcing that he had been awarded the VC. Modestly, in the years after, he said that he had been lucky and that many others did more courageous deeds without recognition. Haslam was awarded the DFC for his part in the action.

West's award went some way to balancing the loss of two VCs during July. James McCudden need not have returned to the Front, but insisted on leaving his training post in Scotland on 25 June. Promoted major, he was appointed to command No 60 Sqn. Before leaving Hounslow in his SE5a on 9 July 1918, he asked a friend to 'look in on the mater and my sisters. You know a fellow can't say all he feels, and I always want to cry inwardly when I leave them.' That morning he said goodbye to his widowed elder sister Mary (Cis), leaving his decorations with her. He had recently completed a memoir of his service, which would be published posthumously. En route to his new squadron, he put down at Auxi-le-Chateau to check his position in hazy conditions. Scarcely had he taken off again, when the engine cut out. Apparently trying to return to the airfield, he crashed into nearby trees. His brother William had died strapped into his machine, James was thrown clear without being secured. Fatally injured, he died three hours later.

Not knowing exactly how his brother had died, on 31 July Maurice McCudden congratulated his younger sister Kitty on her engagement and thanked her for a letter about 'Jim's end'. Maurice speculated that

> Jim's internal injuries would be caused by the safety belt round his waist. As the machine hit the ground, the sudden impact of hitting could tend to throw the pilot forward, but the safety belt would prevent this, hence causing internal injuries. If Jim had not been strapped in, he would have been thrown forward on the front of the seat and his head and face would have been an awful sight.

When writing, Maurice evidently did not know that his brother had perished because he had not been strapped in.

On 11 July, a letter reached James McCudden's father from Mrs E. Alec-Tweddie, who had encouraged McCudden to compile the memoir of his Service life for publication:

> I can't tell you how sorry I feel for you. No doubt you know I have seen a great deal of your son lately, and I have learnt to appreciate his honesty and charm ... Please tell your wife how very, very deeply I sympathise with her as a mother in this her third loss. I lost a dear boy myself near Loos so know what it all means. It is a cruel blow for you both, and a cruel loss to the nation.

A piece appeared in the *Evening News* from Miss Elsie W. Copping, when McCudden's book *Five Years in the Royal Flying Corps* was serialised in the paper. She referred to 'poor little Jimmy McCudden – I must call him "little Jimmy". I can't seem to realise that he ever grew up'. Miss Copping had taught him at 'a small prep school in Gillingham, when he was about six years of age, and can only think of him as a chubby little blue-eyed, fair-haired fellow with an abundance of mischief and a great admiration for his big "bruvver".' She added a tribute, the first verse of which ran: 'He is not dead/Such spirits never die/They are unquenchable/He only sleeps.' James McCudden's death affected a circle of friends and acquaintances far beyond the immediate family.

On 22 July 1918, Maj Edward Mannock, a former pupil of James McCudden at Joyce Green in Kent and OC of 85 Sqn, was officially credited with bringing down his fiftieth enemy machine. Four days later, he may have claimed another before falling victim to ground fire as he re-crossed the front line (one later estimate put his total successes at seventy-three). His father would subsequently attend Buckingham Palace to accept from the King not only the VC, awarded to Mannock posthumously, but the DSO and two Bars, MC and Bar, which his late son had gained but not formally received. Writing to his sister a month before he died, Mannock showed signs of the strain admitted by others: 'Things are getting a bit intense just lately and I don't know how long my nerves will last out. I am rather old [32] now, as airmen go, for fighting. Still one hopes for the best.' Mannock would never enjoy the relaxation of a forthcoming leave to which he referred in this letter.

In the days after Mannock's death, British troops with French forces on their right continued to probe forward east of Amiens, as the Germans carried out a series of tactical withdrawals. Further north, on 19 August British, Belgian and American troops counter-attacked around Ypres aiming to recapture the ground lost in April. Lt Frank Marsh flying a No 149 Sqn FE2b was part of the RAF support operations. It had taken him almost four years to get to the Front. At the outbreak of war, he went to a recruiting office to be told that he must wait until his seventeenth birthday. When that arrived, he was told to come back after his eighteenth birthday. Early in 1915, walking down the Strand in London, he saw one of the famous Kitchener posters. As he stood looking at it, a recruiting sergeant approached and on learning that Marsh was under age, said: 'Don't worry about that, I'll get you in'; and he did. Rapidly promoted sergeant, then commissioned into The Hertfordshire Regiment, Marsh was hugely disappointed at not being sent to France. He responded to a request in battalion orders early in 1918 for volunteers to join the RFC. Having passed a medical and completed a month's training at Reading, Marsh went to a training squadron at Marham and duly passed out as a pilot.

However, he must now prove himself proficient at night flying. During one exercise, he was assured that four designated emergency landing grounds would have 'the landing path … shown up by hurricane lamps, at each side of which a petrol flare could be ignited if needed'. When the engine of Marsh's machine began to overheat, he decided to make use of one of these facilities and did a dummy run overhead to alert those below to light the landing equipment. There was no reaction, so he landed in the dark; 'rather hazardous', he ruefully noted. As he came to a halt, 'two very elderly men' emerged from the gloom, and Marsh asked them for water. They had petrol and oil, but no idea that aero-engines were water-cooled. Eventually, the necessary liquid was procured, the flares lit and Marsh took off again.

After further night flying instruction, he was posted to No 149 Sqn formed on 3 March 1918 at Yapton, near Bognor. The OC, Maj B.P. Greenwood, insisted on his pilots having 'at least 100hrs' in their logs before going overseas, which the Squadron did on 2 June. The

Frank A. Marsh. Enlisted under age in 1915, he was commissioned into The Hertfordshire Regt. Still in England and with no prospect of front-line action, he volunteered for RFC in 1918. Flew FE2b night bombers with the RAF in Flanders. *(Mrs M. Lee)*

machines were flown over the Channel to Marquise and on to Quillen, where the ground crew and transport, which had travelled by sea from Southampton, joined them on 4 June. Twelve days later, the squadron moved to Alquines, near St Omer, from which it raided 'generally railway sidings and dumps of stores and later when the enemy was in retreat, bridges over rivers'. However, 'very poor weather with most nights with big mists [often] made flying impossible'. The crews had to stand by after dinner in case improvement occurred. If not, it was 'well after midnight that we were allowed to dismiss'. The main target was the railway junction at Lille, where the searchlights 'increased considerably which showed how much the enemy was concerned at our success'.

Marsh counted himself lucky that his observer, Lt R.D. Linford, had previously served in the infantry in this part of the Front and knew the terrain well. Linford had also been detached for a time to the RNAS for submarine spotting and after fifty hours on this 'hazardous job' was recommended for a decoration. He could not be given a naval medal and the Army refused to reward his work with another Service, so Linford was awarded the MBE. This, he declared, was given to civilians at home engaged in war production. He sent the medal back with a note: 'Give it to some profiteer'. Not guaranteed to enhance his promotion prospects.

After Marsh had dropped his bombs on a target, Linford would often doze, which once nearly proved fatal. 'On our third show', Marsh also nodded off and when he came to the FE2b was flying north and just crossing the North Sea coast. Marsh rapidly turned south and found the aerodrome with his observer still asleep. There was another hazard apart from a dozing observer: crossing the line in darkness, Allied anti-aircraft guns frequently opened up. Marsh explained that each night, the bombers were given a different code letter to flash from

Above: Coming home. Aeroplane descending in stormy conditions. (*Peter Jackson*)

Left: German Aviatik biplane. (*Peter Jackson*)

a small light under the machine: 'But the gunners took no notice, and the light merely helped them to get their range. The result was that we did not use this indication.'

Maj R. Graham, commanding No 213 Sqn, revealed another local difficulty. In a somewhat pained communication to a nearby army unit, he expressed his dismay at the aftermath of a Sopwith Camel crash in friendly territory near Bergues, south-east of Dunkirk. 'French soldiers and civilians undoubtedly helped themselves to parts of the machine as one piece of no importance was returned to my mechanic as he was clearing the wreckage away.' Graham accepted that ideally the pilot ought to have made arrangements for a guard to be mounted, but 'he was shaken by the crash so any omission on his part was excusable'. The squadron commander continued waspishly: 'I should be grateful if you would explain to your men that the pilot expected British soldiers to look after his machine and not allow people to pilfer

Crashed biplane with air-cooled rotary engine. *(Peter Jackson)*

with it [sic] … Should such a crash occur again, I hope your men will do their utmost to keep thieves away.'

The plan south of Flanders on 21 August was to attack between Albert and Arras to outflank a German salient further south and close on the line St Quentin–Cambrai. The immediate objective on the first day was the Arras-Albert railway, followed two days later by a more general attack north of the Somme by the Third and Fourth armies. For the initial attack, No 6 Sqn was detailed to co-operate with the Cavalry Corps, No 8 Sqn the Tank Corps, which could also call on No 73 Sqn of Camels for low-level work against anti-tank guns. Nine other squadrons, including two American, were allocated in direct support of the attack. In addition, four fighter squadrons were ordered to fly high-level offensive patrols over the battlefield; day and night bomber squadrons would be made available for targets beyond the fighting zone.

On 19 August, orders were issued to RAF squadrons reminding them that success of the Army's plan depended on surprise and that no unusual air activity should be undertaken to alert the enemy in advance. To conceal the noise of tanks manoeuvring during the night of 20/21 August, aeroplanes were to fly along the front of the Third Army. To confuse the Germans, similar flights would take place over the lines of the Fourth and First Armies. For the attack itself, detailed orders were issued to cover battlefield targets, tank, infantry and cavalry co-operation, reconnaissance flights, the bombing of aerodromes, railways and communication centres.

Ground mist and light rain during the preceding night and until after 10am on 21 August disrupted the air effort. To some extent, the overcast conditions worked in favour of the ground troops whose activity was concealed so that by the time aeroplanes appeared, consid-

John C. 'Paddy Jo' Quinnell transferred from The Royal Artillery to the RFC. He served on the Western Front and in Mesopotamia before commanding No 104 Sqn RAF of DH9 bombers under Sir Hugh Trenchard in France during closing months of war. Retired from RAF as air commodore in 1945. *(Mr J. Craig)*

erable progress had already been made. Zero hour was 4.55am, but many machines did not get airborne until 11am. During the afternoon, long-range bombing attacks on railways and aerodromes took place with variable results. Better conditions on 22 and 23 August brought more successful raids on transport targets, though German machines also attacked British airfields, which in turn led to retaliatory raids by day and night bombers against enemy air bases.

Even before the threat to Paris had lifted or plans for the battles of Amiens and Bapaume been perfected, a significant development occurred on 6 June 1918. The lukewarm view of French airmen towards it was expressed by Gen Maurice Duval: 'If we are defeated on land, the bombardment of Cologne is without interest'. In London, Maj Gen Sir Hugh Trenchard had clashed with his political master, the Secretary of State for Air (Lord Rothermere), and resigned as CAS. In June 1918, Trenchard found himself back in France at the head of bomber squadrons of the new Independent Force tasked with attacking industrial targets in Germany. After reinforcements arrived, two months later he commanded two wings together totalling eighty-six bombers in five squadrons: two of the squadrons flew DH9 machines, one DH4s, one the HP O/100 or HP O/400 and a fifth the pusher FE2b. By the end of August, another three Handley Page squadrons had arrived, plus one flying DH9s. In all, the new force could therefore deploy nine squadrons for long-range day and night bombing unconnected with the armies on the Western Front. In the three months, from June to August 1918, it dropped 246 tons of bombs and took 2,297 reconnaissance photos. Over the same period, 52 men were missing and 119 wounded.

Maj John Quinnell, a 'genial Irishman' known to his family and service colleagues as 'Paddy Jo', commanded No 104 Sqn of DH9s stationed at Azelot, near Nancy, one of the original five Independent Force squadrons. While serving in The Royal Field Artillery, Quinnell had been seconded to the RFC in February 1915. As a reporter for the *Irish Times* pre-war, he had been photographed wearing a leather helmet in a stationary machine. At his interview, he made considerable play of the fact that, although he had not actually flown, he was familiar with an aeroplane. Flying as a pilot on the Western Front, Quinnell was wounded when a bomb which had failed to release, exploded on landing. After recovery, between December 1916 and June 1917 Quinnell commanded a squadron in Mesopotamia before returning the Britain, where he raised No 104 Sqn at Andover and took it to France as part of the new bombing force.

Shortly after his arrival, he received an apology from the Independent Force commander, Sir Hugh Trenchard, explaining that due to pressure of work he was unable to visit individual squadrons. Trenchard added: 'Everyone should remember that the bombing of Germany is considered, and I believe it is, a means of winning this war and it is up to all of you to show this by doing your utmost to bring this about during the summer months.'

On 11 August, Quinnell led twelve DH9s to bomb Mannheim, 110 miles (176km) over the lines. Twenty miles (32km) into enemy territory, fourteen hostile machines appeared and opened fire, causing two of the British aeroplanes to lose altitude and fall behind. Quinnell reduced speed and descended to 9,000ft so that the formation could close up. Even then, one DH9 was forced down and the remaining eleven were continuously attacked. 'A thick sheet of cloud' obscured Mannheim, so Quinnell decided to make for Karlsruhe, 40 miles (64km) due south of Mannheim. Flying over the clouds by compass, a convenient gap exposed Karlsruhe, where the 'principal railway station' was bombed. It later emerged that a direct hit killed twelve officers going on leave, two other strikes on a crowded train at the platform killed all the passengers in one carriage.

German fighters pursued the bombers almost to the Allied lines, three of the enemy being destroyed, another driven down, according to the post-operational report. Trenchard signalled Quinnell: 'A great day for you and No 104 Sqn. It will help the battle up North. It showed determination, pluck and good leadership. Well done all.' On 22 August, a more sombre message was received from the Independent Force commander: 'I deeply regret to hear you have lost so heavily in your raid this morning ... but please remember the Squadron did its job. Bomb Mannheim and a squadron which does this materially assists in the progress of the war.'

The last airship raid on Britain occurred during the night of 5/6 August 1918. Five Zeppelins approached East Anglia and thirty-five defensive sorties were launched. Visibility was not good. Two DH4s went up from RAF Yarmouth; one piloted by Lt R.E. Keys, the other by Maj Egbert Cadbury, who deserted a nearby charity concert at which his wife was singing in response to an emergency call. Cadbury had another experienced pilot, Capt Robert Leckie, as his gunner. In an attempt to gain speed, Cadbury jettisoned his two 100lb bombs, as Leckie discovered that his Lewis gun had no sight. Emerging from thick cloud, the DH4 crew saw L.70 behind them and Cadbury turned for a head-on attack. Pomeroy explosive bullets fired by Leckie ignited the airship, which broke into two and crashed close to Wells-next-the-Sea on the north Norfolk coast. Cadbury then located and attacked L.65,

Major-General Sir Hugh Trenchard (centre). Commanded RFC on Western Front 1915–17. RAF's first Chief of the Air Staff, January 1918. Commanded Independent (Bombing) Force and Inter-Allied Independent Air Force in the field during closing months of War. Chief of the Air Staff 1919–29, retiring as Marshal of the Royal Air Force. Here with officers in France 1918. *(IWM Q 62965)*

but after one burst, Leckie's gun jammed and he had to break away. Writing later to his father, Cadbury described how the next thirty minutes had been the worst of his flying career to date, as he became utterly lost in cloud. His anxiety was not helped by having been told that the DH4 'could not land at night'. Eventually, he managed to put down at Sedgeford, Norfolk, after narrowly missing another machine in the air, where a further shock awaited him. The two 100lb bombs were still attached, which explained the aeroplane's sluggish performance.

There was an interesting postscript to this episode. Keys, who experienced engine trouble and landed at Kelstern, Lincs, also claimed the destruction of L.70 and an attack on L.65. It is quite possible that both DH4s did carry out simultaneous attacks unknown to one another in the swirling cloud and troublesome wind, but Cadbury and Leckie got the credit for the last destruction of a Zeppelin over England during the war.

As Autumn 1918 approached, in France heavy fighting still lay ahead. By the end of August 1918, though, on the ground a breakthrough had undoubtedly been made, with the Germans being pushed back steadily towards the Rhine. Air superiority had been maintained and the growing bomber strength of the Independent Force promised a separate, major contribution to Allied operational achievement in the closing phase of the war.

Breakthrough, September–November 1918
'Great confusion of (enemy) troops and transport'

During the night of 1/2 September 1918, RAF bombers attacked defended villages, enemy barracks and aerodromes east of Bapaume, roughly 10 miles (16km) north of the Somme and 20 miles (32km) south-west of Cambrai. When British troops launched an assault at dawn the following morning, other RAF squadrons were poised to deal with enemy anti-tank guns, co-operate with their own armour, support the cavalry, give close support to the attacking infantry divisions and seek out German troop formations. Between 6.30 and 9am on 2 September, day bombers mounted a concentrated effort against railway targets and bridges over the Sensée river.

The previous day, although badly shot up after clashing with German fighters, Rhodes and Pithey of No 12 Sqn were commended for completing their patrol and bringing back 'a most valuable report'. On 2 September, Rhodes accounted for a two-seat LVG, bringing his and Pithey's total to ten aeroplanes and two balloons destroyed. Both men now received a Bar to their DFC gained in June. Rhodes explained: 'When you went into action, you had to wait and wait and wait' until the enemy came within lethal range. In later years, Rhodes would recall their 'numerous forays, tempting would-be executioners to try their arm with us to their own destruction'. Although the RE8 was 'very slow, we had a perfect understanding and once we got them in the position we wanted them, it was easy'.

So swiftly did British troops advance on 2 September that, as intense aerial activity took place over the battlefield, by noon they had broken through the formidable Drocourt-Quéant Line, running across the front six miles south from the Sensée river in the north to join the formidable Hindenburg Line at right angles near Quéant, two and a half miles into enemy territory. Low-level bombing attacks that morning were carried out predominantly by Camels. At one point patrols overlapped, as single-seat machines engaging enemy infantry, artillery batteries and transport in front of the Canadian Corps of the British First Army. Eight tons of bombs were dropped and almost 50,000 rounds of machine-gun ammunition fired. German aeroplanes were not idle, though, and the RAF's two-seater reconnaissance squadrons in particular suffered. From the four squadrons directly involved with the First Army, fifteen aeroplanes were missing or wrecked.

Despite such losses, aerial reports helped to build up an accurate and invaluable picture of the battlefield, as crews assisting the XVII Corps of the Third Army demonstrated. With their observers briefed to drop messages by bag to denote progress, two RE8s of No 13 Sqn took off at 5am, requiring the pilots to fly low through the British artillery barrage covering the infantry advance. Their Squadron recorded that 'the reports they dropped at Corps headquarters were concise, accurate, and clear', and as a result, XVII Corps went forward to

Salvage or Scrap? Ground crew take away damaged aeroplanes. *(Peter Jackson)*

capture Quéant, Pronville and Inchy. The OC of No 13 Sqn recorded that, on the evening of 2 September, the corps commander rang him 'and told me that the success of the operations depended very largely indeed on the information obtained from the air'.

There were also a number of multiple air clashes that day. At about 9.30am, a group of SE5a, Camel and Bristol Fighter machines encountered a formation of Fokker and Pfalz scouts. Six aeroplanes, three from each side, were shot down. An hour and a half later, ten SE5a machines escorting four Bristol Fighters on a low-level operation were attacked by fifteen German machines. Some opened fire, while others kept watch above. As nine American Camels and RE8s joined in, other enemy aeroplanes appeared, and soon a melee developed. Five German and four American machines went down. Two other Americans returned badly damaged, and one of the RE8s force-landed on the British side with a wounded observer.

The American pilot and future author, Lt Elliott W. Springs, described part of this combat in which 'about 25 enemy aircraft [were] seen … Fokker pilots very good, but poor shots'. Patrolling the Arras-Cambrai road at 11.45am, Springs and three other pilots engaged four Fokker machines. He explained that 'three more came down out of the clouds and we were forced to withdraw. Seven more enemy aircraft came up from the north-west, and after some manoeuvring I attacked another enemy aircraft south-east of the road, but we, in turn, were attacked by a large number'. As the American top flight dived, a dog-fight ensued. 'We were badly outnumbered', Springs wrote, 'Saw one enemy aircraft attack an RE8 and attacked him. Assisted by a Bristol, attacked another enemy aircraft very low. We succeeded in preventing enemy aircraft from attacking RE8, and eventually drove them east', into cloud over Cambrai.

On 2 September, the RAF had thirty-six machines lost or written off, twenty-two officers missing and fourteen wounded. During the night of 2/3 September, enemy troops fell back, and a contact patrol flying at 300ft over the battlefield early on 3 September reported that no Germans remained west of the Canal du Nord. Later aerial reports showed that bridges over the canal were being blown up. Nevertheless, by 5 September British troops had crossed the canal and advanced three miles (5km) into enemy territory.

Further south, between 12 and 16 September the Americans launched a successful offensive against the St Mihiel salient jutting into the Allied line on the Meuse river, 60 miles (96km) south of Sedan, taking 16,000 prisoners and 443 guns. Col William 'Billy' Mitchell, commanding the air component, decisively committed a large force of aeroplanes in reconnaissance, bombing and ground-support roles. Mitchell could call on 1,481 Allied aeroplanes; 49 American and French squadrons with a further 9 British bomber squadrons on standby. Mitchell's plan was to deploy one third of this force in close support of ground troops, the rest against the German rear areas. When its machines were called upon, poor weather interrupted some of the Independent Force operations. However, flying through heavy rain, No 207 Sqn did attack Le Cateau station with a 1,650lb bomb, forty-eight 112lb and thirty 25lb bombs during the night of 13/14 September. Two nights afterwards Nos 207, 83 and 58 squadrons hit enemy aerodromes.

Mitchell had transferred from the infantry to the Aviation Section of the US Signal Corps after witnessing the Wrights demonstrate their machines. Dismissive of staff officers, who he said knew as much about the air 'as a hog knows about skating', while acting as an official aviation observer at the front before the USA entered the war, he was impressed by Trenchard's long-range bombing philosophy and supported similar action when appointed to the staff of the American commander, Gen John J. Pershing. His role during the St Mihiel offensive led to promotion to brigadier-general and command of over 1,000 aeroplanes in other battles before the Armistice.

At the extreme north of the Allied line, at 5.30am on 28 September Belgian forces under King Albert and the British Second Army, commanded by Gen Sir Herbert Plumer, advanced on Ghent, with the RAF providing extensive air support. Eight squadrons (three Camel, two DH4, one DH9, one Handley Page and one FE2b) were allocated to the Belgian force; sixteen squadrons to the British Second Army (three of RE8, DH9 and SE5a; two Armstrong-Whitworth and Camel; one each of Sopwith Dolphin, Bristol Fighter and FE2b).

Abnormal air activity was curtailed before the attack, and complete surprise therefore achieved. By the end of the first day, British and Belgian ground forces had made substantial gains. RAF bombers successfully hit railway targets and ammunition dumps from Thourout to Roulers, reporting three trains and three dumps destroyed without loss. Low-flying machines attacking targets, troops, artillery and transport in the immediate battle zone faced particular peril. Visibility varied from poor at best to downright dangerous, especially when a violent rainstorm occurred in the late morning. On 28 September, twenty-seven RAF aeroplanes engaged in low-level attacks failed to return. The following day, further wet weather restricted aerial activity and slowed down the ground advance.

The experiences of 2/Lt Thomas Dodwell illustrated not only the frequency of inhospitable weather, but the strength of enemy defences in the coastal region in the weeks leading up to the Allied assault. During the late spring and summer of 1918, as a DH9 observer with No 211 (former RNAS) Sqn at Petite Snythe, near Dunkirk, Dodwell survived three crash landings, had his machine mauled by fighters and damaged by 'Archie' ('deuced unpleasant time') during bombing and photographic operations. On one raid, he was 'stunned by piece of shrapnel, which cut my helmet'. During an operation against Bruges, the engine began to misfire 5 miles (8km) east of Ostend, so the pilot fired a green Very light to signal leaving the formation and turned 'for home'. The DH9 then 'dropped pills on Ostend' only to be 'shot up in four places by Archie'. Rapidly losing height, the bomber put down on a beach after crossing the lines. The tide was rising and as the pilot dashed off to phone their base, Dodwell persuaded nearby French soldiers to haul the machine to safety. A squadron maintenance party found blocked fuel lines, rectified the problem and laid boards on the beach for the aeroplane to take off before the tide turned once more.

Back from leave, on 13 August flying with 1st Lt Allan F. Bonnalie, an American pilot, on a photo operation Dodwell's machine ran into serious trouble. Bonnalie explained that 'despite the presence of hostile aircraft … in the district south of Bruges, [Dodwell had] succeeded in taking the required photographs … [then] on the way back, six Fokker biplanes made a determined attack.' The guns of both the DH9's escorts malfunctioned, leaving Dodwell to cope alone with the enemy fighters. Bonnalie wrote that 'Lt Dodwell used his gun so effectively that he managed to keep all the enemy aircraft engaged and prevented their attack from destroying either of the two helpless machines,' in which one observer had been killed and a pilot wounded. Bonnalie struggled to retain control of the DH9 as he dived to protect one of the escorts. Nevertheless, his pilot reported that Dodwell 'continued to engage three enemy machines that were attacking him and eventually drove them off, an operation that called for great coolness and skill, as the shooting platform was most unsteady.' As they made for base, Bonnalie experienced more trouble with the DH9:

> Realising that the machine was out of control owing to the loss of lift in the tail plane, half of this being shot away, he [Dodwell] left his cockpit, and, climbing onto the wing, lay down along the cowling in front of the pilot, enabling the latter to obtain partial control of the

Thirsty machine. German ground crew fuelling an aeroplane. *(Peter Jackson)*

machine and head for home. When nearing the ground, he climbed back into his cockpit to allow the nose to rise, and the pilot succeeded in safely landing.

Bonnalie believed that Dodwell's 'presence of mind and cool courage … undoubtedly saved the machine and deserve the highest praise'. Both pilot and observer survived unscathed, but there were over 250 holes in the fuselage. Thomas Dodwell discovered 'eight in my cockpit', and reflected 'we were very lucky getting out of a tight place'.

Two days later, he wrote, 'very hot Archie owing to clear visibility. Hit in six places, one piece went through the back of my skipper's seat. A lot of Huns knocking about were engaged by the Camel escorts, who shot three down'. On 16 August, Dodwell's luck ran out. 'Hit in three places by Archie … Attacked by Hun scout. Engine stopped and bottom wing shot in two close to fuselage. Managed to dodge the Hun and landed in sea 2½ miles from coast'. An hour afterwards, Dodwell and the pilot Capt C.S. Wynne-Eyton were picked up by a neutral Dutch vessel. Dodwell's left arm had been badly injured close to the shoulder and that afternoon was amputated. Between 21 April and 16 August 1918, excluding a short leave in England, he had flown fifty-eight operations.

Almost two months later, on 17 October, Dodwell returned to England 'in an old tramp steamer', shortly afterwards being invested with the DSO for which he had been recommended by Lt Bonnalie due to his 'extraordinary heroism' on 13 August, and he received a separate Mention in Despatches for his work during other operations.

While the advance into Flanders progressed in September 1918, further south three British armies supported by 1,058 aeroplanes were committed to assaulting the Hindenburg Line. A thrust towards Cambrai on 27 September was followed, after two days of preliminary bombardment, at 5.50am on 29 September by the main attack towards Bellenglise-Vendhuille, near St Quentin. As close-support squadrons saturated the battlefield, bombers hit more distant targets. By 4 October, the line had been breached and British troops were through to open country.

Aeroplane losses in Flanders and in the Bapaume area showed, however, that the German air force was by no means spent. The highly-manoeuvrable Fokker D.VIII single-seat fighter (nicknamed 'Flying Razor Blade' by the British), with two Spandau machine-guns, maximum speed of 202 kph (126mph) and ceiling of 21,000ft, proved a formidable acquisition. Fortunately for the Allies, it did not come into service until August 1918 and initially suffered teething problems from which the American Elliott Springs may have unknowingly benefited on 2 September, when he criticised its defective gunnery.

In mid-September, as Allied troops in the area advanced, No 12 Sqn moved forward to Vrau Vraucourt, 5 miles north-east of Bapaume, where Croye Pithey and Hervey Rhodes continued to carry out contact patrols, photo reconnaissance and artillery spotting tasks. On 26 September, Rhodes received his 'ticket' to train as a pilot on Sopwith Snipes in England. Superstition decreed that once a 'ticket' had arrived the individual concerned should not fly again. Next day, however, was the big attack on the Hindenburg Line, as Rhodes put it, 'the beginning of the end'. Arguing that on such 'an important show' Pithey would not want a strange observer in the rear cockpit, Rhodes persuaded his flight commander, Capt Castles, much against his own judgement ('you're a bloody fool', he told Rhodes) to let him fly. Rhodes would later admit to being 'Headstrong and young and impetuous'.

That evening, he saw soldiers resting on the edge of the airstrip on their way to the front for the dawn assault. He and other members of the mess dragged the squadron water carrier across the grass and offered refreshment. Rhodes was astonished to find a friend from his own street with whom he had grown up. He walked some way with him before turning back, wondering whether as Castles had said he was being foolish. Waking at around midnight, he decided that he had been silly, put on his leather jacket and sought out Castles. Far from being annoyed, the flight commander commended him for seeing sense and agreed that he should not fly. It was soon Rhodes' turn to be shaken, however, when about three hours later Castles woke him, 'I've got bad news', he said. No 12 Sqn provided support for VI Infantry Corps, which would take part in the forthcoming attack. Over the previous months, the crews had become well-known to the soldiers and Castles told Rhodes that the corps commander had asked for Pithey and Rhodes to be on duty that morning.

They duly flew their dawn patrol, had breakfast and then went back to the hangar. Another machine landed, its pilot wounded before completing his reconnaissance, and not waiting for orders, Pithey and Rhodes went up to finish the task. Flying over the Canal du Nord, they saw German field guns being towed away, and immediately the RE8 dived to scatter men and horses with repeated machine-gun bursts from 100ft before turning for home. Crossing the Bapaume–Cambrai road, Rhodes saw a puff of blue smoke rising from a crossroads shortly before shells struck the machine. Pithey suffered an arm wound, Rhodes was severely hit in the legs and buttock. With his observer rapidly losing blood, Pithey managed to land back at base, where willing hands gently extracted the unconscious Rhodes from his shattered cockpit. Before he passed out in the air, Rhodes dimly heard a mechanic calling, 'your aerial's hanging out, sir', and thinking, 'my life's hanging out let alone the aerial'. Rhodes came round in a Casualty Clearing Station and would remain in hospital for two and a half years. Unlike many less fortunate families, though, he and his two brothers survived the war.

During October 1918, as their armies attempted to rally, German squadrons concentrated on preventing British day bombers from attacking the railway network. Their particular concern was to protect the bottleneck through Namur and Liège necessary for the safe withdrawal of enemy troops from Belgium and northern France. To achieve their aim, the Germans amassed large formations, sometimes totalling fifty machines, with which to attack the bombers and their fighter escorts. On 30 October, an enormous aerial scrum ended with claims of sixty-seven enemy aeroplanes shot down, forty-one RAF machines either lost or written off with twenty-nine airmen killed or missing and eight wounded.

The RAF gained two more VCs during October. South African Capt Andrew Beauchamp-Proctor, who would also secure a Bar to his MC and a DSO before the Armistice, flying a No 84 Sqn SE5a was awarded the VC for his achievements over a two-month period. Between 8 August and 8 October 1918, he shot down ten aeroplanes, drove down four more out of control and accounted for twelve observation balloons. On 8 October, after destroying a two-seater near Maretz, Beauchamp-Proctor was wounded in the arm by machine-gun fire as he flew low but contrived to land safely at base and to make his report before being taken to hospital.

Maj William 'Billy' George Barker, already the holder of the MC and two bars, DSO and Bar, French Croix de Guerre and Italian Silver Medal while on the Italian Front, brought Canada its third VC in the air. Born in Manitoba, Barker had served in the trenches with the Canadian Mounted Rifles before becoming attached to the RFC as an observer then qualifying as a pilot. During the morning of 27 October 1918, flying a No 201 Sqn Sopwith Snipe he shot down an enemy two-seater over the Forêt de Mormal, but was then himself attacked by a Fokker biplane. Despite being wounded in the right thigh, he managed to shoot down this machine as well. However, Barker was soon surrounded by several more enemy machines, was hit in the left thigh, yet drove down two of his opponents out of control before briefly losing consciousness. On coming round, his aeroplane was still under attack, but he accounted for a third enemy, suffered a shattered left elbow and fainted once more. Regaining consciousness yet again, in spite of his injuries, he despatched a fourth German attacker.

Now thoroughly exhausted, Barker broke away and made for base, only to be confronted by further enemy machines, which he evaded to crash over the British line. His tally of four aerial victories, which brought his overall total to fifty, was according to the citation, 'a notable example of the exceptional bravery and disregard of danger, which this very gallant officer has always displayed throughout his distinguished career'. Barker was one of fifteen VCs awarded to members of the British air services in North West Europe.

As Allied divisions on the ground, covered by their air components, advanced in Autumn 1918, the Independent Force continued to execute its own operational programme. From 22 September, with the arrival of another Sopwith Camel squadron, its strength had risen to ten squadrons. Availability of the 1,650lb bomb greatly increased the force's destructive capacity, and one of these weapons reputedly wiped out a whole factory at Kaiserslautern. Specifications were drawn up for a long-range bomber, powered by four 375hp engines in tandem, with a top speed of 90mph and crew of between five and seven. Depending on the bomb-load and number of machine-guns carried, there would be provision for up to five machine-guns and a maximum bomb-load of 7,500lbs. First flown in May 1918, the Handley

Page (HP) v 1500 had the ability to reach Berlin and three of the machines were standing by to do so from Bircham Newton in Norfolk in November 1918.

Lt Anthony Kilburn was one of the pilots ready to bomb the German capital. He had first taken up an HP v 1500 on 29 July 1918 and declared that it 'flew beautifully'. Kilburn remained involved in the test programme, though not without alarms. On 22 September, he set out from Andover for Shrewsbury carrying 'a DW directional wireless – new invention for the bombing of Berlin'. Bad weather caused him to land at Malvern. A week later, for some unexplained reason, he flew to Malvern with only one crew member and 'landed in a large field to pick up the rest of crew'. As Kilburn attempted to get airborne again, the throttle broke, 'swinging machine into large tree. Crashed, no one hurt'. Then, on 2 and 3 November 1918, he flew from Bircham Newton as second pilot on preparatory flights for 'the bombing of Berlin'. During the second of these, the bomber was forced to land at Martlesham Heath 'owing to bad weather'. An unsubstantiated belief has survived that the sandwiches were already cut for crews prepared for the Berlin raid, when it was cancelled after pressure from the Foreign Office. So the HP v 1500 did not fly operationally before the war ended, although Kilburn's association with it had by no means finished.

While the HP v 1500 crews prepared for their ambitious operation, Independent Force bombers pressed home attacks on targets in Germany, despite raids during September being severely restricted. An official report explained:

> On nineteen days and eighteen nights no operations were carried out owing to adverse weather conditions … During the period of the useful phases of the moon, conditions for night flying were particularly bad. Strong winds, low clouds, and much rain prevented many of the long-distance objectives being reached.

A pilot, who through his many later publications would have an immense influence on perceptions of aerial fighting during the First World War, flew with No 55 Sqn of the Independent Force in 1918. William Earl (known to contemporaries as Bill) Johns had joined The King's Own Royal Regiment (Norfolk Yeomanry) in 1913 and been mobilised at the outbreak of war. In September 1915, Pte Johns found himself embroiled in the Gallipoli disaster, and after the withdrawal from the peninsula, he transferred to The Machine-Gun Corps. Following a spell at home, he sailed for the Salonika enclave, where Allied troops were engaging Austro-Hungarian forces. In fever-ridden Greek Macedonia, his unit suffered more fatalities from sickness than enemy action.

Recovering from malaria back in England, L/Cpl Johns volunteered for the RFC: 'It seemed to me there was no point in dying standing up in squalor, if one could do so sitting down in clean air', he explained. So on 26 September 1917, 2/Lt Bill Johns found himself at an Oxford college for a month-long introductory course, and almost precisely a year later, on 15 September 1918, flying one of the twelve DH4s of No 55 Sqn to bomb Stuttgart and survive a determined attack by enemy fighters on the way back. Johns was not impressed with the DH4, which he claimed was 'an unpopular machine' and a potential 'flaming coffin' because the main petrol tank was positioned between the pilot and observer. He also claimed the constant roar of the aero-engine during a prolonged flight frequently gave crews painful headaches.

The next day, Johns flew one of twelve DH4s ordered to the Lanz works and railway yards at Mannheim. Six machines aborted the operation, but Johns was in the formation which flew on to attack the target. On the way back, near Hagenau, Johns fired a green light indicating engine trouble and fell behind. He failed to return and was duly posted 'missing in action'.

Unknown to his family, already damaged by anti-aircraft fire, Johns' bomber had been shot down by an enemy fighter. The observer died, Johns himself was wounded in the crash and destined to spend the remaining weeks of the war in captivity; apparently, not without incident. He twice briefly escaped from different camps and shortly after his capture, was reputedly put on trial and sentenced to death for bombing civilians. Johns weighed 11 stone (69kg), when he became a prisoner, and 7 stone (44kg) on release.

Johns was only one of many airmen to be lost or posted missing in the closing phase of the conflict, causing anguish and dismay among their relatives. Mrs J. Bishop from Worthing, Sussex, learnt that her son had been reported missing in September 1918. She wrote to his squadron commander two months later and wondered whether, as it went unanswered, previous correspondence had 'gone astray. I should esteem it a great favour if you could possibly send me any further news about our poor lad, as we have heard nothing from the Red Cross or the Air Board.' A letter from south-west London reached No 56 Sqn following 'the death of my son Lt J.A. Pouchot ... Naturally, I am anxious to know how he came by his end and should esteem it a favour if you would give me all the particulars you can'. From Cottisbrooke, Northants, another distraught letter went to that Squadron. 'I am writing on behalf of my father to ask if you have any news of my brother, A. Vickers, who has been missing since September 3rd. If you will kindly have all his kit collected and sent home. We were hoping to hear some news of him.'

Such despair was not confined to the United Kingdom, again underlining the diverse origins of RAF crews. In Toronto, a cable had been received revealing that Lt Jas C. Crawford had died of burns received in a crash. His father penned a letter to Crawford's Flight Commander:

> We would be greatly indebted to you, if you would send us full particulars whether accident or shot down and when it happened and where he is buried. Hoping that is not asking too much of you. I am making this as short as possible. I know your time is taken up ... from a lonely mother, father and brother.

From Omaha, Nebraska, the grandfather of Lt Jarvis J. Offut, an American officer killed while attached to a British squadron, wrote asking that the effects of 'our dear boy' could be forwarded to his mother, whose address was appended. As Victor Yeates, who flew 248 hours in Sopwith Camels, crashed four times and was shot down twice, reflected: 'It's rotten for women. It's worse to stay at home than go and get on with the war.'

Away from this grief, in the penultimate month of the war, agreement was reached to expand the British Independent Force into a powerful international bombing organisation. On 3 October 1918, a Heads of Agreement document was drawn up between the British and French governments and submitted to the Italian and American governments for approval to establish an Inter-Allied Independent Air Force (IAAF) under Maj Gen Sir Hugh Trenchard as C-in-C. For operational purposes, the IAAF would be responsible to the Supreme Allied Commander, Marshal Foch. Its 'object' would be 'to carry war into Germany by attacking her industry, commerce, and population ... Air raids must be on a large scale and repeated, forming part of a methodical plan and carried on with tenacity'. On 17 October, the British contribution comprised 10 squadrons totalling 140 machines. It would not, in practice, be swelled by aeroplanes from other nations, and effectively the IAAF remained the Independent Force by another name, whose targets were officially to include urban concentrations as well as industrial and commercial centres.

At dawn on 4 November, along a 30-mile (48km) front from Oisy on the Sambre to Valenciennes, the British First, Third and Fourth armies launched the last major assault of the

First World War. RAF squadrons attacked transport concentrations beyond the battlefield and enemy troops on it with bombs and machine-guns as they fell back, even though weather conditions were not always favourable. On 9 November, a large formation of DH9, Camel and SE5a machines carrying bombs were escorted by Bristol Fighters and Sopwith Snipes to Enghien, near Brussels. The raid leader reported that 'there was great confusion of troops and transport of all descriptions on the roads, trains on the railways and in the station, also two aerodromes with machines on the ground'. Hangars and aeroplanes were wrecked on both aerodromes, and twenty direct hits were observed on the station, where one train was set on fire. Along roads leading to the town, troops and transport were badly disrupted:

> Lorries were seen to collide, one being set on fire, many others being destroyed by direct hits and others ditched. Horse transport was seen stampeding in all directions, and in numerous cases troops endeavouring to get into houses for cover were shot at and many casualties caused.

The end was clearly in sight. That day, 9 November, the Kaiser abdicated and a German Republic was proclaimed. Fighting, though, did not cease for another two days when the Armistice came into force at 11am.

On 10 November the Anglo-Irish pilot Ewart Garland living in Australia and back in action as a flight commander after several months in England recovering from nervous exhaustion, flew No 104 Sqn's only twin-engine DH 10 to bomb an ammunition dump. He was luckier than Capt Charles Brown, who had returned to action with No 46 Sqn in October after a lengthy spell in England also recovering from exhaustion. That day, too, Brown flew a Camel on a 'reconnaissance of back areas', but according to his log book, was 'wounded in the leg whilst strafing some motor transport on the road between Sauvage and Chinay'. As a result, he spent Armistice Day in hospital. Lt Frank Marsh, who had enlisted in The Hertfordshire Regiment under age in 1915, remained in England and three years later joined the RFC seeking action at the front, was in the air in a FE2b during the night of 10/11 November, when he realised that the Armistice had been agreed. He turned back as 'coloured (red and white) lights were being fired all along the line and we had quite a job to find our way home'.

A letter to Brown's parents from Maj Gerald Allen, OC No 46 Sqn, provided yet another example of a thoughtful squadron commander. 'Your son, Capt C.A. Brown, put up a very good performance this morning, and displayed great devotion to duty'. Carrying out a reconnaissance at low level, he located 'a lot of Hun transport' but 'got a rifle bullet in the right thigh'. It would have been easy for an 'experienced pilot like him' to land as soon as he crossed the line or at the first available aerodrome. However, 'realising his information was very important', he made for his home base and executed a perfect landing. He was unable to walk unaided, but insisted on making his report to Allen in person. As a result he 'sent out a bombing raid, which was very successful'. The bullet hole was clean and the bullet was 'probably out now', because Brown had been taken to a nearby Casualty Clearing Station. Maj Allen concluded: 'I have written, as I thought a mother generally likes to have an outsider's opinion, if her son is hit', and he assured both of Brown's parents that the Squadron wished Brown 'a speedy recovery'.

When the guns fell silent, the RAF on the Western Front numbered 99 squadrons and seven separate flights with a total of 1,799 aeroplanes. This was a far cry from the sparse force, which in August 1914 according to Maurice Baring 'went gaily as to a dance'.

Conclusion

Peace at Last
'Lit-up cities'

Shortly after the Armistice, Maj Ranald Reid, commissioned into The Argyll and Sutherland Highlanders in August 1914 and now in the RAF at Dunkirk, visited the Waterloo battlefield south of Brussels, until November 1918 behind enemy lines. En route, he found 'the lit-up cities … fantastically beautiful after the long darkness of the blackout'. Further south, Capt Hugh Chance, who joined The Worcestershire Regiment in March 1915 and the RFC the following year, experienced a strange encounter at Gouzeacourt, south-west of Cambrai. He came across a French peasant ploughing in a field, who remembered a particular incident during the war: 'Yes, brave French aviators dropped bombs on a German troop train. The engine was hit and a bomb fell on the last two coaches, which contained ammunition and blew up. There were over forty casualties and I was ordered to help to clear the wreckage'. The farmhand was surprised, when Chance told him that the attack took place on 15 September 1917, the airmen were British and he was the pilot of the bomber. Lt Frank Marsh, who had enlisted in The Hertfordshire Regiment under age after a chance encounter with a recruiting sergeant in The Strand, went with No 149 Sqn to Namur, where to his amazement all of the sixteen machines fitted into a Zeppelin hangar. 'And the FE 2b was not a small plane [wing span 47ft 9ins, length 32ft 3ins, height 12ft 7½ ins]', he wrote.

Reid, Chance and Marsh were now part of an organisation unrecognisable from that of August 1914, when aerial warfare had been an unknown quantity, a military leap in the dark. Two small forces attached to the British Army and Royal Navy with little prospect of operating over long distances or far from the native shores had been transformed into an independent third service. The combined strength of the RFC and RNAS in August 1914 was 2,073 officers and other ranks; all stationed in Britain. When hostilities ended, the RAF comprised 291,175 personnel serving with the fleet, in training, deployed for home defence and in the operational theatres of Europe, the Near and Middle East and East Africa. The service included men from many nations, like Norwegian Tryggve Gran and at different times, some 300 Americans such as Lt Allan F. Bonnalie, the pilot in No 211 Sqn who commended Thomas Dodwell's bravery, and Lt Norman H. Read, who survived the crash which killed William McCudden in Gosport. Much has been written about the Lafayette Squadron of Americans serving with the French before the United States entered the war, comparatively little about Americans who served in the RFC at the same time. On 1 March 1918, approximately 25 per cent of men serving in the British air arms on the Western Front were Canadian, three of whom won the VC.

Assertions that British authorities were inept and negligent pre-war, unduly stubborn in refusing to recognise the military potential of air power, should be treated with some caution. Sefton Brancker's contention on 25 July 1914 that the RFC was not ready for action represented a light-hearted response from 'a short, dapper and monocled' officer 'with a cheerful approach to life', energetic and enthusiastic but often 'tactless'. The number of aeroplanes available at the outbreak of war was undoubtedly inferior to the front line strength of France and Germany, but their strategic responsibilities differed markedly from those of Great Britain. Like Britain, both countries had faced opposition from senior military figures, a press campaign for action and pressure groups such as the German Air Fleet League and the French National Aviation League. Germany had been further hamstrung by friction between the War Ministry and Army General Staff and an initial preference for airships. Like Frank McClean at Eastchurch, a German industrialist Dr Walter Huth sponsored military aviation, yet by the close of 1911 only thirty pilots had qualified to fly, and Helmuth von Moltke's aim of six aeroplanes attached to each army and corps HQ by 1 April 1914 proved a pipe dream.

Where France, and to a lesser extent Germany, had a distinct advantage was in the size of their aeronautical design and manufacturing base. France, once war commenced, exerted considerable indirect influence over the operational capability of the RFC and RNAS. Inability of the two British air arms to co-operate in matters of design and manufacture, by each having its own dedicated producers at home and competing procurement agencies in Paris created further serious problems. Attempts by the JWAC of 1916 and two later Air Boards, all of which lacked executive power and the political status of a ministry, to resolve this unsatisfactory scenario provided one major reason for creation of the unified air force.

In terms of doctrine, the seed corn of belief that bombing an enemy's homeland could adversely affect industrial production and civilian morale was nurtured by the German raids on Britain. During the war, 103 airship and aeroplane attacks took place, killing 1,414, injuring 3,416 and causing approximately £3 million of damage. Beyond these bald statistics lay instances of panic, serious interruption to factory work and evacuation of urban areas. Postwar, Trenchard would claim that the moral to the physical effect of bombing was twenty to one. The experience of Britain, which the uproar following the two daylight raids on London in 1917 underscored, gave weight to this argument.

Trenchard was on less firm ground when assessing the achievements of long-range bombers from eastern France. Between June and November 1918, the Independent Force and IAAF flew an impressive 12,906 hours in day and night operations and dropped 543 tons of bombs. In reality, the bombers merely nibbled at the edges of German industry, restricted by the limited accuracy of attacks and range of the aeroplanes. The father of Albert Speer, future Nazi Minister for Armaments and War Production, moved his family just thirty miles from Mannheim to Heidelberg to escape Allied bombers.

For four years after the war ended, the RAF had to fight for its existence as the other two services sought return of their air arms: in effect, recreation of the RFC and RNAS. Trenchard restored as CAS in 1919 had strenuously to defend the independence of the new force in personal confrontations, lengthy memoranda and dreary committee rooms. He used the RAF's peculiar contribution to warfare, long-range bombing quite separate from tactical support to the Army and Royal Navy, as a powerful tool. In the timely words of a leader in the *Manchester Guardian*: 'Air power … is a revolutionary force upsetting established conventions everywhere, creating new precedents … not a trailer on existing military and naval theory.' Until August 1919, RAF personnel retained the ranks of their original Service (RFC or RNAS). That month, introduction of a new structure (2/Lt, Lt, General/Admiral becoming Plt Off, Fg Off and Marshal respectively) gave an appearance of permanence. Ultimately, after a favourable official enquiry in 1923, the RAF was saved, but it had become virtually wedded to the concept of strategic (long-range) bombing as a raison d'être.

The personal lives of airmen and their families were dominated by the war and its aftermath. Apart from the 9,000 dead or missing, over 7,000 were wounded; many permanently disabled. Those who signed on only for the duration of the war or failed to secure a permanent post later found themselves in a depressed labour market. Peace came after a prolonged period of living for the present and concentrating on mere survival. Re-adjustment, especially for those who had joined up straight from school and had known no other adult life, would prove difficult, often nigh impossible. Harold Balfour dubbed them 'the untrained graduates of war', a designation equally applicable in Germany. When the Richthofen wing was disbanded, its last commander, Hermann Göring, had no job. A biographer has observed: 'He was trained for nothing save only soldiering and flying, and for men of that craft there now seemed to be no place whatever in the defeated Reich.' Before he pursued his notorious political career with another First World War survivor, Adolf Hitler, Göring eked out a living as a commercial pilot, instructor and stunt flyer.

At first glance, Manfred von Richthofen's collection of cups to celebrate his aerial triumphs, the striving of Immelmann, Boelcke and Voss to outscore one another and the practice of German airmen describing their separate victories in family correspondence distinguishes them from their British counterparts. Yet British airmen frequently referred at length and in detail to their exploits in letters home. Nor were trophies and ambitions disregarded. Noting his 49th victory, Edward Mannock wrote: 'If I have any luck, I think I may beat old Mac [James McCudden]. Then I shall try and oust old Richthofen.' In August 1917, Mannock despatched a parcel to James Eyles, with whose family he had lodged pre-war while working for the Post Office. It contained 'boots which belonged to a dead pilot … [and] goggles belonging to another pilot', together with a cigarette holder and case, field dressing and piece of fabric from other downed machines. McCudden took home as a trophy the silk cap from a pilot he shot down.

There were other parallels between British and German airmen. James McCudden and Max Immelmann gratefully acknowledged food parcels from home. Immelmann thanked his mother for sending him boots, McCudden asked his for warm 'cycling stockings'. Oswald Boelcke and Manfred von Richthofen steadfastly denied suffering from 'nerves', but there was ample evidence on both sides about the effects of prolonged periods in front line action. Battle fatigue, or nervous exhaustion, may well have contributed to the deaths of Boelcke, Richthofen, Ball and Hawker.

Concern about crippling injury, fire and death, whether use of seat belts saved lives and the benefit of riotous parties to relieve tension were common threads in correspondence, journals and dairies. Franz Immelmann, a pilot like his famous brother, pondered 'was it war we loved or flying', opting for flying, a sentiment echoed by among others Robin Rowell, Ewart Garland and Tryggve Gran. Manfred von Richthofen likened aerial warfare to the hunting of wild boar, but saw his quarry as an aeroplane, not the man who flew it.

Cecil Lewis agreed: 'They were simply "the enemy", their machines had black crosses, and it was our job to bring them down.' Garland wrote, 'I would not go so far as to say that flying men on both sides felt less personal antagonism towards their antagonists than, say, footballers in the heat and excitment of play,' but he held that the term 'Hun' was meant to be 'derogatory not derisory'. In old age, Hervey Rhodes' memories of his days in action, and one encounter in particular, haunted him. He had intermittent nightmares about the image of a pilot he shot down and the fact that their eyes locked briefly before the German spun away to his death. Dedicating his memoir of the war to British airmen, Algernon Insall added, 'in some strange way to the memory also of our enemies'. As individuals, British and German aviators had much in common.

The experiences of British airmen who survived the war inevitably varied. William Leefe Robinson, awarded the VC for bringing down the airship at Cuffley in September 1916, had been harshly treated as a PoW and in his weakened state, succumbed to Spanish flu seventeen days after returning to Harrow Weald, Middlesex, where he was buried with full military honours on 3 January 1919. The South African VC, Andrew Beauchamp-Proctor, was killed during an air display at RAF Upavon on 21 June 1921.

Victor Yeates, Sopwith Camel veteran and author of the semi-biographical novel *Winged Victory*, died in 1934 from tuberculosis, allegedly caused by 'war strain' and technically classified as 'Flying Sickness D'. Yeates himself believed that inhaling gas after a crash upside down in a shell hole on 29 March 1918 brought on his condition. Sefton Brancker, first recipient of the Air Force Cross (AFC) in June 1918, left the RAF in January 1919 to promote civil aviation. He was subsequently gazetted air vice-marshal on the retired list and appointed KCB. Brancker returned to the Air Ministry as director-general of civil aviation in 1922 and eight years later perished in the crash of the experimental civilian R101 airship near Beauvais in France, en route to India.

Some of the First World War participants who remained in the Service would hold influential posts in and after the Second World War. Charles Portal, John Slessor and Sholto Douglas became Marshal of the Royal Air Force; the first two CAS. Arthur Tedder also reached five star rank, was appointed Deputy Supreme Commander to Gen Dwight D. Eisenhower during the Normandy invasion and in 1950 CAS.

Despite having one false leg, the result of amputation following the injury sustained when winning the VC, Freddie West lobbied the former commander in France Sir John Salmond and his squadron commander, Trafford Leigh-Mallory, for support to remain in the RAF. His persistence paid off and he secured a permanent commission. But a desk job was not his aim. Surreptitiously he began to fly again and eventually re-qualified as a pilot. At the outbreak of the Second World War he was in command of No 50 Army Co-operation Wing of Blenheims, which joined the Advanced Striking Force in France, where with characteristic ingenuity West turned a Nelsonian eye on reports that one of his squadrons had arranged to have its washing done at the local brothel.

Invalided home with a perforated ulcer, West recovered to be appointed air attaché to Italy. After its declaration of war in 1940, he took up a similar post in Switzerland, where he became closely involved in assisting Allied servicemen to escape via France to neutral Spain. He left the RAF in 1946 as an air commodore to join the Rank Film Organisation in an executive role and played golf until he was eighty. West counted himself fortunate to have survived two world wars ('to be old you have to be lucky'), especially as he narrowly avoided death in 1944. His former squadron commander, Air Chief Marshal Sir Trafford Leigh-Mallory, had been designated Air Officer Commanding in the Far East and invited West to be his Senior Air Staff Officer (SASO). West declined on the grounds that he knew nothing about the Far East, knowledge which he considered essential. Leigh-Mallory and his staff were killed when their aeroplane crashed into a Swiss mountain en route to the appointment.

West's wartime observer, Alec Haslam, secured a permanent commission in the RAF and qualified as a pilot. An accomplished rugby full back, he represented the RAF against the Royal Navy post-war. Professionally, he served in Germany and on the North-West Frontier of India before leaving the RAF as a flight lieutenant in 1927. After completing an engineering degree at Cambridge, he worked for the Aviation Department of the Asiatic Petroleum Company before returning to Cambridge to do research, all the time taking every opportunity to fly. In 1938, Haslam went to the Air Ministry in a reseach capacity before two years later rejoining the RAF as a flight commander at No 18 Operational Training Unit, where he taught Poles to fly the single-engine Fairey Battle bomber. He was soon back at the Air Ministry, investigating engine failure among twin-engine Blenheims on take-off. After spells at the Ministry of Aircraft Production and as SASO to No. 44 Training Group, Gp Capt Alec Haslam finally retired from the RAF in 1945. He returned once more to Cambridge to lecture, before resigning at the age of fifty-three to be ordained as a Church of England clergyman.

Harold Balfour, who had served in the infantry at the Front before transferring to the RFC, left the RAF in 1923 to work as a journalist before entering politics and ultimately becoming Under-Secretary of State for War. Hervey Rhodes would also have a distinguished political career, after one as a successful businessman. Rhodes had recovered sufficiently from the wounds he received on 27 September 1918 to leave King's College Hospital, London, in February 1921. However, for the rest of his life shrapnel would remain in his body and he would need to wear an uncomfortable leg brace. Aged twenty-five, he had no job and little money. Going back to the only industry he knew, weaving, he set about building up a business by refurbishing a loom discarded on a rubbish tip and fulfilling commissions from firms secured by persistence and hard graft.

One legacy from the war years still troubled him, totally unconnected with his physical condition. He and Croye Pithey, his pilot, had made a pact that, if one were not to survive, the other would make contact with his parents. Pithey had quickly recovered from his wound, remained in the peacetime RAF but been lost in a flying accident in the Irish Sea. Busy making a living, Rhodes had not fulfilled his promise. However, in December 1936, he at last felt able to do so.

He made his way to Capetown in the liner, *Stirling Castle*, and up country by train to Pithey's home. A tall man stood on the station platform. Alighting, Rhodes approached him: 'Are you Mr Pithey?' 'You must be that so-and-so Rhodes', came the unpromising reply. Outside was a large motor car and two hours later, with Rhodes on board, it drove through the gates of an impressive colonial-style mansion. Dinner was a tense affair, after which Pithey's 87-year-old father retired and his daughter apologised for his taciturn behaviour; he had not mentioned her brother since his death. Next morning the atmosphere thawed, and Rhodes offered to tell Mr Pithey about Croye's wartime exploits. There was no need, the old man said. He could recite the contents of every one of his son's letters. It was a moving demonstration of both the anxiety and the grief of a parent separated from his offspring, whose hopes for his safety in a far-off land had been cruelly dashed.

Back in England, Rhodes' manufacturing enterprise flourished before he entered Parliament, became a government minister, life peer and Knight of the Garter. During the Second World War, he commanded the 36th West Riding Home Guard. Rhodes would always be grateful to the RFC, though, for giving him the confidence to compete in a harsh commercial and political environment, pointing to the pivotal realisation during his training course at Cambridge that he could match others better educated and more experienced than himself. In a sense, his RE8 crew epitomised the ability of the flying service to bring out the best in men of different social upbringing: the pilot from a vast mansion in South Africa, the observer from a small terraced house in Yorkshire.

Ranald Reid also remained in the RAF after the war. Among his subsequent appointments were commands in Egypt, Sudan, Aden and as air attaché to Washington, 1933–5. During the

Second World War, he held senior administrative posts before retiring in 1946 as an air vice-marshal and KCB. Harold Wyllie, who had skilfully sketched enemy positions and aeroplanes at the front, would become a distinguished painter living in Portsmouth. The eldest son of the celebrated marine artist W.L. Wyllie, who lost two of his five boys in the war, Harold left the RAF in 1919 to which he had been seconded with an OBE and the following year the Army. Five years later, he joined the RAF Reserve of Officers, qualified as a pilot and secured a commission in the RAF Volunteer Reserve in 1939. While serving at sea as a liaison officer, he transferred to the Royal Naval Volunteer Reserve being demobilised as a lieutenant commander at the end of the Second World War. He had thus been commissioned in all three Services. Louis Strange, the pilot involved in early aerial gunnery in France and reputedly Christmas Day festivies over Lille airfield in 1914, also served in the RAF during the Second World War and survived to fly a jet fighter afterwards.

In the post-war Service, Maj J.C. 'Paddy Jo' Quinnell spent time in Iraq, was SASO to the Advanced Striking Force in France 1939–40, and commanded an RAF group and a bomber base during the Second World War. He retired as Air Cdre in 1945 to become a prize-winning yachtsman. Toby Watkins remained in the RAF after the first conflict as well and left the Service as a wing commander.

Lt Arthur Kilburn's post-war service was less prolonged. On 6 May 1919, he was one of two pilots and four crew members of an HP v 1500 four-engine bomber, who left RAF Manston in Kent for Madrid. Over France, the machine ran into severe hail and rainstorms, which damaged one engine. Flying south of Tours, the pilots strove to climb above the clouds, failed and dived through them in an attempt to identify a landmark. The bomber now found itself in a valley surrounded by mountains, none of which, in Kilburn's words, 'by a miracle' it struck. Round and round the HP v 1500 went, as its crew anxiously sought a way out of their predicament. Suddenly, 'the clouds parted for a moment or two … [and] through a small valley', the sea appeared. With extreme relief, the crew guided their machine through the gap to land on the beach at Biarritz.

After the engine had been repaired and more petrol 'scrounged', the HP v 1500 eventually reached Madrid on 12 May. There it took up Spanish passengers for 'joy flips', before leaving for Barcelona with press representatives on board. Once more, several 'joy flips' were carried out before a four-and-a-half hour return flight to Madrid, with the additional press passengers still on board and only ten minutes petrol to spare on landing.

Following an eventful flag-waving exercise, the RAF machine took off on 30 May 1919 for a non-stop flight back to England. Not long after leaving Madrid, while over mountains part of an engine exhaust came apart 'and hung on by a wire, causing considerable agitation owing to the awful country we were going over'. To Kilburn's immense relief, the crew managed to negotiate the Pyrenees and were 'all set for home'. Then the rear starboard propeller sheered off 'jarring the whole machine terribly and taking two of the engine struts with it also making great gashes in the wings'. Kilburn admitted that the aeroplane was 'more or less out of control'. The two pilots decided to get down on 'some piece of the shore', but were unable to keep the machine straight and finished in the sea. The crew members were rescued by a rowing boat, though Kilburn lost his camera, his photos of the trip and a great deal of personal kit. Shortly after reaching England once more, Kilburn was demobilised. In his journal, with evident warmth he wrote: 'No more flying for this Child!'

Following the Armistice, John Jeyes remained at Worthy Down, from which he had set out on his excursion to Micheldever earlier in the year, testing and ferrying aeroplanes, until demobilisation in 1919. He returned to the family firm, P. Jeyes & Co of Northampton, before qualifying as a pharmacist and in the 1920s, becoming prominent in gliding competitions. Hugh Chance joined his family's glass firm, Chance Bros. The former Rolls-Royce fitter Edwin Bousher, whose operational career had begun and ended during the Battle of Passchendaele, was discharged from the RAF on 19 May 1918 and shortly afterwards joined the Department of Aircraft Production as a technical examiner.

Roy Brown, credited with shooting down Richthofen, returned to Canada post-war and became a successful businessman. Wilfred May, the Red Baron's intended eighty-first victim, won a DFC before pursuing a career in civil aviation. Stuart Keep, when a test pilot with the Westland Aircraft Company at Yeovil, Somerset, lost both legs below the knee in 1924 after crashing the cantilever monoplane Dreadnought in taking off for its initial flight. Fitted with two artificial legs and aided by sticks, he recovered to act progressively as factory superintendent, business manager and general manager before retiring in 1935.

Sgt Harold Taylor, who had been shot down and wounded in 1917, had his damaged leg amputated in 1960. By then, he had discovered that his machine was the twenty-eighth victim of Lt Kurt Wolff of Jasta 11. In his 70th year, musing on 'all the horrors of war' he wrote: 'I do know that when men are faced with death they can establish a comradeship which is never present in civil life in peacetime.'

Men like Rhodes, Reid, Quinnell, Keep and Taylor did not have their wartime exploits publicised. But a cult of personality contributed to a misleading presentation of aerial warfare during the inter-war years. The term 'ace' was a press invention, the first on the Allied side after achieving five 'kills' being the Frenchman Adolphe Pégoud in 1915. The Germans, while not officially using the word, initially awarded the *Pour le Mérite* (Blue Max) after eight successes, then later, after sixteen. The British authorities did not formally acknowledge aces either, though allegedly a DFC was sometimes awarded after eight victories. If the French criterion of five 'kills' had been followed, over 500 RFC and RAF airmen would have qualified. By definition, aces were likely to be fighter pilots, and this focus on one aspect of aerial operations detracted from roles like reconnaissance, close support for troops, co-operation with artillery and tanks, tactical and strategic bombing. Fighters evidently dominated the skies; a fiction perpetuated by illustrated volumes like W.E. Johns' *Fighter Planes and Aces*.

Edgar Ludlow-Hewitt, at one stage James McCudden's pilot during the war and who, as Air Chief Marshal, would be Air Officer Commanding-in-Chief Bomber Command at the outbreak of the Second World War, had reservations about undue accent on the exploits of VCs for psychological reasons. Publication of their feats prompted civilian and Service exhilaration, but news of their deaths triggered corresponding depression. Maurice Baring admitted to being acutely downcast on learning of Albert Ball's loss, and Johns confessed that McCudden's death could not have shocked him more than revelation that the Kaiser was in Paris.

Johns also wrote somewhat disparagingly, 'so hero-worshipping youth turns his eyes upwards and visualises himself in the cockpit of the fighting plane that wings its way across the sky'. Yet, whether intentional or not, like other contemporary writers William Earl Johns helped to foster an unrealistic, romanticised impression of fighting in the air. Writing to an old school friend, the author Henry Williamson, Victor Yeates complained: 'I read an awful book the other day called *The Camels Are Coming* [by Johns]: it was about Camels in the War and it was super-bunk'. Ludlow-Hewitt deplored the way his former observer James McCudden was portrayed in volumes about wartime figures. Stating that McCudden was 'a quiet, unassuming, essentially modest person … far from the glamorous, fire-eating hero of fiction'.

It was common practice for German airmen to be buried with part of a propeller. In the centre is the grave of Lt Hans Kirchstein who held the *Pour le Mérite* and was credited with twenty-seven victories. *(Peter Jackson)*

Apart from fears, like incineration in the air or in accidents on the ground, airmen writing memoirs and personal journals showed intense preoccupation with being trapped in a doomed machine, as parachutes were provided for balloons, but not aeroplanes. The container fixed to the side of the balloon basket had the parachute inside, which was pulled clear as the balloonist jumped and opened by the air current caused by his fall.

A belief has arisen that parachutes were forbidden in British aeroplanes in case they undermined 'the spirit of aggression'; airmen being likely to bale out prematurely. However, there were practical problems about using a static system in aeroplanes, such as operating at heights higher than those attained by balloons or need to avoid a mass of wires, struts and whirling propellers. One further consideration involved weight; the available parachute equipment being 40lbs. Indirectly, German aviators proved the validity of some negative points, when using static parachutes from aeroplanes in the closing months of the war. Several men were lost, when the apparatus became entangled in the structure or machinery of their aeroplane. Experiments involving a parachute, with the airman pulling a rip-cord to open it, had been carried out in 1912, but not for another ten years would the Irvin free-fall parachute be developed. It was rumoured that Edward Mannock, the VC lost in July 1918, carried a revolver for personal use should he be involved in an inescapable fire.

Flying in the First World War reinforced the need for teamwork. Shortly before his death, James McCudden reflected: 'I often look back and think what a splendid squadron No 3 was. We had a magnificent set of officers, and the NCOs and men were as one family.' Another aviator, Hubert Griffith, pondering his wartime experiences focused more closely on the crew of two-seaters. 'Within the squadron', he wrote, 'the pilot-and-observer relationship was more binding than that of a marriage ... It was, I suppose, the most personal relationship that ever existed.' An exaggeration, perhaps, but the example of Freddie West and Alec Haslam supports the general thesis. Both were born in 1896 and lived to the age of 92. Throughout their long lives, different careers and interests – West addicted to horse racing, Haslam in middle age an Anglican priest – they remained in close touch. Both retained an enduring respect for one another and until West died, they spoke on the phone on the anniversary of the action on 10 August 1918 when West won the VC and Haslam the DFC.

The grief of Amelie McCudden represented the lingering effect of the air war on many families, which like hers showed a closeness and affection for one another in their correspondence. Having lost three sons as pilots, on Armistice Day 1921 Mrs McCudden was chosen to represent British mothers and lay a wreath at the burial of the American Unknown Soldier in Arlington Cemetery, Washington DC. In July 1920, she had suffered more personal tragedy when returning to their Kingston home from his job in the Air Ministry in London, her husband had been killed in a railway accident at Clapham Junction. Her youngest son Maurice survived the war, but failed to become a pilot, and four months before his father's death had been discharged from the RAF. He subsequently qualified for a civil flying licence and tested new aircraft at Farnborough, dying from bowel inflammation in 1934. The squadron with which his brothers William and James went to war, No 3, supplied the funeral party.

Lloyd George's flowing rhetoric 'cavalry of the clouds' could perhaps be justified by referring to fighters as light cavalry skirmishers and bombers as heavy cavalry shock troops. But it is the concept of a 'knighthood' in the sky, with its overtones of chivalry, which has had the greater impact. In his poem, 'The Pioneer', Neil East captured this mood with an image of 'new knight-errants' riding on 'broad-winged shining cars'; a concept roundly condemned by Victor Yeates. Similarly, Franz Immelmann referred to 'honourable knightly combats', and the text chosen by the pastor at Oswald Boelcke's funeral service ran, 'so let us die in knightly fashion for the sake of our brethren'. To some extent British actions, like burying Richthofen with full military honours and dropping of a wreath, 'to the memory of Captain Boelcke, our brave and chivalrous opponent', reinforced the myth.

In 1933 Harold Balfour, decorated wartime pilot and future government minister, firmly dismissed this seductive fantasy: 'Of the chivalry of the air, which is so fatuously and ignorantly written about, neither side could afford to indulge in.' Conscious of the number of British airmen he had killed or maimed, Edward Mannock once reputedly declined to raise a glass to Richthofen with the words: 'I won't drink a toast to that bastard.'

There were examples of pilots waving at one another, when they ran out of ammunition or guns jammed during combat. In his early days as an observer, Harold Taylor recorded that the crews of British and German machines patrolling their own side of the line did sometimes salute one another without opening fire. But he soon came to realise that 'this was total war' in which he had 'to kill or be killed'. In the words of Manfred von Richthofen: '[War] is not as the people at home imagine it, with a hurrah and a roar; it is very serious, very grim.' As Freddie West VC MC put it: 'You survive, I survived, by being the first to shoot.'

Appendix A

Significant Dates

1900

2 July   German rigid airship *Luftschiff Zeppelin* (LZ.1) flies

1903

17 December   Orville Wright's initial flight

1908

16 October   S.F. Cody makes first recognised aeroplane flight in Britain

1909

28 January   Report of Esher sub-committee of the CID on 'aerial navigation'
25 April   Formation of unofficial Parliamentary Aerial Defence Committee
25 July   Blériot's cross-Channel flight

1910

8 March   First Aviation certificate awarded by Royal Aero Club

1911

1 April   Air Battalion of Royal Engineers formed
25 April   Balloon Factory, Farnborough, renamed Army Aircraft Factory (later Royal Aircraft Factory)
November   Italian airmen bomb rebels in Tripoli

1912

28 February   Report of Haldane's sub-committee of the CID on 'aerial navigation'
11 April   Seely sub-committee recommends establishing RFC
13 April   Royal Warrant creates RFC with Naval and Military wings
19 June   Central Flying School opens at Upavon
1 September   Brig Gen David Henderson appointed Director-General of Military Aeronautics

1914

28 June   Assassination of Archduke Franz Ferdinand at Sarajevo
1 July   Naval Wing of RFC renamed RNAS

27 July	RNAS on war footing
3 August	Germany invades Luxembourg and Belgium, RFC mobilised
4 August	United Kingdom at War
7 August	Lt Col H.M.Trenchard takes command of RFC (Military Wing) and depot at Farnborough
9 August	BEF crosses Channel prior to deployment in north-eastern France
13 August	Commanded by Brig Gen Sir David Henderson, RFC squadrons begin to cross Channel
16 August	Four RFC squadrons operational close to BEF
19 August	First RFC aerial reconnaissance flights
22 August	German columns threaten Anglo-French positions
23 August	Battle of Mons, followed by Allied retreat
3 September	RNAS assumes aerial defence of UK
6–10 September	First Battle of the Marne, Paris saved
7 September	Field Marshal Sir John French, British C-in-C in France, formally praises RFC
12 September	Violent storm devastates RFC in the field
15 September	First aerial photos taken in battle by RFC
19 September	Term 'archie' coined for German anti-aircraft guns
22 September	RNAS aeroplanes raid Zeppelin sheds on Rhine
8 October	Second attack against Zeppelin sheds on Rhine
10 October	Antwerp formally surrenders
19 October	First Battle of Ypres begins
November	RFC in the field organised into two Wings
21 November	Three RNAS machines raid Zeppelin works at Friedrichshafen, Lake Constance
22 November	First Battle of Ypres ends
21 December	First aeroplane raid on Dover
24 December	Second aeroplane raid on Dover, first bomb hits land

1915

19 January	First airship raid on Britain against East Anglia
3 March	3rd RFC Wing formed in France, fourth created in England
10–13 March	Battle of Neuve Chapelle
22 April	Second Battle of Ypres begins: first use of gas
26 April	2/Lt W.B. Rhodes-Moorhouse wins posthumous VC for bombing Courtrai
25 May	Second Battle of Ypres ends
31 May	First airship raid on London
7 June	FSL R.A.J.Warneford destroys Zeppelin over Ghent: awarded VC
25 July	Capt L.G. Hawker wins VC patrolling Ypres Salient
29 July	Admiralty declares RNAS 'an integral part of the Royal Navy'
31 July	Capt J.A. Liddell wins posthumous VC in Belgian coastal area
19 August	Col H.M.Trenchard assumes command of the RFC in France, replacing Maj Gen Sir David Henderson.
25 September	Battle of Loos begins
8 October	Battle of Loos ends

7 November	2/Lt G.S.M. Insall wins VC for action near Bapaume
6 December	Allied conference at Chantilly plans for 1916
19 December	Gen Sir Douglas Haig replaces Field Marshal Sir John French as C-in-C in France

1916

15 February	Joint War Air Committee (JWAC) established under Lord Derby
16 February	Aerial defence of the United Kingdom taken over by RFC
21 February	Battle of Verdun begins
March	RFC in field reorganised: one Brigade to support each Army
22 March	Accusations of 'Fokker fodder' and murder in Parliament
31 March	Derby resigns and JWAC collapses
11 May	Air Board established with Lord Curzon, Lord Privy Seal, as its president
5 June	Lord Kitchener (Secretary of State for War) drowned, when cruiser *Hampshire* strikes mine
18 June	German airman Max Immelmann killed
1 July	Battle of the Somme begins, Maj L.W.B. Rees wins VC while on lone patrol, No 3 (Bombing) Wing RNAS operational under Capt W.L. Elder: to attack industrial targets
3 September	Lt W.L. Robinson brings down airship at Cuffley, Herts, to win VC
15 September	First British use of tanks on the Somme
13 October	Anglo-French bombing raid on Mauser arms factory at Oberndorf in Germany
28 October	German airman Oswald Boelcke killed
18 November	Battle of the Somme ends
23 November	Maj L.G. Hawker VC killed
7 December	David Lloyd George becomes Prime Minister
18 December	Battle of Verdun ends

1917

7 January	Sgt Thomas Mottershead posthumously awarded VC for saving blazing machine
6 February	Two months after Curzon joins the War Cabinet, Lord Cowdray appointed president of new (second) Air Board
6 April	USA declares war on Germany
9 April	Battle of Arras begins, Vimy Ridge taken
16–20 April	Nivelle Offensive on the Aisne fails
May	No 3 (Bombing) Wing RNAS disbanded
7 May	Capt Albert Ball killed, awarded posthumous VC
16 May	Battle of Arras ends
25 May	Cloud prevents Gotha aeroplane attack on London but Shorncliffe and Folkestone bombed
2 June	Aerial action earns Capt W.A. Bishop a VC
7 June	Battle of Messines Ridge begins
13 June	Daylight Gotha raid on London resulting in heavy casualties, political and public uproar
14 June	Battle of Messines Ridge ends

2 July	War Cabinet approves expansion of RFC to 200 squadrons
7 July	Second daylight raid on London; renewed outcry
19 July	First Smuts report on aerial defence
31 July	Battle of Passchendaele begins
19 August	Second Smuts report on bombing strategy and air force organisation
21 August	Flying a Sopwith Pup off HMS Yarmouth, FSL Bernard Smart shoots down German airship off Denmark
2 September	Series of night raids against London and south-east England commence
23 September	German ace Werner Voss shot down
1 October	Memorandum by Minister of Munitions, Winston Churchill, on loss of industrial production during airraids
11 October	41st (Bombing) Wing RFC established under Lt Col C.L.N. Newall to attack targets in Germany
29 October	Lloyd George praises 'cavalry of the clouds' in Parliament
6 November	Passchendaele village captured
10 November	Battle of Passchendaele (3rd Ypres) ends
20 November	Battle of Cambrai begins: use of massed tanks
23 November	Lord Rothermere replaces Cowdray as president of Air Board
29 November	Air Force (Constitution) Act receives Royal assent
7 December	Battle of Cambrai ends
24 December	Strong British bombing raid on Mannheim
28 December	Last meeting of Air Board

1918

3 January	Establishment of an Air Ministry: Rothermere Secretary of State, Maj Gen Sir Hugh Trenchard CAS
18 January	Trenchard hands over command in France to Maj Gen J.M. Salmond
28 January	Severe bombing raid on London; 233 casualties
1 February	41st (Bombing) Wing RFC upgraded to VIII Brigade under Brig Gen C.L.N. Newall
5 February	Order-in-Council provides for Independent Air Force
19 February	Title 'Royal Air Force' approved
3 March	Russian peace treaty with Germany and Austria-Hungary at Brest-Litovsk
21 March	Ludendorff Offensive begins against British in Somme region
26 March	Doullens Conference: Gen Ferdinand Foch created Supreme Allied Commander Maj Gen J.M. Salmond orders RFC to 'bomb and shoot up everything you can see'
1 April	Formation of RAF
2 April	Capt J.T.B. McCudden awarded VC after accounting for 54 enemy machines
5 April	First phase of Ludendorff Offensive checked
9 April	Second phase of Ludendorff Offensive launched in Flanders
11 April	Sir Douglas Haig's 'backs to the wall' message
13 April	Trenchard's resignation as CAS accepted
14 April	Maj Gen F.H. Sykes appointed CAS
21 April	German airman Manfred von Richthofen killed
22 April	British bombers hit targets from Liège to Mannheim

27 April	Sir William Weir replaces Rothermere as Secretary of State for Air
30 April	German advance in Flanders halted
1 May	2/Lt A.A. McLeod awarded VC for action over Albert
27 May	Ludendorff mounts third offensive on the Aisne
5 June	Attack halted on the Marne, but Paris at risk
6 June	Maj Gen Sir Hugh Trenchard appointed to command Independent (Bombing) Force, replacing VIII Brigade
9 June	Germans advance on the Oise
12 June	Oise attack defeated
9 July	Maj J.T.B. McCudden VC killed in air crash
15 July	Second Battle of the Marne begins
22 July	Maj Edward Mannock claims his fiftieth victory, leading to award of the VC
26 July	Mannock shot down and killed
5 August	Last airship raid on Britain against East Anglia
4 August	Second Battle of the Marne ends: Paris saved again
8 August	Battle of Amiens begins 'Black Day' of the German Army
10 August	Air battle against heavy odds, which costs him his left leg, earns Capt F.M.F. West a VC
12 August	Battle of Amiens ends
19 August	Allied counter-attack at Ypres recovers ground lost in April
21 August	Allies advance on Bapaume
29 August	Bapaume falls
2 September	Allies drive east of Bapaume
3 September	Germans fall back towards Hindenburg Line
12–16 September	Americans win Battle of St Mihiel
26 September	Major Allied assault towards the Hindenburg Line
28 September	Anglo-Belgian attack in Flanders
3 October	Hindenburg Line breached; Allies agree Trenchard to assume command of new Inter-Allied Independent (Bombing) Air Force
8 October	Culmination of two months aerial success brings South African Capt A.W. Beauchamp-Proctor a VC
9 October	Allies take Cambrai
20 October	Belgian coast in Allied hands: Ostend, Zeebrugge, Bruges freed
27 October	Maj W.G. Barker awarded VC after shooting down four machines unaided that day
4 November	Allies commence last major thrust
9 November	Kaiser abdicates
11 November	Armistice effective 11am

Appendix B

Sources and Acknowledgements

I am particularly indebted to Dr Neil Young and Roderick Suddaby (Imperial War Museum), Peter Elliott (RAF Museum Hendon), Andrew Orgill (Central Library, RMA Sandhurst), Robert Owen and my son, Mark, for their valuable help and advice.

The staff of the following libraries and archives have also supplied me with material and patiently answered a multitude of questions: British Library, Department of Aviation Records, RAF Museum Hendon, Imperial War Museum: Department of Documents and Department of Photographs, Ministry of Defence, Air Historical Branch and Royal Military Academy Sandhurst. I readily acknowledge permission to use the information that they have reproduced. I thank, too, the Controller of Her Majesty's Stationery Office for allowing reproduction of photographs and to quote from records under Crown copyright, the Trustees of the Imperial War Museum and of the RAF Museum Hendon for permitting reproduction of photographs and to quote from documents held at those locations.

National Archives, Kew

To avoid a long procession of separate items, such as those of individual squadrons, only the relevant document files are noted to give researchers a starting point.

Air 1 Air Historical Branch Records 1862–1959, Series 1, includes RFC, RNAS and RAF squadron records, and casualty returns

Air 5 Air Historical Branch Records 1914–1959, Series 2

Air 6 Records of Meetings of the Air Board and Air Council 1916–1945

Air 8 Chief of the Air Staff Papers 1916–1945

Cab 2 Minutes of Meetings of the Committee of Imperial Defence (CID)

Cab 14 Minutes, Memoranda etc of Air Committee of the CID 1912–1914

Cab 16 Ad Hoc Sub-committees of CID 1905–1922

Cab 17 Correspondence and Miscellaneous papers of CID 1902–1918

Cab 21 Registered Files 1916–1939

Cab 22 War Council, Dardenelles Committee and War Committee 1914–1916

Cab 23 Minutes 1916–1939

Cab 24 Memoranda 1915–1939

Cab 63 Collection of Official Papers by Lord Hankey 1908–1943

Imperial War Museum, Department of Documents

I am grateful for permission of the undermentioned copyright owners to quote from the following papers: Mrs J.I. Blundell (H.A. Blundell), Mr H.K. Dodwell (T.B. Dodwell), Mrs

A.V. Pockney (A.S. Keep), Mrs M. Lee (F.A. Marsh), Mr J. Craig (Air Cdre J.C. Quinnell), Lady Elisabeth Rowell (Sir Robin Rowell), Mrs J. Watkins (S.R. Watkins), Mrs N. Wyllie (H. Wyllie).

Every effort has been made to contact the copyright owners of these papers: G. Allen, O.L. Beater, E.V. Bousher, Sir Sefton Brancker, C.A. Brown, H.A. Buss, C. Callender, Sir Hugh Chance, E.J. Garland, T. Gran, A.E. Horn, J.T.P. Jeyes, B.R.S. Jones, D.G. Joy, A.C. Kilburn, F.E. Rees, Sir Ranald Reid, B.A. Smart and H.G. Taylor. The Department of Documents at The Imperial War Museum would be grateful for any information, which might help to trace them.

The following papers held in the Department have also been studied: Gp Capt R.J. Bone, J.G.H. Chrispin, A.H. Curtis, C.W. Davyes, G. Donald, Gp Capt D. Gilley, J. Gilmour, A.W. Hawkins, B.A. Isaac, J.K.A. Jeakes, J.G. Kingsbury, E.D. Kingsley, W.C. Knight, J.B. Lacy, R.M.W. Loudon, L.W. Mason, Air Cdre C.R. Samson, K.H. Tilley, A.M. Vickers, C.E. Wilkins, S. Wyborn, Miscellaneous 2013 (anonymous account of No 6 Sqn RFC/RAF), Special Miscellaneous Z (combat reports from A. Ball, W.A. Bishop, W.J. Douglas, A.T. Harris, J.I.T. Jones, H. Kelly, E. Mannock, J.A. McCudden, J.B. McCudden, J.C. Slessor, A.W. Tedder).

Peter Jackson, distinguished film director and aviation enthusiast, has most generously provided me with copies of letters from the German pilots Manfred von Richthofen and Max Immelmann and the British VC, James McCudden. He has also made available a multitude of photos, due to space only a few of which could be selected. I remain deeply in his debt both for forwarding and for allowing me to make use of this material.

I am grateful to Adam Sutcliffe for providing me with sound recordings made by his grandfather Lord Rhodes, for permission to quote from those and associated written material, making available and giving permission to reproduce relevant photos.

RAF Museum, Hendon
My special thanks are due for permission to quote from the James McCudden Collection held in the Aviation Records Department.

Other Material
I have drawn on correspondence or interviews with the following: Sir Barnes Wallis, Air Chief Marshal Sir Ralph Cochrane, Marshal of the Royal Air Force Sir Arthur Harris, Gp Capt J.A.G. Haslam, Herr Albert Speer, Air Cdre F.M.F. West. Use has also been made of appropriate volumes of Hansard Parliamentary Debates together with specific reports and items from Parliamentary Papers.

Previous research in the undermentioned manuscript collections has provided additional background information and clarification: Asquith Papers, Beatty Papers, Cowdray Collection, P.R.C. Groves and R.M. Groves papers, Henderson Papers, Lloyd George Papers, (Lord) Montagu Papers, Robertson Papers, Smuts Papers, Sykes Papers, Trenchard Papers, (Henry) Wilson Papers.

Bibliography

Unless otherwise stated, all books published in London

Air Ministry, *A Short History of the Royal Air Force* (1929)
_____ *Four Lectures on the History of the RAF* (1945)
Arthur, M., *Symbol of Courage: A History of the Victoria Cross,* (2004)
Ashmore, E.B., *Air Defence* (1929)
Aston, G., *Sea, Land and Air Strategy* (1914)
_____ *The Biography of the Late Marshal Foch* (1929)
Atkin, G.F., *Winged Victor* (VM Yeates) (2004)
Balfour, H.H., *An Airman Marches* (1933)
_____ *Wings Over Westminster* (1973)
_____ *An Airman Marches: Early Flying Adventures 1914–1923* (1985)
Baring, M., *Flying Corps Headquarters* (1920)
Barker, R., *The Royal Flying Corps in France: From Mons to the Somme* (1994)
Bickers, R.T., *The First Great Air War* (1988)
Blake, R., *The Private Papers of Sir Douglas Haig 1914–1919* (1952)
Bowyer, C., *Albert Ball VC* (1977)
Boyle, A., *Trenchard: Man of Vision* (1962)
Bruce, J.M., *The Aeroplanes of the Royal Flying Corps (Military Wing)* (1982)
Burrows, W.E., *Richthofen: A True History of the Red Baron* (1970)
Butler, E. & Young, G., *Marshal Without Glory: The Life and Death of Hermann Göring* (1973)
Casirella, P.J., *Who Killed the Red Baron?* (1974)
Chamier, J.A., *The Birth of the Royal Air Force: The Early History and Experience of the Flying Services* (1959)
Chapman, G., *Vain Glory* (1937)
Charlton, L.E.O., *War From the Air* (1931)
_____ *War Over England* (1936)
Churchill, W.S., *The World Crisis: 1916–1918,* vol 2 (1927)
Clarke, T., *My Northcliffe Diary* (1931)
Clodfelter, M., *Warfare and Armed Conflict,* vol 2 (North Carolina, 1992)
Cole, C., *McCudden V.C.* (1967)
Cole, C. & Cheesman, E.F., *The Air Defence of Great Britain 1914–1918* (1984)
Collier, B., *Heavenly Adventurer: Sefton Brancker and the Dawn of British Aviation* (1959)
_____ *A History of Air Power* (1974)
Cooper, B., *The Story of the Bomber 1914–1945* (1974)
Creagh, Sir O'M & Humphris, E.M. (ed), *The V.C and D.S.O.,* Vols 1–3 (1923)
Cuneo, J.R., *The Air Weapon 1914–1916* (Harrisburg, 1947)
Dean, M., *The Royal Air Force and Two World Wars* (1979)
Douglas of Kirtleside, Lord, *Years of Combat* (1963)

Drew, G.A., *Canada's Fighting Airmen* (Toronto, 1930)

Duffy, C., *Through German Eyes: The Battle of the Somme 1916* (2006)

Dugdale, B.E.C., *Arthur James Balfour, First Earl Balfour, 1906–1930* (1937)

Edmonds, J.E. (ed), *Military Operations France & Belgium 1914–8, with maps and appendices* (1925–1935)

Ellis P.B. & Schofield, J., *Biggles: The Life Story of Capt W.E. Johns* (1993)

Franks, N., *Under the Guns of the German Aces* (1997)

Fredette, R.H., *The Sky on Fire: the First Battle of Britain 1917–1918, and the Birth of the RAF* (New York, 1966)

George, D.L., *War Memoirs, Vols 1&2* (1936)

Gibon, M., *Warneford VC* (Yeovil, 1979)

Gibbons, F., *The Red Knight of Germany: Baron von Richthofen* (1930)

Goodspeed, D.J., *Ludendorff* (1966)

Grider, J.M., *War Birds. The Diary of an Unknown Aviator* (1966 ed.)

Hankey, Lord, *The Supreme Command 1914–1918*, vols 1&2 (1961)

Harris, A.T., *Bomber Offensive* (1947)

Hearn, P., *Flying Rebel: the story of Louis Strange* (1994)

Henderson, D., *The Art of Reconnaissance* (3rd ed., 1914)

Henshaw, T., *The Sky Their Battlefield* (1995)

Higham, R., *Air Power, A Concise History* (1972)

Holmes, R., *The Little Field Marshal* (1981)

Höppner, E. von, *Deutschlands Krieg in der Luft* (Leipzig, 1921)

Huxley, L. (ed), *Scott's Last Expedition*, vol 1 (1913)

Immelmann, F., *Immelmann: 'The Eagle of Lille'* (1934)

_____ *Immelmann: 'The Eagle of Lille'* (revised ed., 1984)

Insall, A.J., *Observer: Memoirs of the RFC 1915–1918* (1970)

Jackson, A.J., *Avro Aircraft since 1908* (1965)

Jackson, R., *Fighter Pilots of World War I* (1977)

Jane, F.T., *Jane's All the World's Aircraft* (1918)

_____ *Jane's Fighting Aircraft of World War I* (1919)

Johns, W.E., *Fighting Planes and Aces* (1932)

Jones, H.A., *The War in the Air* (official history, Great War), vols 2–6 (Oxford, 1935–7)

_____ *The War in the Air, appendices* (1937)

Jones, I., *King of Air Fighters* (E Mannock) (1934)

Jones, N., *The Origins of Strategic Bombing* (1973)

Joubert de la Ferté, P.B., *The Fated Sky – An Autobiography* (1952)

_____ *The Third Service: The Story Behind the RAF* (1955)

Joynson-Hicks, W., *The Command of the Air or Prophecies Fulfilled* (1916)

Kerr, M., *Land, Sea and Air* (1927)

Kiernan, R.H., *Capt. Albert Ball* (1933)

Kilduff, P., *Richthofen: Beyond the Legend of the Red Baron* (1993)

Lanchester, F.W., *Aircraft in Warfare: The Dawn of the Fourth Arm* (1916)

Lawson, E. & J., *The First Air Campaign* (Pennsylvania, 1996)

Lee, A.S.G., *No parachute: a fighter pilot in World War I* (1968)

Lewis, B.A., *A Few of the First* (1997)

Lewis, C.A., *Sagittarius Rising* (1936)

Lewis, P., *The British Bomber since 1914* (1980)

Liddell Hart, B.H., *Foch: The Man of Orleans* (1931)

Low, A.M., *Parachutes in Peace and War* (1942)

Ludendorff, E., *Meine Kriegserinnerungen* (Berlin, 1922)

MacBean, J.A. & Hogben, A.S., *Bombs Gone* (1990)

Mackersey, I., *The Wright Brothers* (2004)

Macmillan, N., *Sir Sefton Brancker* (1935)

_____ *Wings of Fate* (1967)

Mason, F.K., *Battle Over Britain* (1969)

Mawson, P., *Mawson of the Antarctic* (1964)

McCudden, J.T.B., *Five Years in the Royal Flying Corps* (1919)

Mills, J.S., *David Lloyd George, War Minister* (1924)

Morris, A., *First of the Many: The Story of the Independent Force, RAF* (1968)

_____ *Bloody April* (1967)

Morris, J., *The German Air Raids on Great Britain 1914–1918* (1925)

Morrow, J.H., *The Great War in the Air* (1993)

Munson, K., *Bombers 1914–1919* (1968)

Neumann, G.P., *The German Air Force in the Great War* (1921)

Nicholson, G.W.L., *Canadian Expeditionary Force 1914–1919* (Ottawa, 1962)

Norris, G., *The Royal Flying Corps: A History* (1965)

Parkinson, R., *Tormented Warrior* (E. Ludendorff) (1978)

Pemberton-Billing, N., *Air War: How to Wage It* (1916)

Pollard, A.O., *The RAF: a concise history* (1934)

Probert, H., *Bomber Harris* (2001)

_____ *High Commanders of the RAF* (1991)

Raleigh, Sir W., *The War in the Air* (Official History, Great War)

vol 1 (Oxford, 1922)

Reid, P.R., *Winged Diplomat: The Life Story of Air Commodore 'Freddie' West* (1962)

Richards, D., *Portal of Hungerford* (1977)

Richthofen, M., von *Der Rote Kampfflieger* (Berlin, 1933)

Riddell, Lord, *War Diary 1914–1918* (1933)

Roberston, W., *Soldiers and Statesmen, 1914–1918* , vol 2 (1926)

_____ *From Private to Field Marshal* (1921)

Rock, W., *Mr Lloyd George and the War* (1920)

Roskill, S.W. (ed), *Documents relating to the Naval Air Service 1908–1918* vol 1 (1969)

Rowell, E. (ed), *In Peace and War: memoirs of Robin Rowell* (1996)

Saundby, R., *Air Bombardment: The Story of its Development* (1961)

Saunders, H. St G., *Per Ardua: The Rise of British Air Power, 1911–1939* (Oxford, 1944)

Scott, J.D., *Vickers: A History* (1962)

Segrelles, V., *Early Aircraft* (1984)

Shores, C., Franks, N. & Guest, R., *Above the Trenches* (1990)

Slessor, J.C., *The Central Blue: Recollections and Reflections* (1956)

Smith, A.M., *Knights of the Air* (1959)

Smuts, J.C., *The Coming Victory* (1917)

Spaight, J.M., *Beginnings of Organised Air Power: A Historical Study* (1927)

Steele, N. & Hart, P., *Tumult in the Clouds: War in the Air 1914–1918* (1997)

Strange, L.A., *Recollections of an Airman* (1933)

Sueter, M., *Airmen or Noahs* (1928)

Sykes, F.H., *Aviation in Peace and War* (1922)

_____ *From Many Angles* (1942)

Taylor, J.W.R., *Central Flying School. Birthplace of Air Power* (1958)

Tedder, Lord, *Air Power in War* (1948)

Thompson, Sir R., *The Royal Flying Corps* (1968)

Till, G., *Air Power and the Royal Navy 1914–1945* (1979)

Turner, J.F., *VCs of the Air* (1960)

'Vigilant', *The Red Knight of the Air* (1934)

Walbank, F.A., *Wings of War: An Air Force Anthology* (1942)

Walker, P.B., *Early Aviation at Farnborough: The History of the Royal Aircraft Establishment* (1971)

Werner, J., *Boelcke: der mensch, der flieger, der führer der deutschen jagdfleigerei* (Leipzig, 1932)

_____ *Knight of Germany: Oswald Boelcke, German Ace* (1933)

_____ *Knight of Germany: Oswald Boelcke, German Ace* (revised ed., 1985)

Weintraub, S., *Silent Knight: The Remarkable Christmas Truce of 1914* (2001)

Whitehouse, A., *The Zeppelin Fighters* (1966)
Williams, C., *Pétain* (2005)
Wise, S., *Canadian Airmen and the First World War* (Toronto, 1980)
Wright, N., *The Red Baron* (1976)
Wright, P., *At the Supreme War Council* (1921)
Yeates, V.M., *Winged Victory* (1934)

Unpublished
Leigh-Mallory, T.L., *History of Tank and Aeroplane Co-operation* (1919)

Periodicals, Journals and Newspapers
Aeronautical Journal
Aeroplane
Air Clues
Air Force List
Aircraft Illustrated
Army List
Army Quarterly
Car Illustrated
Cross & Cockade
Daily Chronicle
Daily Express
Daily Graphic
Daily Mail
Daily Telegraph
Dictionary of National Biography
Flight
Illustrated London News
Journal of the Royal United Services Institution
London Gazette
Manchester Guardian
Morning Post
Navy List
New Dictionary of National Biography
News Chronicle
Observer
Pall Mall Gazette
Pall Mall Magazine
Popular Flying
Punch
Purnell's History of the First World War
Quarterly Journal of Military History
The Times
United Service Magazine
Weekly Despatch
Westminster Gazette

Index